Gasper Tringale

Patricia J. Williams, a recipient of the MacArthur "genius" award, is a columnist ("Diary of a Mad Law Professor," *The Nation*), and a professor of law at Columbia University. Her previous books are *Seeing a Color-Blind Future*, *The Alchemy of Race and Rights*, and *The Rooster's Egg*. She contributes regularly to *Ms.* and *The Village Voice*.

Open House

Open House

Of Family, Friends,

Food, Piano Lessons,

and the Search for

a Room of My Own

Patricia J. Williams

PICADOR

FARRAR, STRAUS AND GIROUX · NEW YORK

www.picadorusa.com

Picador® is a U.S. registered trademark and is used by Farrar, Straus and Giroux under license from Pan Books Limited.

For information on Picador Reading Group Guides, as well as ordering, please contact Picador.
Phone: 646-307-5626
Fax: 212-253-9627
E-mail: readinggroupguides@picadorusa.com

Grateful acknowledgment is made to the conceptual artist damali ayo for permission to quote on pages 208–209 from her Web site www.rent-a-negro.com.

Designed by Debbie Glasserman

Library of Congress Cataloging-in-Publication Data

Williams, Patricia J., 1951–
    Open house: of family, friends, food, piano lessons, and the search for a room of my own / Patricia J. Williams.
        p. cm.
    ISBN 0-312-42459-0
    EAN 978-0-312-42459-6
    1. Williams, Patricia J., 1951– 2. Journalists—United States—Biography. 3. African American women journalists—United States—Biography.
    I. Title.

PN4874.W625A3 2004
070.92—dc22   2004004925

First published in the United States by Farrar, Straus and Giroux

First Picador Edition: November 2005

10 9 8 7 6 5 4 3 2 1

TO MY PARENTS

Then said the Interpreter, Come in, I will show thee
that which will be profitable to thee.

—JOHN BUNYAN, *The Pilgrim's Progress*

Contents

Open House

1

The Fourth Wall

It was the dinner from hell. I'm not sure why I went; I was trying to be polite, I think. I wanted to be open-minded, to show myself an engaged citizen, a lover of the debating arts. Besides, it began so innocently.

"My wife and I like the kind of trouble you've been stirring, Miss Williams," he said, with a smile and a challenge. He had an avuncular, wizardy twinkle, very Albus Dumbledore. It made me feel feisty and smart, like Hermione Granger. They *liked* my kind of trouble. But let this be a lesson: When a woman of my great dignity and years loses her sanity and starts imagining she's one of Harry Potter's magical little friends, you can be sure that the cosmic gyroscope is wobbling off its center . . .

It was only after I'd accepted the invitation that the host, a courtly old-school conservative, added that he wanted me to come because he thought it would be interesting to have me "take on" his friend J.B., an aggressive, much-published neo-conservative with a reputation for sheer meanness. I should have pleaded my dead grandmother right then. But instead I got dressed up, bought a bottle of overpriced but understated red wine, and presented myself at their doorstep, feeling vaguely penitent.

My host and his wife were rich old conservatives, no middle-brow barbecue-throwing conservatives they, and so the dinner was more of a dinner *party*, small and formal, with four staid couples in tasteful attire. I came uncoupled, unhitched, free-floating as a dandelion puff, but they had thought ahead. They paired me with the head of the local Federalist Society, a states' rights organization whose positions on legal issues fly as far to the opposite extreme of everything I believe in as is possible under the cosmos. He was young; passionately Con-federate; energetic; sharp of mind, tooth, and tongue—the kind whom no one would mistake for a vegetarian. He stapled himself to my side and proceeded to grind me down over drinks: Had I ever heard of the great legal philosopher J. L. Austin? (It was a very condescending question. It's rather hard to graduate from law school without having heard of J. L. Austin.) Was I a Christian? (God knows . . .) Explain why lib-erals hate everyone. (Huh?)

Over the first course, a delicate chilled soup of pureed ap-ple and watercress, my host started gnawing at me from the other side. What year had I graduated from law school? 1975? Ah, yes, he was teaching at Yale back then and never did he encounter a worse group of students. The affirmative action students were not just badly prepared, they really didn't have the ability, you know . . . He used to read *The Nation*. When did I start writing columns for them? 1997. Ah, well, then, no wonder he hadn't read me; that was the year he canceled his subscription. More potage?

The main course was veal, pale and pink as a baby's bot-tom. "J.B. likes his meat," laughed his champagne-suited, champagne-colored wife. J.B. himself was all glistening knives as he slashed into the innocent flesh. He was a tall, hearty man, very much the gruff colonial administrator, straight-talking and speed-talking right on past the stop signs of ordinary conversational exchange. He was full of plans for the world; he knew just what was what. Head Start was a complete waste of tax dollars. Affirmative action was corrupt. If civil rights activists were so keen on integrating they'd stop trying to glad-hand their way into jobs they weren't qualified for and go back to the ghetto where the real problems were. Genes were everything, you either had it or you didn't. Environmentalists were fanatics. Young black men who had children out of wedlock should be put in jail. When he learned that I had adopted my son as a single parent, he opined that women who raised children without a husband were engaged in child abuse. Anti–hate speech advocates were the real haters.

Two years later I am still coming up with snappy answers for that evening, witty retorts, little barbs that would have made me seem above it all, as dry-humored as a stiff martini, cynical even, please-God-less-earnest. At the dinner, however, I was hopelessly earnest. I cited statistics, studies, books—until J.B. cut me off as being elitist and out of touch. After that, I sat tongue-tied and sweaty, feeling even more powerless than he assumed I was. I could feel a deep roiling in my gene pool, a gurgling eddy in the mitochondrial stream I share with Grandfather Orangutan—I could feel the ancestral monkey blood grow red-hot and unkind, plotting sad little scenarios of revenge. I wanted to walk out but didn't have the courage to—it would be so rude—until after dessert was served, whereupon I turned down coffee and excused myself. Take *that!*

This is who I am. A soft-spoken, fiftysomething mush of a minority, deferential but strong, really I am. I confess to a tendency to collapse under rightish pressure, but I try to compensate by writing brave, leftish articles for *The Nation* under the Joan of Arc byline "Diary of a Mad Law Professor." I teach courses in contracts, consumer protection, history of civil rights, theories of equality, and general issues of law and public policy. My hair is so unruly that new students get mesmer-

ized by it before they finally manage to wrestle themselves
back down to eye contact with me. I am an anxious mother, a
worrier by habit, and therefore a pretty decent lawyer. My skin
is a soft custardy, mustardy brown, with lots of freckles and im-
perfections. I am punctual. I am good at math. I wish I had
found someone to marry so I wouldn't always have to go to
dinner parties by myself—to say nothing of avoiding arrest for
child abuse should J.B. ever become president—but I have no
regrets. I like the independence. My life is good. When not
consumed by my many official duties as a politically correct,
feminazi black single mother, I like poetry, walking on the
beach at sunset, and traveling to new places.

It was not just the dinner from hell that brought home the reality that the shock jock ethic of AM radio was no longer simply a ratings game, but a party game. Or that the beat-'em-up
political snarl-fests that on TV looked so much like XXX-
treme entertainment were beginning to bleed over into daily
social encounters. Although that evening was the first time I
had had to suffer through such an excruciatingly intimate bal-
let of confrontation, it was predictable that something like the
game of guess who's coming to dinner would become sport.
Years of shouting shock jocks and tabloid TV have had a slow
but sure sedimentary effect on the political discourse of the
world at large.

Such attacks—on civil rights activists, or on feminists, or on
the Left, or on the "liberal media"—have less to do with specific disagreements about issues, I think, than with unresolved
ambition, an ethic of no holds barred. There is a virulent resentment abroad that is taking us backward in time, exploiting
divisions that go back a hundred years or more—the Confed-
erate South versus the elitist North, freethinkers versus the
cult of true womanhood, evolution versus creationism, and so
on. The resentments have no necessary grounding in sub-

stance or reality; they're not even consistent. After all, it's kind of hard to be an unruly white-hating Afrocentric anarchist and a sappy bleeding-heart integrationist embracer of human rights at the same time. But this is the nature of propaganda, and I do fault those who, like J.B., give life to their resentment by projecting, describing, inventing the embodiment of their most pornographic dreams. It's how prejudice has always given undue agency to stereotypes.

W.E.B. DuBois coined the expression "double consciousness" to convey the experience shared by so many African Americans of trying to negotiate the space between one's humanity and one's stereotype. "It is a peculiar sensation," he wrote in *The Souls of Black Folk*, ". . . this sense of always looking at one's self through the eyes of others, of measuring one's soul by the tape of a world that looks on in amused contempt and pity. One ever feels his two-ness—an American, a Negro; two souls, two thoughts, two unreconciled strivings; two warring ideals in one dark body, whose dogged strength alone keeps it from being torn asunder."

I would tweak the notion a little farther and describe it as a sense of "double being." It isn't just about feeling split inside; in today's culture, where visual media can replicate your image and blast it everywhere, it's more like having two entirely separate bodies. The force DuBois described as "the eyes of others" today has lights! camera! action!—as well as scriptwriters on very large budgets.

For those who do not completely understand what it is to be marked by the hierarchies of color or ethnicity, let me make an analogy in the nonracial context. I think being stereotyped is a bit like living in a state of perpetual victimization by identity thieves. The novelist Paul Auster, in his little collection of vignettes titled *The Red Notebook*, describes coming across a letter written by a stranger who had apparently set himself up as Auster, using his name, address, and identity as literary critic: it was rendered ". . . in a bombastic,

pretentious style, riddled with quotations from French philoso-
phers and oozing with a tone of conceit and self-satisfaction . . .
It was a contemptible letter, the kind of letter I would never
dream of writing to anyone, and yet it was signed with my
name." Auster ends the account by remarking on the odd
sense of watching something like oneself operate indepen-
dently, a phenomenon reminding him "that the world I live
in will go on escaping me forever."

It is intriguing, the theme of escape. Perhaps one of the
most important features of modernity is mobility. We want to
escape the world, the world escapes us. In a way, escapism is
the cornerstone of antifeudalist notions of freedom. America
was founded on the ability to escape the status of serf; we are
committed to the notion that it is possible and desirable to
step out of one's place in a given society, go where one wishes,
and be governed by nothing but individual ability and free
will.

But mobility is premised on dislocation as much as escape
and therefore might lead to its own extremes, its own backlash
of unfreedom. Certainly it was nostalgia for "place" and the
anxiety produced by industrialism's upheavals that fueled Fas-
cism and Nazism in pre–World War II Europe. I worry that
today we live in a similarly precarious moment: We are sub-
merged in an image-driven culture with no long-term memory, as well as in a diasporic world full of wandering refugees,
displaced by violence, searching for simulacra of home. Too
many of us are weary pilgrims, nostalgic for a place where we
are known but that we have never known, a place where the
static is less a prison than an idealized source of peace.

And so we invent our homes, with inventive desperation.
New York University film scholar Manthia Diawara writes of
an excruciating encounter with a Parisian taxi driver. "Your
accent is rather Parisian . . . Where are you originally from?"
asked the cabbie, with such piercing intrusiveness that Diawara sought to shield himself immediately by saying that he

was from New York. "The cabdriver had walked right into my fantasies, and I felt no shame in presenting to him the new identity I had fabricated for myself." In actuality, Diawara is Malian but has lived in the United States for many years. He speaks "such good French" because he is Malian and has lived in Paris for many years as well. But the subtext of the encounter was a complex one. In questioning him about his origins and accent, the cabbie was really asking if he was a French colonial. "I knew that he was fascinated with me because I was a black American man, powerful and free. The image of the West African in Paris, on the other hand, was that of unwanted illegal immigrants, called *les sans papiers*." By claiming to be an American, he was refusing to be colonized, he was trying to play against the taxi driver's stereotypes. But eventually the cab was stopped by a police officer who demanded to see his passport and who revealed him as Malian, not American—in very condescending terms. Humiliated before both the officer and the cabbie, "I had lost twice."

To be conquered and colonized is always to feel humiliated, betrayed. And betrayal introduces the psyche to the hopeless, brutal truth that we live half our lives in the dreams, imaginations, prayers of others. We are just that ephemeral. In a convoluted way, the "lie" that Diawara told was an attempt to communicate the truth of his humanity. It was a fictionalizing of the self designed to generate brick walls of respect; it was a cipher for the idealized, admirable, "really" valuable self, as most likely to be understood by a class-conscious cabbie in urban French culture. Communication at this level is pure art, I think. It presents a core dilemma in the ethics of translation and representation, begging the question of reality itself. I remember hearing Studs Terkel interview painter David Hockney once upon a time. Hockney described watching two television programs about elephants: One was a documentary in which elephants were filmed roaming about their natural habitat; the other was a Disney cartoon. To Hockney, the cartoon somehow better captured the true elephantness of elephants than the straightforward but dry documentary.

Of course, Diawara's so-called lie also proceeded from the more general desire to protect ourselves from the presumption of nosy strangers. *Who am I? None of your damn business!* Sometimes we meet the obsessive pull for information with an engrossing invention, some magical words that don't rebuff people harshly but merely redirect them to some reassuring, opaque wall of a banality. A friend says that whenever she's in a taxi or on public transportation and a stranger tries to ask her questions that are too intimate, she tilts her head back, closes her eyes, and says, "If you don't mind, I'd like to pray quietly now." As she begins to mutter not-so-quiet incantations, people edge away just as nicely as you please.

Most of us tend to invent a bit, perhaps to preserve privacy, perhaps to conform to the safest status, the highest ground in a flood of negative presumptions, however irrational: bigger muscles, the better car, the more interesting accent, the larger house, the more popular brand of T-shirt. We are all tyrannized to some extent by the power of snobbery on the one hand and the yearning to be respected and well liked on the other. I once pretended to be Guyanese, for example, because a Guyanese pizza delivery man in the elevator of my building said that I looked so much like his daughter he could cry. I didn't want to see him cry. Besides, I had just come from a particularly bruising faculty meeting and longed like an orphan to fit in, just any old place. We must be related! he said rather passionately—do you have family in Guyana? Why, yes, could be, I said vaguely. On my father's side, I ventured recklessly, heady with the promiscuous need for belonging, and prayed for the elevator to get to the lobby before he started quizzing me about exchange rates for whatever the Guyanese currency might be.

Diawara's story made me think of all the ways I have imagined myself over the course of my life. When I was growing

up, I imagined myself one of the Jackson Twins. The Jackson
Twins were not real; they were cartoon characters, the hero-
ines of a syndicated comic strip by Dick Brooks that we read
in *The Boston Globe*. It featured two adolescent girls who led
exceptionally conventional lives, as I recall, but for the fact
that people were always mixing them up. All the action of that
comic centered on setups for misidentification, predictable
twin-girl dilemmas. Both my sister and I were fascinated by
the stories, I think partly because we ourselves looked so
much alike that people frequently mistook us for one another
even though we are two years apart. "We started off being one
set of twins," remembers my sister, "and then it sort of multi-
plied to the point where everyone in the family was a twin."
And so we would play, making up plots, conversations, negotiating our sibling rivalry by pretending we were identical and
testing our parents by forcing them to distinguish us: "Can
you tell us apart?" and "How can you tell?" Our real parents
gave the right answers. The evil twins of our real parents always liked the other sister better.

Beyond sibling rivalry, there was another element in the
play, at least for me: I was fascinated by the ease with which I
believed twins could trade places. I thought of them as being
a single person, I suppose. Two whole halves and thus able to
be in two places at the same time. One twin could witness an
event, clandestinely yet openly, while people thought it was
the other to whom they were speaking. To me it seemed as
though the real you could huddle up and hide while someone
else took over. It was simultaneously a rest from oneself, an
excuse for oneself, an eavesdropping on oneself.

All this is to say that the night after the dinner party from
hell, I had a redemptive, Harry Potterish sort of dream. I was
very small, pigeon-sized, perhaps. I was floating among the
rafters, hidden in the eaves of my host's home. My host bore a
surprising resemblance to General Robert E. Lee. He and his
whole family, including children, grandchildren, great-grand-

children, and great-great-grandchildren, were gathered for a
feast in the dining room below me. It was the culmination of
a holiday celebrating what they kept referring to as the South's
victory at Gettysburg. The first course was goose. Each person
received a whole goose, sized from the biggest to the smallest
family member. For the next course, each person received a
whole turkey, again ordered from biggest to smallest. The next
course was a whole duck for each, then a whole chicken, then
a whole mourning dove, then a whole wren.

I sat perched in a hidden corner of the ceiling beams looking down on these perfectly calibrated carcasses, this carefully
ordered progression of fowls, so precisely sized for each consumer and yet so excessive. Oddly, I was enjoying the sights
and sounds of the feast and enjoying also some strips of meat
taken—yes, stolen—from the kitchen. I had collected rich
drippings, crisp skins, gooey strings of meat fallen into the
gravy, globs of the fruit sauce used to glaze the ducks, tiny
pearl onions and prunes that had dropped into the pan and
been left behind. There was even a leftover sweet potato. I
stuffed handfuls of purloined bounty into my mouth and nestled into my warm, dry aerie, as deeply involved in their lives
and as curious as if I were watching the Fox Network.

Then the family went to sleep, and in a misty little trail,
my dreams entered theirs and, through dreams, I reproduced
myself inside them. In the morning, dozens of mes came
spilling, spinning, bursting out of their mouths and wombs
and fingertips, overflowing, rushing out of the house, running
past the front gates, racing toward the horizon to escape and
melt like butter back into the world. With the morning, my
body grew too heavy to float, too large to roost in the rafters,
which creaked beneath my weight. I came down from the secret place and slipped into the cool of the world and joined
the little band of selves I had created.

Somewhere in the background of this dream, and of my
childhood "twinning" play, there lingers the fear, perhaps the

reality, of being alone. Of losing not just others but also myself. Of disappearing, evaporating into space. A desire for extra versions of me, to dodge, feint, fool, and survive. Like so many African Americans, or like many immigrant families who came to this country having known great oppression, I have a family history wrapped in reinvention. Quite a few of my relatives are hard to trace not only because record keeping was so careless when it came to black people, but also because they disguised themselves, were always afraid of being chased by their past. We Americans are unique in our ability to "just forget about it." We embrace oblivion like no other people on earth. We are always changing our names, hiding religions, suppressing mother tongues, riding the ambition of pure self-aggrandizement. If there is a measure of release in that, there is also great loss.

Growing up, I listened to my father's stories of being raised in Georgia, when lynchings took place at a rate of about one a week. Such constant tyranny bred secrecy, he says, and ultimately duplicity. I listened to my mother's passionate protectiveness in the wake of a police scandal that was one of my earliest introductions to Boston's bitter race politics: A thirteen-year-old black girl was found strangled only a few blocks from our house. When the police got there, one of the officers reportedly said, "Oh, it's just a nigger girl."

The traumatically induced determination not to speak hobbles our ability to grasp or heal those most painful bits of our history. The impenetrability of that past creates a portal for ghosts, if ghosts are a way of representing what we do not know. Thus we are shaped not only by the hard science of what happens in the world but also by the fairy tales and the half-truths, the willed ignorance and the escapism, the parables and the myths with which our desperate forebears cushioned us as we fell into the world.

I think a legacy of violence against and among one's people, tribe, group, always engenders a certain preparation for

death, a magnification of life by planting lots of yourselves in
many different guises and forms. I am a this, not a that. I am
here, not there. You live life as though you were writing your
own obituary—so that others will know, so that no one will
ever mistake you for "just" a this or a that. But it's hard to keep
up in a world where the struts are knocked out from underneath any stable structure of community with such ruthless
frequency. Time keeps sprawling forward, a rushing mess, the
roots torn and washed away.

At the root of integrity is an Aristotelian notion of being one
self. Much like our understanding of an integer in math, it
conveys a sense of being undivided, not split into fractious
parts. To have integrity is to be whole.

We often think of integrity only in its simplest, little-kid
sense: George Washington chopped down the cherry tree and
that's the truth. William Jefferson Clinton didn't have sex with
that woman and that's a lie. Anything more or less is commonly denounced as wretched relativism.

The concept of integrity is more complex than that, however. In the law, for example, there are—or had been until
recently, when the USA Patriot Act put much of this in
question—lots of rules designed to protect certain zones of
privacy or intimate community. Since September 11, 2001,
many Americans tend to think of the law almost exclusively as
a bulwark against terrorism. But the legitimate fear of terrorism from beyond our borders has had the unfortunate side effect of emboldening the snoops within our borders, the
busybodies among us, the paranoids whose entire lives are
dedicated to the extraction of "truth" from the unwilling. We
forget at our peril that the law also serves to protect certain re-
gions of truth from public scrutiny, as when the knowledge is
too private, too personal, too close to the heart, or when the
extraction of information would require undue state violence.

It's why we have the Fifth Amendment, or are exempted from having to testify against spouses or other intimates. It's why lawyers, priests, brokers, or others who work as fiduciaries testify only at the will of those whose confidence they guard. All such rules are designed to make sure that citizens can remain "true" to themselves—or whole within themselves—particularly against the power of the state. Having such protection ensures that the government cannot "dis-member" you or your family or designated surrogates, literally or figuratively, an interest that outweighs even the pursuit of certain justice interests. It is, after all, a primal challenge to the notion of liberty: the tension between the security of the citizenry as a collective body and the security (or integrity) of the individual citizen's body.

This notion of integrity allows at least some space for the placing of close confidences in others. Since no one is truly an island, we recognize in our public policy the role of close family members and trusted advisers. I use the word "role" advisedly, for there is a surprising amount of overlap between civic roles and what we commonly think of as theater. Fiduciaries, like actors, are charged with subsuming their own interests so as to become a vessel or vehicle for the interests of another. Families, we assume, do this fairly automatically. Other categories of fiduciary are bound by ethical codes. Lawyers become the "mouthpieces" for those who cannot speak for themselves in the foreign language of the court. Doctors become stewards of the broken body regardless of whether they like the person inside. Penitents confess to priests not because the priest is literally a man they want to chat with, but because the penitent seeks peace within himself and accomplishes that by seeking God in the guise of a priest. The God-and-Freud wars notwithstanding, this much is very similar to the role played by psychotherapists. One pours out one's heart not really to "share," despite popular disparagement to that effect. The ultimate goal of most therapy is to allow the individual to confront the self and to experiment with alternative ways of behaving. What worries me most about the new plethora of security guards and computer police and official monitors, seen and unseen, is that they are positioned as voyeurs, privy to our most intimate actions and transactions, thumbing through our wallets, feeling us up for the pocketed coins and foil-wrapped candy bars that might set off the metal detectors. And yet there is no clearly defined responsibility to represent us carefully. There is no shared ethical understanding about who knows, or why me, or what is done with the information.

Representing the interests of another is thus part art: It is a healing art, whose end is to repair alienation and restore integrity. Perhaps it would help if we wore masks or face paint or wigs to accomplish this end, like witch doctors or shamans or British barristers. I don't want to suggest that we routinely don uniforms for these functions, but I think it would be useful, every now and then, to remind ourselves of the delicate boundaries, to mark the difference between the ordinary self and the role on behalf of another. These roles are vital not just to our integrity but also to our dignity, and dignity is essential for the health of our civic life.

Perhaps this concern is more easily addressed as a species of public theater. I'm thinking in particular of the kind of work done by the performance actress Anna Deavere Smith. Smith is perhaps known most widely for her roles in the popular television series *The West Wing* and movies like *The Human Stain*. But Smith's most remarkable work is revealed in one-woman shows where she takes on social issues like the Crown Heights clash (*Fires in the Mirror*), the Rodney King beating and subsequent riots (*Twilight: Los Angeles*), or the presidency of the United States (*House Arrest*). Smith researches her topics by interviewing hundreds of subjects, then performing their actual words, sequencing the quotes into constructed dialogues. Smith is a marvelous actress (Al Sharpton doesn't do Al Sharpton any better than she), but the brilliance of her work is in the juxtaposition of voices. People who would never talk to one another in real life are brought together in Smith's multiple personalities. The title of one scene in *House Arrest* captures the essence of it: "These people said these words, but not in each other's presence." But there is no doubt that they should have.

I suppose it is wishful thinking to imagine the day on earth when the lamb and the lion will sit down long enough for a good listen to each other, but Smith's stage pieces are the sort of vehicle where that is exactly what happens. Tough-as-nails L.A. police chief Daryl Gates is juxtaposed with sad, illiterate young street kids from South Central. Studs Terkel fades into George Stephanopoulos. A stoic Hasidic housewife's musing on the complexities of her neighborhood dissolves into an utterly absurd yet oddly moving soliloquy by Al Sharpton on the subject of his hair.

Smith's work has made me wonder what it would mean if, as in certain traditions, artists were more highly regarded in governance—not merely as propagandists but as real collaborators in the civic process. My favorite of Anna Deavere Smith's projects is one that attempted to do just that. For three consecutive summers, Smith coordinated a project in Boston and Cambridge called the Institute on the Arts and Civic Dialogue. It brought together actors, scholars, journalists, community activists (and passives), politicians, the homeless, blacks, whites, Latinos, dancers, Vietnam vets, Democrats, Republicans, children, and musicians. She set these disparate characters to work on collaborative cross-disciplinary projects, trying on each other's words, roles, perspectives. What if, she began by asking, what if instead of applause, the audience were to say, "What can we do?" And what would the actors say in return?

I was lucky enough to be a fellow at the institute during those three summers. Cartoonist Art Spiegelman worked on an opera about the comic-book censorship codes of the 1950s. Impresario Ping Chong created a multimedia show on the complications of Asian ethnicity and identity. Choreographer Donald Byrd staged Petipa's *Snow White* with a black princess and a white prince. Boston politicians conferred with Judy Baca, a Chicana muralist from Los Angeles. Members of the audience—from a twelve-year-old cellist to a fiftysomething fireman—wrote down their prayers and submitted them to singers Maggie and Suzzy Roche, who then set them to music (resulting in the gorgeous CD *Zero Church*). Artists Brad McCallum and Jacqueline Tarry created an installation at King's Chapel documenting the toll of gun violence. A troupe of Broadway actors interviewed diverse members of the audience and then staged and performed the gathered stories. The Girls Choir of Harlem teamed up with psychologist Carol Gilligan. Filmmaker Isaac Julian made a film about talk radio shock jocks. Robert Brustein, director of the American Repertory Theatre, got into dustups at discussion groups over his views of "political correctness." We all got to create, perform, observe. We all got to be critics. We argued a lot.

There was also a so-called core audience, a group of people from literally all walks of life who committed themselves to come to a minimum number of events over the course of the institute's life, who followed those events all over the greater Boston area and beyond, from Cambridge to Chelsea to Chinatown, from Roxbury to Lincoln, from theaters and museums to churches, schools, living rooms. I call them remarkable, even though they represented a diverse cross section of "ordinary" people. Yet they wrote songs too, they created scripts, they gave voice. They maintained a vibrant long-term conversation, a true civic engagement. The spirit of that commitment is summed up in one of my favorite songs on the Roche sisters' *Zero Church*; it began as a list of guidelines for student council presidents written in the 1960s by Kent Keith, then a student at Harvard. It has floated around in several different versions, one of which was erroneously attributed to Mother Teresa. The faux–Mother Teresa version was submitted to the Roche sisters by a member of the core audience and they set it to music:

People are often unreasonable, illogical and self-centered,
    Forgive 'em anyway.
If you are kind, people may accuse you of selfish ulterior
      motives,
    Be kind anyway.
If you are successful, you will win some false friends and
      some true enemies,
    Succeed anyway.
If you are honest and frank people may cheat you,
    Be honest and frank anyway.
What you spend years building someone may destroy
      overnight,
    Build anyway.
And if you find serenity and happiness they may be jealous,
    Be happy anyway.
The good you do today people will often forget tomorrow,
    Do good anyway.
Give the world the best you have, it may never be enough,
    Give the world the best you've got anyway . . .

Journalist friends of mine are always wondering how to encourage candor in their interviewees, but watching that core audience grapple with unfolding levels of self-revelation convinced me that real candor across race and class boundaries simply doesn't emerge without a great deal of time, effort, anger, and, ultimately, trust. For example, the third summer, during a discussion after one of the shows, a black woman in the audience volunteered that a perplexed white man sitting next to her had just leaned over and asked her what she had made of some complexity in the performance. It was a small, casual, offhanded question, she said, "but it struck me because in all my life I don't recall a white man asking me what I thought about anything." As of this writing, some five years later, about fifty members of the institute's core audience still meet, still party, and still discuss things by e-mail—they represent the most fruitful result of the institute's work: the seeding of ideas and the incentive, the space, to keep on working things out.

Anna pushed everyone to do something they wouldn't do under ordinary circumstances. In the first week of the first summer, she paired me up with the legendary jazz saxophonist Oliver Lake and told us to get busy.

And so we set to work.

"We think of the theater as a three-walled place," read my notes of Anna's instructions to us. "We think of it as the proscenium stage, but to me, the theater has a fourth wall, and that wall is held up by the core audience. Traditionally, the fourth wall is invisible, and we think of 'using the fourth wall' as a way of . . . giving [actors] a focus . . . without being disturbed by the presence of the audience. The idea of the institute is that the presence of the audience is crucial and that the important moment is exactly when the artist acknowledges their presence. Ultimately, I think there is a moat between the stage and the fourth wall, and in the institute we're trying to fill that moat with vigorous discussion, inquiry, and struggle."

I swam at the end of the moat filled with struggle. I tried so hard to be an artist. I do have my talents, but let's just say that there is little of the relaxed, jovial ham in my heart and no discernible grasp of the musical arts. Anyone who can find a beat beneath my voice is a genius. Luckily for both of us, Oliver Lake is a genius.

Over the course of those years of the institute's existence, we produced three works: *An Evening of Words and Jazz*, *Obstacle Illusions*, and *Y2K*. I attribute the success of those pieces—and successful they were—entirely to Oliver. Oliver has a very cool, loose jazzman's kind of personality, and he filled the stage with spilling, intense, magically improvised riffs. I am very tight and teacherly. I stuck to my text. But somehow it worked, if in an eccentric, gently comic way. The contrast of our styles formed a dialogue all by itself: his complex, expressive, saxophoned poetry versus my prim, lady-lawyer, eternally lecturing, lectern-clutching delivery. It was a weird model of diplomacy in action, an unlikely harmony achieved with two completely different vibrations—his improvisational stream of colorful motifs dancing around the immovable column of my atonal solemnity. (It is a collaboration that has lasted, by the way, in case you wish to book us. We do the conference circuit and are available for the birthdays and weddings of the extremely serious minded.)

What did we get from this experience? Or as Anna put it, "What does the artist gain and lose in coming out of the studio to engage with the world? And what does the public gain by trusting the fools and the clowns of the world with these issues?" Personally, I was humbled by the experience of trying to present my thoughts in a different idiom, another world. But working with Oliver gave me firsthand observation of someone to whom that fluency across idiom comes much more easily. For example, we would each have an idea. I would put my idea out as a formal premise, neatly ironed into subject-verb-predicate. He would take his idea and break it apart like a prism. His idea would have a bass line to keep you riveted and a flute part to make your spine sing, and a poem to connect it to your imagination and some body language to keep your feet tapping. Then he'd craft it so that all I had to do was float my grammatical battleship on top. He dressed up our political conversations with the complexity of a jazz concerto. This is a tremendously interesting phenomenon, particularly for a lawyer, and it is a tribute to his creativity and patience that he was able to render us a team.

In the end, what we accomplished is all too rare: a sustained political discussion, a kind of civic dialogue. Plus some good music. Despite the grim misfortune of my Nixonian performance style, we both gained new audiences. I learned my own limits while simultaneously expanding my range. Most of all, I learned that beyond the invisible wall and deep in the invisible moat there lurk invisible alligators. And so I learned about building good strong bridges.

II

The Outhouse

W hat hand gestures do you have in common with your mother?" Merry Conway had asked. I was thinking furiously, the camera rolling. She and her associate, Noni Pratt, are two of the artists I met at the Institute on the Arts and Civic Dialogue. They do things like make witty film documentaries of people's unrehearsed answers to odd, intriguing questions, and I was stuck. Everyone else they'd interviewed had shared memories of his or her mother's hands engaged in domestic rituals: cooking and cleaning, more cleaning, then a little extra cooking. There were hands patting tortillas, pinching gnocchi, rolling rice balls, punching bread dough, pounding herbs. There were sweeping hands, polishing hands, wringing hands, and washing hands. Perhaps Conway and Pratt had anticipated this industrious slant; the film was, after all, part of a larger installation they had assembled, titled *A Woman's Work Is Never Done*—a monumental collage of found and donated objects, reenactments, and graffiti.

My mother was an affably casual housekeeper by comparison. My father went out into the world and earned money and dealt with all that that entailed as best he could. My mother stayed home and kept us amused. She had been a school-teacher and had quit her job in order to raise my younger sister and me. Not a day went by that she didn't remind herself how lucky she was not to be filling out an endless stream of administrative reports but rather curled up comfortably in the big armchair, reading with her two perfect offspring, reading long novels aloud, with both patience and passion. She was not in any sense a traditional homemaker, which is not to say our life wasn't orderly. It's just that we had few domestic rituals apart from reading.

We passed long happy afternoons chatting and snacking and reading. It was blissful. I understand Proust's madeleine through my own palate of happily conjoined recollections: J. D. Salinger and Langston Hughes are summoned for me by the taste of radishes and cream cheese. Ralph Waldo Emerson and Superman comics float upon the scent of cinnamon toast and tea.

My mother is funny and kind and a marvelous storyteller, just the kind of mother my sister has become, always upbeat and optimistic. My sister gestures like my mother; whenever they are about to say something, their hands whip the air like eggbeaters or the propellers on a twin-engine plane. It's a pity I didn't inherit more of that internal combustion, but I am definitely on the grim end of the family spectrum, always weighed down with the events of the world, not at all flecked with bright spots or levity.

The camera was still rolling.

Merry and Noni are patient artists, very encouraging. Merry was actually trained as a clown—a real circus clown—and Noni can stand on her head. That alone is enough to make them friends to brag about. Besides, they are also among the few nonlawyer friends I have, and I am unduly grateful when I drop references to their latest unorthodox adventure at bar association functions. I remember the first time I saw an exhibit of theirs, embodying what they billed as "the practice of community." I heard that description a little too offhandedly and was expecting something along the lines of an art-themed Quaker meeting. So I was taken off guard. I walked unsuspectingly from the dark impersonal loneliness of Manhattan's SoHo district at night into what felt like some combination of a small city and my mother's brain. It was like entering an attic world of endless dress-up games—but one where all the memories had come alive.

There were collections of love letters, heaps of old clothes, meticulous arrangements of cosmetics I hadn't seen in years. (Evening in Paris perfume! Pomatex Hair Dressing! Sweetheart Soap!) A great part of it was a memorial to the twentieth century's ideal of domesticity, but it was no mere higgledy-piggledy heap of nostalgia. It was also a living organism, a whirl of an event, an active witnessing of actual women's lives. After all, the exhibit was not culled from secondhand shops or estate sales; rather, Merry and Noni had borrowed each of the items—each of the thousands and thousands of objects—from real mothers and real daughters. All those possessions and mementos were painstakingly cataloged, all lovingly placed in masterfully overwhelming profusion, hidden, spilled, exposed, a constant play between what should and should not be seen.

And so there were walls with peepholes and cracks through which one could spy actors performing all the little rituals of private anxiety about appearance and femininity: applying lipstick, trying to see if the back of one's skirt is smooth, worrying and patting and preening in front of the mirror. There were little living rooms about the size of a child's playhouse in which actors read scripts of real domestic discord, little kitchens in which women cooked perfect Betty Crocker meals, little boudoirs spilling over with hundreds of hand-crocheted doilies. There were smiling hostesses proffering platters of cocktail franks on toothpicks, a ceaseless procession of brides unto the altar, scraps of paper with jotted anxieties, and a dark hall filled with "women's depression." (I'm sure it must have been the lighting, or the thermostat, but it certainly felt as though they had managed to pump depression into the very air of that room. You could breathe the madness, like chilled ether.)

Hours after I entered the gallery, I went back out into the emptiness of SoHo's backstreets, but with a bright noise inside me. I was exhilarated, confused—a laser show of memories blazed in my head. I wondered what had happened to my confirmation dress. It was beautiful, a rich yellowy cream, with stitched-in pleats and little red roses embroidered at the top of each pleat. It was my first really grown-up dress, and it precipitated a huge fight with my parents because I wanted to wear nylon stockings with it to church. But this was 1963. They made me wear white wool knee socks instead.

I wondered what had happened to those letters from my first boyfriend and my lucky chain made of Juicy Fruit gum wrappers and my Beatles cards. For years I kept a stash of Beatles cards and fan magazines hidden under my mattress. I had a crush on Paul McCartney, which embarrassed me terribly. I was "the colored kid" in an all-white class and knew well where the line was. In fourth grade I'd made the mistake of telling an indiscreet friend that I liked a boy best known in that class as "the Italian kid." He was repulsed by my affection, and the other children used it to make cruel fun of him. I learned early that having a crush on white idols was not something one confessed to easily or at all.

I wondered what had become of the industrial-sized compact of original Max Factor Pan-Cake makeup I had borrowed—well, sneaked—from my great-aunt's dresser and forgotten to return. It was an unnatural undertaker's-orange kind of color and she used it generously—"foundation," she called it, in tones that implied all Rome rested thereupon. It came in round oily cakes the size and heft of fruitcakes, and when my miserable adolescent visage erupted in the glowing, pustular protuberances that won me the nickname "Headlights," that tub of foundation was the only thing I could see being up to the job. I slathered it on thick as bricks, a wall behind which I hid to make it through the day. Years later when Kermit the Frog sang his lonely little anthem, "It's Not Easy Being Green," I wept, remembering that it also wasn't easy being orange.

My wave of nostalgia took me back to the days when all girls wore slips. We had an overflowing dresser drawer full of slips (the straight kind that always hung just a half inch too long as well as the stiff puffy ones that you wore beneath the bell-shaped poodle skirts of the 1950s. I remembered Jeannie, the red-haired girl who lived across the street. She had a slip with a little plastic inner tube around the perimeter that you had to blow up so it stood out in a perfect circle, like a hula hoop stitched into the hem. We were all so envious until she tried to sit down in it.

I thought of my prized tube of lip gloss, my treasured Ouija board, my mood ring. My bride doll—she was among the last of the entirely flat-chested bride dolls, a fact I remember well because I acquired her just around the time Barbie was becoming popular. My parents viewed Barbie's conical plastic breasts as much too sexually suggestive. And so I suppose it's no surprise that they found me a bride doll who wore little white knee socks and carried a missal.

I left Merry and Noni's exhibit with my grandmother's smell of lavender and pine needles suddenly in mind, with my mother's warnings about using potholders warm in my heart. I left with a hundred little memories of growing up a girl in a certain era, with a thousand recollected intimacies of all it has taken to turn me into this, a woman of a certain age.

The truth is I don't understand conceptual art on any but this most instinctive level. I am intrigued by artists like William

Pope.L, who has been known to chain himself to a Chase bank with sausage links while dressed only in a skirt of dollar bills as he handed free money to the bank's clientele. His contribution to the Whitney Biennial consisted of crawling on his hands and knees through all five boroughs of New York, to symbolize the humility and labors of the workers who made the city great. It took him months to do the entire circuit, but apparently he'd timed it carefully, so as to arrive at the Whitney's threshold just in time for the gala opening and cocktail party. For a future biennial, I advised Merry and Noni, they ought to enter a documentary of women careening through all five boroughs in that urban tank known as an SUV, from home to office to gym, while simultaneously dropping off and picking up hundreds of random children from school, play dates, soccer, music, and tennis—to symbolize the excessive labors of the modern professional female. Performances twice daily.

"Your mother's hands?" they prompted gently. And I told them instead about my grandmother's.

When I was very little, my grandmother told stories like my mother's, although hers were more in the way of strange cautionary tales about what to do in case of accidental enslavement, or how to cure the influenza with kale juice and crushed walnuts, or how to build a house on a desert island with only a hatpin, a hairpin, and a box of onions. I would sit close beside her, she would hug me, and I would lean into her and listen.

When I was seven, she suffered a stroke and sank into silence. Although I still sat beside her and she would still hold me with one arm, she would lean with her weight on the other elbow, as though in resignation, cupping her chin with her hand, fingers across her mouth, eyes half closed, entirely turned inward, lost in dreams.

My mother says I grew to imitate that gesture perfectly, and to this day, whenever I am pensive I lean into my hand, mouth covered, as though retrieving the curious comfort of her wordless love.

"Cut!" said Merry.

"How perfect," said Noni. They are very gracious friends.

The image of my hand supporting the lower half of my head played on a loop in an anteroom of *A Woman's Work Is Never Done*. It seemed a very still picture beside all the busy, deft flutterings of other people's signaled recollections. But with this small testament, other memories came undone—the rest flying not from my hands but from my mouth. For months thereafter, I dreamed of ticker tapes of text issuing from my mouth, of spaghetti streams of stories, lists, and thank-you notes.

My mother says that when she was growing up, my grandmother was a large, fierce person who baked bread and cleaned house and grew turnips and beat rugs. She wasn't entirely typical of the women of her generation, in that she'd studied for two years at Rust College in Mississippi, one of the all-black colleges set up in the hopeful times immediately after the Civil War. Going to college was particularly unusual for a black woman in those days, but Rust was also the alma mater of the remarkable journalist and antilynching activist Ida B. Wells, and while I do not know if they knew each other personally, my grandmother and mother often cited her accomplishments, and we were instructed to be like her. It was only as an adult that I began to realize how privileged I was to grow up in a house where that kind of open political strength in women was appreciated, even taken for granted.

In her twenties, my grandmother worked as a receptionist and executive secretary for the staunchly reputable Boston portrait photographer David Bachrach, whose family business remains to this day the preeminent iconographer of Boston society. My mother describes him as "a fine old gentleman" who always treated my grandmother "as one does a first-class citizen. She was respected. And well paid." Bachrach paid her on a par with white employees, in other words. By all accounts, my grandmother stood up for herself. When one of Bachrach's clients told racist watermelon stories, she "took him right on," according to my mother.

What does that mean—took him on—I asked.

"She looked him straight in the eye and demanded, 'Why are you saying such things in my presence?' " (If only I'd had the presence of mind to tongue-lash J.B. with that one!) My mother explains demurely, "We Ross women"—Ross was my grandmother's maiden name—"have always been feisty."

My grandmother left her position at Bachrach's establishment when she met the quiet, good-natured man who became my grandfather. She married in her thirties and had four children, the last well into her forties. My mother was the second of these—"the middle child," she always called herself. "I was the reliable one," she says with rueful pride. Her reliability was always a kind of shadowy second to the legendary beauty of her elder sister, Elizabeth. When Aunt Elizabeth was about twelve, she was hit by a speeding taxicab and hovered near death for a very long time. During the awful hours after the accident, my mother remembers standing on the front porch, listening as the news spread among the neighbors. "Which one was it?" asked a voice. "The pretty one," replied another. "Oh, no!" responded the first.

To my mother, little in life ever rivaled the unkindness of that comment. No comparison with either of her two other siblings ever came close. Even many years later, when I was growing up, the same neighbors were still referring to Elizabeth's looks, or to my mother's younger sister's academic brilliance, or to her little brother's charming but devilish ways. And so the sense that she was a dull gosling haunted my mother, a fear that she was drably utilitarian and vaguely dispensable. But there were other layers to the power of "pretty," particularly in the mouths of those neighbors: It meant more than just a ranking of the sisters. While it must be acknowledged that my aunt Elizabeth, now in her late eighties, is still by all measures a strikingly handsome woman, in that time and place (perhaps no less today), the people on my mother's street used "pretty" as code to signify who in the family was "the fairest"—as Snow White's evil stepmother put it—who was the least ethnic, who had the straightest hair, who had the greatest chances for social acceptance among them and in the wider world.

Mine was the only African-American family in the area for the first half of the twentieth century; the neighbors were working-class immigrants from all over Europe. They were from Ireland, Germany, Russia, southern Italy, and Portugal. They had a multitude of good reasons for wanting to escape to the United States and carried their traumas with them. They prospered in this neighborhood of "workmen's cottages"— small wooden-frame houses built by the great New England breweries of that era, like Haffenreffer and Reingold. The post-1950s analysis that might call this "upward mobility" was not a prominent feature of their thinking as I recall it. Rather, the dynamic was pointedly calibrated toward rebutting the humiliations of peasant status. "Peasant" was an epithet equivalent to what in other parts of the country might have been phrased as "white trash." Fighting words.

Eventually, this self-consciousness emerged as the full-blown anxiety about middle-classness that today marks much of American social life, but at that time I remember my neighbors being more fully intent upon erasing every last ethnic marker they could. They were so extremely focused on how they might be "seen," so worried about how to wrap themselves in the symbolic trappings of America as a means to escape the oppressions of the Old World. They laughed at their elders' accents. They studied Shirley Temple movies. They anglicized their names. They cringed at stories about jovial

Italian organ grinders as much as my family shuddered at stories about grinning banjo-picking slaves. They hated their noses or their brothers' ginger hair or their fathers' crinkly black mustachios. They looked down upon anyone whose large toe exceeded the length of the second, for an elongated second toe was an unquestioned indicator of elegance and royal blood. There were people in my neighborhood who proudly and loudly traced their lineage to disgraceful degrees of royal bastardy, people who looked to Cinderella as allegorical redemption. They—we all—yearned so much to "pass."

Luckily, everyone in my family is blessed with long, elegant second toes.

My sister and I were always "the Negro children" or, in warm fuzzy moments, "the colored kids." Yet I'm not sure that any of those recent-immigrant neighbors ever fully thought of themselves as truly white until the beginning of the great migration of blacks from the South to the North, the migration that peaked in the early 1960s and that transformed urban centers into inner cities.

One way of looking at it is that America's own rural population, the dark-skinned serfs and abused peasantry of home-grown origin, flooded into the workmen's cottages and factory jobs of the industrial North as had hopeful Europeans a generation or two before. But when the first black family other than ours, a family of former sharecroppers from Mississippi, moved into the neighborhood, they weren't greeted as just part of another aspiring migrant wave. They had two little boys who took the same route to school that we did. I can remember walking some distance behind them, observing the adults on my street observe the boys. It was alarming watching face after face, house after house, peer from behind a busyness of curtains. It made my stomach hurt with fear to see these people I had thought of as friends so constricted with tight, frowning disapproval. I would like to think that those neighbors saw something of themselves in the black laborers who came to settle in their midst. "They lope like farmers!" sneered one haughty neighbor who was herself the grandchild of potato farmers. It is the most forgiving interpretation I can attach to the panic that characterized the wholesale exodus that was white flight.

Times have changed since I was a child, as has the demography of the American landscape. Ethnicity is fashionable, even for blacks, particularly now that we have hyphenated ourselves into African-American personages. The rape-qua-breeding system that enhanced slavery's profits has been reconstructed as eternally unconsummated, star-crossed love, like Evangeline, or Romeo and Juliet. Tragic mulattas like Sally Hemings have been reconfigured as irresistibly fetching, made-for-TV soap-operatic minxes who lead good men astray. Tiger Woods is the new everyman—well, not exactly the new white everyman; more like the new brand of idealized black everyman—not really black but mixed, diluted, watered down if you will, or "whited up," as the Brits so crudely put it. Less potently fearsome. Exotic. Refined. Cablinasian.

Recently, Conway and Pratt installed *A Woman's Work Is Never Done* in a warehouse in my old neighborhood. They invited the neighbors, new immigrants from new parts of the world—Haiti, Bangladesh, Dominican Republic—to come in and share their stories, contribute to the organic jumble of artifacts that told of how women were raised and with what rituals. Over the course of just a few days, the objects began to mount—the Bibles, the prayer cloths, the photos ("taken the week before we fled"), the haunting bits of correspondence ("There are some things I can say to you only in Persian . . .").

Back in my own home, I dug through old storage boxes to find an unsent thank-you note I once penned to my great-aunt

Mary, to whom my mother has always compared me when she's in a bad mood. Aunt Mary was a sardonic personality whose gifts to us children had a daunting, old-school quality that made them seem like punishment.

January 3, 1962

Dear Aunt Mary,
Thank you so much for the grey wool suit you sent for Christmas. It is beautiful and I am looking forward to wearing it to church. I particularly liked the rabbit-fur muff. I also liked the white gloves and ankle socks. My sister liked hers too. She is writing a thank you note of her own. We have always wanted to look like twins. And you are quite right that if I can't have a dog, a grey wool suit is the next best thing. Thank you so much.
                              Your loving niece,
                              Patricia

My mother made me rewrite the note, leaving off the last three sentences. Finding this draft made me smile. Dogs were literally for farmhands, according to Aunt Mary. Young ladies wore gloves. But then, among the litter of old correspondence, I found another letter, one that made me frown, this one from the fifteen-year-old daughter of a friend. It was a complex message, one that made me feel that perhaps I had become Aunt Mary, after all, true to my mother's chastening comparison.

January 5, 2001

Dear Tanty-Pat,
Thank you so much for the box of your favorite clothes before you put on the weight. Although school requires that I wear an unadorned navy blue uniform, I shall enjoy wear-

ing them to chic parties and charity events. As your letter
indicates, the rage for pleated silk suits is not unknown in
my age group . . .

Kids have such smart mouths these days. Wherever are
their editors?

My grandmother was one of five sisters, born into a family of
so-called house servants. House *slaves* would be more precise,
but when people have only a peephole onto the landscape of
human dignity, I guess they still put curtains up to make the
view more pleasing. They were born in Bolivar, Tennessee,
but all migrated to Boston as soon as they came of age. Bolivar
was where a white landowner named Austin Miller had impregnated his slave, my great-great-grandmother Sophie. Sophie's child by him was my great-grandmother, named Mary.
It was a sentimental touch, I suppose; Mary was Miller's wife's
name. Indeed, over the ensuing years, Miller's generous wife
busied herself with the instruction of slave children, particularly the light-skinned ones. She made sure they were all
raised to be chaste, obedient, church-going Episcopalians,
and, after the Emancipation Proclamation, hurried them into
respectable arranged marriages.

So it came to pass, in an act comprehensible only within
the complicated pathology of those times, that Sophie's
daughter, my great-grandmother Mary, named her own eldest
daughter—my great-aunt—Mary too. She named another of
her daughters Mattie, after one of Austin Miller's white
daughters, whose actual name was Martha. The black Mattie,
who was my grandmother, never liked her name; she considered it a nickname and therefore demeaning. It was only as an
adult that I began to see her resentment as more complexly
related to slavery than the simple indignity of "nickname."
The incestuous underside of slave-naming practice, so com-

mon in the Old South, was a cipher for much deeper patterns of disrespect and extreme dysfunction in slave-owning families.

When my great-aunt Mary was only five years old, one of Miller's white daughters married and moved with her husband to the big city of St. Louis. After the birth of her first child, she apparently became depressed and very homesick for Tennessee. Her father decided to ease her burdened heart by sending my great-aunt, the first generation to be born out of slavery, as helpmate to the new mother. Aunt Mary stayed in St. Louis until she was thirteen, part servant, part beneficiary (for benefit it was to those so recently emancipated) of an education at a local "Indian school," as they were called then, as well as at the knee of the white child's tutor.

"You have to understand," my mother would say years later when Aunt Mary would order us all around like the unsurpassedly arrogant grande dame she had become. "She was taken from her family at age five or six. She was supposed to lend the Miller daughter comfort when she herself was little more than a baby. She grew up without guidance in a household that flattered her with certain privileges but spoke of blacks with great contempt."

And indeed it must have been a rift in my aunt's life. Close to her ninetieth birthday she still spoke with uncertain, half-excited apprehension about the day she left her family and was put on the train to St. Louis. "I remember the little velvet dress I wore," she would begin, never getting much farther with the story.

When she reached puberty, Mary's utility to the Miller family apparently expired. She was packed up and summarily sent back to Tennessee. I wondered if she had ever come home to visit during all those years. I asked my mother, who responded impatiently, "Slavery may have ended, but they still thought of her as chattel. Do you send cats and dogs back to where they were born because you think they miss their families?"

Leaving the bright lights of St. Louis to return to rural Tennessee was not a happy homecoming for my great-aunt Mary. Her siblings seemed "unsophisticated" to her, and she looked down upon them, quite unforgivingly, ever after. When I was little I remember her complaining about how hot and small Bolivar had seemed upon her return, how dusty the streets, how dirty the children. My mother rounds out other details of that time by revealing that Mr. Ross, Mary's father, worried about her. He was a French-Canadian musician who'd grown up in Canada and settled in Memphis to play with a band there. He was not used to the way the South worked and was alarmed by Mary's indenture. He worried about the fate of his other daughters—it was dangerous to have "pretty" black daughters in those days. There was nothing in the way of civil or legal recourse during the early times of the Jim Crow era. They were some of the most violent years of post–Civil War backlash. Mr. Ross committed himself to sending them to school so they could be economically self-sufficient and beyond too-easy approach. He put his two sons to work instead; their wages helped pay for the education of all the girls except Mary, who, as in all things, had already struck out on her own.

Family lore has it that soon after her return from St. Louis, Mary, miserable as usual, had retired to the outhouse to weep. Those were times when newsprint had a dual function, times before the Scott Paper Company had refined the pillowy sheets of rolled softness with which most of us in the industrialized world find comfort today. And so for that function, there hung from a hook an old magazine. My aunt Mary reached for a page and was about to consign it to its end use when she spied an advertisement printed thereupon. Garland Junior College, in Boston, Massachusetts, was offering scholarships to Indian maidens. While it is true that John Ross, the Cherokee leader of the Trail of Tears, was a relation, that was never the dominant cultural influence in her life. But . . . here was a path to Boston! Where abolitionists had conspired!

Thus began my aunt's long life of inspired and ambitious deception.

As a full-blooded Indian princess, my aunt made a most appealing royal exotic. In any event, Garland Junior College was a very proper finishing school for wealthy young ladies of the region, and she made friends among quite a slice of Boston's more rarified classes. She excelled at what was then known as declamation and was soon renowned for her dramatic renderings of long, sentimental soliloquies. She would loosen her hair, don a series of costumes much in the neoclassical style of Sarah Bernhardt, and perform in morality plays with titles like *Everywoman*. She would traipse about the stage in all apparent seriousness, encountering toga-draped sprites that embodied such virtues as Truth, Beauty, and Modesty, unto whom she would confide that

> . . . In my dreams
> I thought myself a flower. And then, anon,
> I was a star, to whom men bowed in worship.
> Yet again, I thought myself a Queen.
> > The dawn hath braver stories far to tell,
> For, see! I am a woman!—and to be
> A woman meaneth flower, star, Queen—
> And much, much more, besides.

In the margins would be little penciled notes to herself with instructions like "Enter fairies. Dance, etc."

Aunt Mary took Boston by storm.

Aunt Mary graduated from Garland with the equivalent of a teacher's certificate. Soon afterward, Booker T. Washington

hired her as governess for his daughter, Portia. Later he employed her to set up a kindergarten at Tuskegee Institute. She
seemed to recognize some of herself in Mr. Washington's relentless assimilationism. At the same time, she, like many
black people of that era, distrusted him as too accommodating
of segregationist policies of "separate but equal." She thought
of him as someone who was unduly "grateful" not to have
been killed in the violence of those times and who therefore
viewed even the barest civility from white people with nothing less than "obsequiousness." To Aunt Mary, it was one
thing to act like one "knew one's place" as a survival strategy;
it was another thing entirely to be grateful just because you
hadn't yet been lynched.

Nevertheless, Washington "was the most brilliant man I
ever met," she often said. She described him as "truly bilin-
gual" in that "he would speak one way to white people and
very differently to Negroes. He had two entirely distinct ways
of being," and she admired that ability. According to Aunt
Mary, Mr. Washington was impatient, emotionally direct,
folksy yet stern with black people. But he grew sonorously eloquent, elaborately polite, and "showed his teeth" to whites.
(Perhaps "showing one's teeth" is not a general enough expression to pass without explanation. It means to smile falsely.
I belong to a book group that read Zadie Smith's *White Teeth*
some time ago. I was startled when all the white members of
the group were mystified by the title, had trouble deciphering
the meaning. It was like stumbling on some hidden cultural
IQ test about the amount of work that goes into forcing smiles
when one is in low-status positions of having to please. Very
few black or brown people—or perhaps anyone with a direct
relation to subservience—would have trouble understanding
the reference immediately, I think.)

In any event, my lifelong opinion of Booker T. Washington's concessionary, separate-but-equal, "fingers-of-the-hand"

recommendations were very much influenced by my initially childish but nonetheless clear political algebra of Aunt Mary's insight into the power of dangerously studied charm.

Under Jim Crow, living separately, however purportedly equally, meant enduring a class system that ranked black people as a race apart, exiles in a homeland whose boundaries would always be fixed by others. Not only was it not really equal, it was never really separate. White people could always go where they wished in black communities; black people moved through white homes and businesses according to strict codes of permission and carefully observed strictures about where to sit, what doors to go through, where to eat, when to speak, and whether they could use the toilet. The power of these invisible lines is illustrated by a story recounted by the great legal historian Leon Higginbotham: A white man and a black man went fishing together during the Jim Crow era. They rowed out to the middle of the lake and fished companionably all morning long. When it was lunchtime, the white man took an oar and laid it across the middle of the boat, thus imposing a "white" and a "colored" section for the duration of the meal.

This condition could be rationalized a number of ways: "Who wants to be around white people anyway?" was one defensive strategy, leading to a kind of investment in segregation as protective. "We can beat them at their own game" was another, often leading to a kind of relentlessly imitative performance of the manners and mores deemed—or ceded—to be the characteristics or privileges of whiteness. Then there was the overlapping strategy of being two-faced, or bicultural, or code switching—of having to be very careful in one world, of being more "real" in the other. W.E.B. DuBois tried to make the mending of that split a political project. Booker T. Washington, according to my great-aunt, maneuvered the divide by telling white people what they wanted to hear—a trait many black people still denounce as unduly concessionary and

servile—as a way of negotiating privileges and funding that
would serve specific interests of the black community. For her
part, Aunt Mary, like hundreds of thousands of others who
looked like her, chose a path of outright duplicity, in "steal-
ing" the protective cloak of nonblackness. Aunt Mary shaped,
honed, polished, and practiced her transformative powers until they glowed. If being "Indian" was regarded as more exotic,
less taboo, in the New England of those days—well, then, she
would employ every potion at her disposal to become Indian.
When she donned that magical cloak, her hindersome African ancestors became invisible; they disappeared as though
by the wave of a wand.

Aunt Mary had a long and lucky life. She outlived all her husbands. She met her first through the wife of Andrew Peters,
mayor of Boston from 1918 until 1922. Mrs. Peters was a close
friend and classmate at Garland; she introduced Mary to Mr.
Joseph Dorsey, who was that rarest of beings, a black realtor in
Cambridge, Massachusetts. Aunt Mary married him quickly.
He was "a good provider" by all accounts, and soon she sent
for her sisters. Their father had always been eager for his
daughters to leave the South; and his now-educated daughters
had been exposed to the ideas of Ida B. Wells, who thought
that migration to the North was the best solution to Jim Crow.
And so they left Tennessee, one by one, and came to stay with
Mary. "Mr. Dorsey was such a wonderful gentleman," remembers my mother. "He always treated Mary and her sisters
with the greatest respect. And those sisters basically took over
his house. He was a good, good man."

Poor Mr. Dorsey. It is overwhelming, the thought of all five
of my beautiful, bickering, strong-willed, and opinionated
great-aunts living under one roof. Soon after their arrival, and
under the aegis of Mr. Dorsey's amiable generosity, all four of
Mary's sisters married and purchased homes of their own. Sis-

ters Rose, Sophie, and Clara stayed close to Mary in Cambridge, where they all lived within a block of one another. Mattie, my grandmother, and her husband moved to our modest Boston neighborhood, the one dominated by breweries, surely the more interesting choice in that it provided a rather substantial and enduring buffer against middle-class pretension.

Their two brothers stayed behind in Tennessee and were trained by their father to play a variety of musical instruments. The sons followed in their father's footsteps and eventually became accomplished jazz musicians and members of W. C. Handy's band. Somewhere in Memphis, my mother tells me, there is or was once a square named for one of those great-uncles, but I have never been able to find it.

Everyone profited from Aunt Mary's marriage to Mr. Dorsey, certainly insofar as the housing market was concerned. The sisters were among a handful of black families in the Cambridge area, most of whom knew each other. Their homes, a mere stone's throw from Harvard and not very far from MIT, Tufts, and the many other great educational institutions in the area, became gathering places for all the displaced, lonely black intellectuals of the era. Harvard University admitted only the occasional black student—almost always because they didn't know the candidate was black—and then, having discovered it, they discouraged him from coming. Even when admitted, black students were not permitted to live in Harvard's dorms, and so, over the years, my great-aunts were among those local black families who hosted teas and dinners for, or let out rooms to, Harvard's students of color and other visiting scholars.

"On Sunday afternoons, everyone would come visiting," says my mother. "Aunt Mary and Aunt Sophie would slice the cake thinner and thinner as more and more people showed up." Wade McCree, the first black solicitor general, was a family friend. The writer Langston Hughes read bedtime stories to the children. The historian John Hope Franklin would drop by to chat. Don Pedro Albizu Campos, who later became the icon of the Puerto Rican Nationalist movement, stayed on the third floor of Aunt Sophie's home. (Years later, in the 1950s, after some members of that movement opened fire upon the U.S. Congress, one of my mother's cousins was denied a passport because the government had a photo of her, at the age of ten, standing on the front steps of the house in the company of Don Pedro. A wise judge reversed that denial, citing her obvious minority. But how the photo ended up in government hands remains a mystery to this day.)

Mr. Dorsey and Aunt Mary had one child, Marjory—my godmother—who very much resembled her father's side of the family, which is to say that she was quite dark skinned. To Aunt Mary's way of seeing things, this was a misfortune. When presented with her newborn, she denied that it could have been hers.

"There must have been some mix-up," she is reported to have said.

"God works in mysterious ways," muttered the aunts for decades thereafter.

Aunt Mary and Mr. Dorsey were divorced when Marjory was quite young. Mr. Dorsey eventually married a childhood friend, a podiatrist with a thriving business. My mother is oblique in her disapproval: "Once you go to a podiatrist, I have observed that you have to go for life. They scrape your foot down to raw nerve, and then apply a little cream, and by the time you walk around your foot is sore again, just in time for the next appointment. So I have never gone to one."

That was my great-aunt's first marriage.

Aunt Mary went off to make her way in the world, this time as an actress, leaving her daughter in Cambridge to be cared for by her sisters.

Aunt Mary had built a modest reputation for herself performing drawing-room soliloquies while a student at Garland.

Now she took that act on the road. She traveled across the country presenting a variety of gentlewomanly monologues in small theaters and churches, sponsored by a myriad of ladies' tea societies and social clubs. In pictures from this period, she was always posed with eyes turned heavenward, one hand upon either her brow (palm out) or her heart (palm in). My favorite photo is one of her reciting Longfellow's *Hiawatha*; she stood gussied up in a full-length beaded doeskin dress with a tropically feathered headband, trailing a stole of little furry creatures with their heads intact.

Aunt Mary supported herself well enough to travel first-class—even though in those days, of course, public transport was segregated. I'll try to give it the nicest spin I can muster: Let us try to imagine that she didn't really mean to deny her heritage when she stepped over the color line and onto the club car. We will constrain ourselves to the observation that there could be no human being less cut out for steerage than she. In this way she became an early pioneer of "don't ask, don't tell" assimilationism and, once emboldened by no one's asking, settled into the comfortable habit of never, ever telling.

And so it came to pass that she found herself seated in the first-class compartment of a Chicago-bound train one sultry summer afternoon. She was musing upon the course of her life and fanning herself languorously (for Aunt Mary always carried a fan and smelling salts), when an elderly woman seated near her struck up a conversation. The woman, whose son had been recently widowed, was impressed by Aunt Mary's comeliness, her genteel comportment. "My son is so lonely . . . ," she confided to my fetching and unstintingly sympathetic great-aunt.

Within a year, Mary Ross Dorsey, born-again white woman, married Frederick Rotch Swift, a wealthy Harvard-educated lawyer from an old New England family of significant social standing. She was welcomed into the family with the warmest possible reception, first and foremost from his mother, who resided in a house that as far as I can determine later became the New Bedford Whaling Museum. It was at this point, according to family consensus, that Aunt Mary truly became unbearable.

Leading a double life is always hard, bound to make one touchy, and Mary was a character and a half to begin with. By the time I was born, the secret nicknames had accumulated within the Ross clan. Miss Scarlett. Miss Anne. Gardenia Petal. Our Lady of the Camelias. Lady Bountiful. Peacock Feathers. That impossible French poodle. Of course she had a name for us too, which she did not trouble to keep secret. To her, we were "the little brown gypsies." This is vocabulary of a different era, I suppose. Given the diplomatic tensions within the family, my great-aunt Mary became the vehicle by which my mother taught us wise little aphorisms. "Never substitute malice for wit," she would warn when the whispered name-calling reached her ears.

Aunt Mary lived very grandly even through the Depression and was listed in the New York and Boston social registers. The family dynamic acquired a complicated double edge of racial disguise: One cautionary tale within the family was about an uncle of mine who, when he had encountered Aunt Mary on a public street, insisted on recognizing and greeting her. It was partly a story about how awful she was for failing to acknowledge her own kin, but it was just as much a story about my uncle's incorrigible impertinence.

In this way, Aunt Mary was a complex example of the pathology, the cruelty, and, yes, the racism it took to deny not only one's individuality but also the connection to one's living, breathing family members. Passing bore the same ugly shape as the psychic denial white owners engaged in when they had children by their slaves but could not see themselves in the faces of those children: Mary's grandfather purchased her slave grandmother and had children by her that he

viewed only as property. Thus when Mary went to St. Louis to
tend the Miller daughter's children, she went as Cinderella,
the literally unacknowledged stepchild. Passing is, by any
other name, the practice of orphaning oneself.

Yet as emotionally costly as it was, Aunt Mary's choice did
not involve the kind of total break of all familial contact that
happened in some families, where brothers, cousins, and uncles went off and disappeared into the Other World. My
mother told me only recently that she thought that Mr. Swift
did have at least some idea that she was not really white. Aunt
Mary told her husband that she was "Indian"—as she had told
Garland—not black. (My mother works hard to lessen the
shame of it all: "Well, she was partly Indian, at least that
wasn't a lie . . .") Under that guise my mother and her sister—
the "poor Indian relations"— actually met Mr. Swift one year,
at his summer home in Kittery, Maine. If he indeed met my
mother's family, surely he must have had some notion that not
everyone was Native American. And if so, he apparently said
nothing, leading my mother to conclude that "he was an aris-
tocrat, a good man, like President Roosevelt." A credit to his
race. Indeed, in some conversations, my mother insists that
Aunt Mary never lied to Mr. Swift about race—a view contra-
dicted by most others in the family—and that she and Mr.
Swift only "kept up appearances" to keep the neighbors at bay.
"They couldn't have moved in his society unless they'd kept it
quiet," she says apologetically.

Among other relatives of my grandmother's generation,
there was an odd pride in Mary's having "gotten" this man to
marry her; it was viewed as a kind of accomplishment. I suppose that's a familiar sensation within any family where a
beautiful daughter marries "above her station," as Jane Austen
might have put it. But Aunt Mary's marriage to Mr. Swift had
its resonance because of race: She was, after all, the daughter
of a woman born into slavery. She was the granddaughter of a
white man who had raped his twelve-year-old slave. All other

white men with whom our family had ever had anything to do had been known only as "the master" or "sir." That Aunt Mary had "gotten" a respectable white man to marry her was seen as the kind of justice meted out by gods in Greek plays, a triumphant kind of vengeance. It was positively operatic: She was not Snow White, and he had no idea.

If there were some in the black community who enjoyed the secret a bit too much, it is also true that the truth was seeded with danger. People kept quiet because revelation risked unimaginable harm, not just scandal. No one feared Mr. Swift per se. But these were the 1920s, after all. Black people feared white retribution in general and as a matter of course; there were daily examples in the news of what happened to those who openly transgressed the racial divide.

If Aunt Mary did not respect her protective siblings as much as might have been desired, she was at least, it seems, devoted to this second husband. And from their correspondence, Mr. Swift (he may not have been "sir," but he certainly wasn't "Uncle Fred" either) comes across as an eloquent and courtly romantic. "My dearest wife," he wrote. "You are a perfect flower . . . How very much I love you."

During Aunt Mary's second marriage, which spanned from before the Great Depression to his death sometime around the Second World War, her blackness was a secret from her husband's family and white people in general but the subject of a great deal of gossip, even envy, throughout Boston's black community.

My grandmother and her sisters took in Mary's daughter Marjory for those years until that daughter left home, entered Boston University at the age of fifteen, and changed her name to Marguerite. She graduated Phi Beta Kappa and, still in her teens, married her math tutor, Carl, a white Floridian graduate student in chemistry at Harvard. This occurred in the late 1920s, so it was definitely one of the more interesting stories of the day. I don't know if it's true—this is rumor whose

substantiation I have yet to see with my own eyes—but supposedly the Harvard *Crimson* ran a story—I paraphrase
loosely—reporting that "Harvard Science Whiz Takes Dusky
Bride." Meanwhile the black Boston press ran a story—I paraphrase just as loosely—reporting something like "Prodigious
Hope for Future of Race Makes Ill-Considered Choice."

Another rumor has it that the marriage was the circumstance under which Marguerite finally met her stepfather,
Mr. Swift. This happened only because Aunt Mary told her
husband that Carl, the Science Whiz, was the child of her
first marriage. (Carl needed a surrogate family, I suppose,
since his parents and all his many siblings disinherited him
immediately upon getting the news.) But of course, in the act
of claiming Carl, Aunt Mary disinherited Marguerite, whom
she now must have presented to the world only as daughter-in-
law. The amount of dissimulation that this ruse must have required boggles the mind. My great-aunts died refusing to tell
me more details of how this might have been accomplished.
It is amazing that anyone came out of this emotional quag-
mire still standing—one too many theatrical Greek plot twists
seemed bound to wind up as tragedy—but in the end Carl
and Marguerite's was a marriage that lasted more than sixty
years, until his death in 1984. I have boxes of their letters to
each other over the decades. "Precious darling," begins each
of his missives to her, echoing, if somewhat more effusively,
Mr. Swift's affectionate letters to Aunt Mary. "Dearest," Marguerite writes back, "I have received your letter and it is a
happy day indeed . . ."

In fact, Aunt Mary's abandoned daughter, my mother's
cousin Marguerite, not only came out standing, she led an extraordinary life whose success was, at least at the emotional
level, very much against the odds. A woman of great resilience
and polymathic intelligence, she worked as an actress for a
short while—she is the "Beautifulest Angel" in the early film
Green Pastures. She earned her PhD in sociology and became

one of the first black professors at Hunter College. She also pursued a career in journalism, publishing regularly in *The Crisis* magazine, the *Chicago Defender*, the *Amsterdam News*, and the *Pittsburgh Courier*, ultimately becoming one of the first United Nations correspondents. She sat on the boards of many institutions, including the Overseas Press Club and the University of Nigeria, and she counted among her friends Golda Meir, Indira Gandhi, and Jomo Kenyatta's daughter Margaret.

Marguerite and Carl never had children. I don't know if that was the result of a particular decision, but among the studies she conducted while teaching sociology at Hunter was one about attitudes toward intermarriage. Among her effects was an entire shelf of index cards containing scores of responses to the question of whether interracial couples should have children. The interviewees, who apparently were her students in a class called American Negro Culture, presented every nutty, superstitious, hateful, hurtful reason in the world not to have children of mixed racial heritage—from its being repulsive and unnatural to fears of "subjecting innocent children to such a life," or of having "no friends," or of its being just plain against God's law. To my knowledge, she never published the results of this data.

Marguerite was also my godmother; I have always considered her the best of guardian angels. She encouraged my writing; she inspired my career.

As for Aunt Mary, by the time I was born she was no longer passing as white—after Mr. Swift's death she had been ignominiously disinherited by the Swifts—and was years into her third marriage, this time to a relatively impoverished pianist (I remember him as German; my mother says he was Dutch) whom she had hired to tinkle in the background of one of the salons she liked to sponsor in her home. He was a good man who raised her consciousness about the American civil rights movement. "He knew her temperament and catered to it," my

mother says. We all liked him, and he became very much part
of the family. He was, if truth be told, much nicer than she.
She died at the age of eighty-nine.

I inherited her dangly white porcelain earrings, a bottle of
smelling salts, and her vanity. Her vanity *table*, I should say—
a spindly affair with anorexic legs like toothpicks. I always feel
very precarious perched before it, my image reflected in the
triptych of mirrors rimmed by no fewer than twenty large
lightbulbs. I remember her gazing into those same mirrors,
looking for all the world like Ava Gardner in bloom. She
smelled of bursting gardenias and ambitious roses with something else, some mysterious spice, a determined undercurrent
that I was never able to decipher.

The roller-coaster genealogy of my mother's family is not terribly unusual among black families in the United States. Very
few of us who can trace our families at all can't also lay claim
to a few romanticized Indian chieftains, Scottish missionaries,
Japanese and Italian war brides, or Red Diaper dads. But the
degree to which racial and cultural mixing has always been a
feature of American society is the degree to which that intergenerational knowledge has been repressed as nonconformist
or embarrassing and, going back not so very far in time, suppressed as illegal. As I write this story of the world in which
she grew up, my mother is adamant that she wants none of
it discussed in public and certainly none of it published.
The whole mess was, after all, a source of some considerable
shame and pain for all concerned. And so, if my enduring image of my grandmother is of her sitting with her hand over her
mouth, my relation to my mother is better captured by the
image of her with her hand over my mouth.

"It's too dangerous," she whispers.

"Mnnglummph," I toss back at her.

But mothers are never entirely wrong. It is hard to get a

story just exactly right, and even then you can never tell how someone else is going to take it.

Which brings me to how I came to be part of the 2000 Whitney Biennial. One of the curators had read a few essays I'd written about my mother and her family. He called me up and asked if I would read several paragraphs that the museum could put on a taped loop with other family chroniclers like Ruth Reichl and Frank McCourt. They wanted to play it in the background of the great cacophony of paintings by Jasper Johns and Jackson Pollock and who knows who. This is an unusual event in the life of a lawyer, and so I told all my law students about it and on opening night hunted all over the museum for my voice. I found it playing in the basement bathroom. Well, bathrooms, actually; it was blaring away in both the men's room and the women's room and there were law students just lined up for days. My name was inscribed on a little plaque on each bathroom wall, so that you could see who was talking even if you couldn't hear it above all the flushing.

My mother, always the hopeful optimist, asked if this mightn't be an exhibit that would rotate to other rooms in the museum.

"You're hoping I'll be upgraded to the cloakroom?" I responded balefully.

An evening at the gallery opening of another of Merry Conway and Noni Pratt's shows, this one titled A *Small Museum of Women's Experience*. The museum was a small storefront space in Chelsea, Massachusetts, a gritty, ethnically mixed community where waves of immigrants have settled in recent years. The museum was dedicated to the ruptures in women's lives and thus focused on experiences of exile, migration, incarceration, loss of loved ones, homelessness, and domestic abuse. But what was particularly fascinating to me was not just the final product as one saw it on the opening night, but the process by which it came into being.

Two months before its opening, it began as an empty room with white paper on all the walls. Noni set her scruffily engaging little dog, Buffalo, out by the front door and chatted with people as they stopped to scratch his ears and belly. Buffalo was quite a people magnet. Children especially loved him, and the next thing you knew, their mothers were inside writing on the walls: anecdotes, remembered fairy tales, grandmotherly and maternal dreams and warnings. "I don't know if I believe in the next life, but I would like to haunt my children. Just to be there saying 'Hmmm.' Not having to evaluate or be responsible but just to be there, letting them be free, but being there."

They brought old letters and weird recovered tidbits like packing lists that read like poems. An urn for gathered recollections / A cashbox of memories / Containing the history of all things / Dried flowers, lost keys / A pin, buttons, small change / The list of things undone.

Soon, the fathers were coming too, contributing stories about how long-departed aunts made the best tortillas or kept their gardens. "Put a melon under a pillow for a night and it will be ripe." Grandmothers were stopping by to lend *their* mothers' rosary beads to display in the window. As the conversations on the sidewalk increased in number, the walls inside grew vines of inscription:

"He beat me when I burned the rice. He'd say, 'Why don't you know how to cook?' I didn't know how. I didn't have any recipes. My mother didn't teach me. I was so terrified of cooking. Much, much later, I realized you didn't have to panic."

"When I was in prison, my children used all my recipes and they said it tasted the same but not the same. That was the best and worst thing to hear."

"Being a refugee you keep moving. Each time you move you shed. Moving and running you don't have the luxury of carrying so much, kind of like a death. Each time mourning losing more and more. I see my refugee status as a yearning for objects."

"You really have to love a person to clean them, to feed them."

"The world happens. It invades your home life and destroys it."

The little room gradually filled with home-grown quotations, family photos, postcards, letters from prison, funeral notices. And, if one but looked up, one could muse upon the dietary conventions and small cultural necessities of contributors, as revealed in hundreds of shopping lists suspended on threads from the ceiling.

"Write to Sister Rachel, make tarts, get prescription, answer email, return dress to Nordstrom's, buy Verna the fruit picker."

"Goat milk, toothpaste, beer."

"Buffalo wings, cereal."

"Three hens, garlic, thyme, whole almonds, chamomile, bread, oranges, dates, white pepper, cardamom."

"Salt, gelatin, toilet paper."

As befitted a museum dedicated to ruptures, its opening night also marked its closing. The closing became a party that in turn became a huge discussion in the round with street artists, college professors, families of women in jail, lawyers, ministers, jugglers, firemen, fathers of "one too many daughters," and several homeless women who had used the museum as a shelter. Let's just say it became the kind of conversation about art, immigration, race, welfare, and social policy that we'll not see in Congress in this lifetime. But if only one could . . .

When I got home from the party, it was long after midnight. My parents, who had been looking after my son, were half asleep in the living room, Fats Waller playing softly on the stereo. They still play records; they still have a stereo. My son was upstairs, tucked into the bed I once slept in as a child. "He did his homework on his laptop, then played something called The Sims for a while," my mother reported.

The Sims is a computer game in which you get to create your ideal of the perfect suburban house and outfit it with weight machines and swimming pools and the happy suburban family of your dreams. My son's ideal of home life is peopled by whole teams of football players with manly names like Cheese Bob and Buttered Toast Bob who lead heroic lives of untrammeled independence but for the little mother in the little kitchen who is always there to slice the cheese and butter the toast. When I played the game, social services took away my children because they all had nervous breakdowns. (I had installed bookcases in every room and wouldn't let them play computer games.) My cyber-husband ran away from home because there was never enough food in the refrigerator. And when you don't pay your bills, the Grim Reaper comes a-calling.

As I explained the game to my bemused parents, I heard the sound of someone crying, an eerie, hysterical sobbing.

Panicked, I ran upstairs to check on my real son. He was smiling in his sleep. I leaned over and kissed his cheek. "My cappuccino maker. Mine, not yours," he responded faintly, from deep within his dream and without ever waking up.

A few moments later I located the sound. A man was crying in the empty darkened street, inconsolable as a new widow. He sat on a fire hydrant and howled. The grief, alarming and desperate, was amplified by the silence of the city. I briefly contemplated calling the police. To say what? That a man was crying loudly? Was he in trouble? Had he gone mad? Is there an emergency number for outsized expression of public grief?

III

The Kitchen

The cappuccino maker was my Christmas gift to myself. When it arrived, I recognized it instantly as a monument to my own gullibility and poor judgment. I couldn't really afford it, I don't really drink cappuccino, and it has a slew of shiny nozzled attachments that look as though they could be used for extinguishing forest fires. It sits in my kitchen taking up an inordinate amount of space because I succumbed to the fantastical notion that one day I would have a houseful of bohemian friends all of whom would want espresso and steamed milk at exactly the same moment. Already it looks dated, conspicuously symbolic of an era, a cappuccino maker being the martini shaker or the Lava lamp of my generation.

I bought it from a glossy catalog chock-full of foolishness, during my catalog-as-bathroom-reading phase. I sat in the tub, warm, relaxed, and much too susceptible to subliminal suggestions of happy transformation. In retrospect, I tell myself that at least I had the strength of character to resist buying the 3-D spherical jigsaw puzzle of the moon that glows in the dark or the chocolate golf balls or the fountain pen that writes in space.

Many of these mailings are devoted to food, odd and extravagant food that speaks directly to the secret libidinal desires of your average Manhattanite: If I were of such a mind, I could have delivered to my doorstep a "corporate-sized" tin of candied popcorn, a ten-pound jar of prunes in Armagnac, a thirty-pound tub of chocolate truffles, and a fifty-pound slab of Japanese beef culled from a steer that has been plumped on a diet of corn, new lettuce, and champagne.

I am smothered with this endless smorgasbord of catalog richesse not because I requested it, but rather because I live in an upscale, relatively recessionproof neighborhood of Manhattan. The catalog fairy judges us neighborhood by neighborhood, block by block, as well as order by order. In contrast, a friend who lives in an upscale suburb in Virginia gets catalogs filled with things like sweatshirts upon which you can have pictures of your pets imprinted, or red plaid mother-daughter dress sets with black velvet buttons and frilly white collars. The bulk of her catalogs have names like Plough and Hearth or Fin and Feather, advertising lots of stuff for playing house, like broom corn centerpieces, hammered-copper log boxes, pool covers, birdbaths, and welcome mats.

My mother and father, on the other hand, no doubt because they are retirees living in New England, receive catalogs for ankle braces, back cushions, neck supports, bathroom supplies, corn removers, smokeless ashtrays, electric blankets, Florida citrus, fruitcakes, and very expensive clothing for very little dogs. Gone, for sure, is the unified, equal-access world according to Sears, Roebuck and Company. These days, it's all about the leveraging of desire.

When my son was just a baby, one of my friends came to visit with her four-year-old. In a quiet moment while I changed diapers, she and her son sat in a corner and read catalogs together. It was such a striking picture, the two of them framed by the big winged armchair, as though embraced by angels. It was so incongruous, their bowed heads and prayerful expressions, and the gentle swooshing of page upon page illuminated with icons of useless gadgets and doodads. I took the moment as a kind of revelation and vowed right then and there never to sit in the angel-winged armchair without serious volumes in hand. And so I spent several years hoisting my son onto my lap to read him classical sonnets and medieval sagas, until he got too old and too heavy and his feet touched the ground and he walked off and found peers with parents who Bought Them Stuff. One day he came home with the J. Peterman catalog in his backpack. "I need a horse," he announced.

More recently, online shopping has surpassed telephone catalog sales for most American middle-class consumers. It's cheaper, apparently, for companies to deal with computer orders than to hire telephone operators. Computers also make it easier to track and predict consumer preferences and thus accumulate detailed profiles of each and every one of us.

The growth of market psychology to "cluster" consumers by region, gender, race, education, and age, as well as the use of computer technology, means that our movements and individual tastes are always being tracked as unerringly as though by a bloodhound. If I wander out of a given geographic range, I receive a call from a stern man at American Express, whose job it is to communicate messages from a tracking terminal named—I kid you not—Mrs. Wilcox. *There has been an unusual use of your card. Please identify your most recent purchase.* Do I have to? *It's for your own protection.* The voice is cross, like a policeman or a parent. Well, er, actually . . . I went to a mall in New Jersey and bought an early recording of the Beach Boys. *That's not like you.* It's a part of myself I had heretofore hidden, I confess. It will never happen again, I promise, feeling miserable and revealed. And resentful. I don't like the feeling of being watched as I meander about the world, trying a little of this, a little of that.

And so I have taken to lying to telemarketers. I absolutely

hate being pigeonholed, and by a machine, no less. I hate the generalizations that the machines generate. I hate being told that this kind of commercial data collection is actually for my own good rather than their profit. I hate the assumption that I am nothing more than a resource pit, to be mined for usable data that some marketing expert will then use in order to sell me back myself. Therefore, when the little pop-up survey boxes on the computer ask me who I am, I tell them I'm a twenty-six-year-old Mormon from Missouri. It makes me feel so free.

Cyber shape-shifting is my modest attempt at resistance. I am not who you think I am. Go away. (Of course, some of those little pop-up boxes enact their own revenge in the form of viruses, worms, and Trojan horses. Recently, I discovered that a computer "infection" was using my e-mail address to spam the world with advertisements for Viagra and solicitations to swinger parties. What was interesting was that only one of my friends saw fit to bring it to my attention. Apparently the rest saw nothing unusual in my being engaged in unsafe business practices.)

But my creative attempts at treachery don't really work anyway, particularly as the government of our newly christened Homeland becomes more and more involved in the enhancement of Total Awareness. One wonders how much Mrs. Wilcox's mentality will constrain this freedom to lie proudly in pursuit of one's privacy. How much will the inventive, the oddball, the curious and spontaneous be constrained by the great bureaucratic spell-checker as programmed by a military strategist? *Subject is crossing bounds of normative behavioral zone* . . . Lights will flash, the gates will close, they'll have to spend a great deal of time and energy to check you out and then, annoyed, they'll throw the bright creative types in the box labeled "loose cannons." Some bureaucratic and corporate employers already do this, as counterintuitive as it sounds: They won't hire those they think "overqualified," or whose IQs are too high. They worry that such people would be out of place, always be thinking outside the box, not following orders.

Then there is the pure literalism of computers as hunter-gatherers of information. They are like smart children in their literalism, but we need smart grown-ups in that business. When my son was much younger, he and I were reading a bright picture book about water safety, as told by a crusty old salt named Captain Bob. In one picture, Captain Bob's sidekick, a grizzled, loquacious cat, stood on the prow of a moving motorboat, leaning out over the water. Underneath the picture, a caption in big jagged capital letters said: "DANGEROUS BEHAVIOR."

"Can you tell me what he's doing that's so unsafe?" I asked my son.

"Yes," said he. "If he leans over the edge much farther he's going to fall overboard and bonk his head on all those sharp letters."

With precisely such determined transparency, computer profiles tend to protect us from the sharpness of letters but without much sense of the complex behaviors to which they actually refer.

This matter of being a creature with both a profile and a price extends even to the Chinese restaurant that delivers my lunch. All I have to do is dial them; my phone number flashes on their caller ID and they know exactly what to bring and where. I try not to think about that student of mine who was cut off from such wonders of modern living because the dorm room she inherited was occupied by someone who didn't tip the delivery people. They put it in the computer.

Being dissed by a computer is like losing your wallet, only worse. When the computer jumbles your stats or loses all track of your identity, you are lost. It's like being inside the brain of someone with no long-term memory and an unforgiving attitude. You are nothing until you prove your existence and then the next day it's all forgotten and you have to prove it all over again. You are a disposable image, an erroneous caption.

A friend of mine went through a terrible divorce recently, during which her mean-spirited husband claimed that her great-grandmother's furniture was his. The dresser brought from Russia. The precious mirror and the silver hairpins. The court asked her for receipts. All she could offer was remembrance of things past. What's your proof? the court demanded. Here's my experience, she faltered. Memories are imaginings. Is there an objective manifestation to ground your claim of ownership?

Anyway, it was my failure to have mastered the complications of my cappuccino machine that drove me into the streets of New York one slushy morning in late December. I had a houseful of bohemian guests from Britain, all jet-lagged and cranky and caffeine deprived. Two of us wended our way to Starbucks for seven cups of House Blend to go. We passed an old man leaning into his reflection in the soaped-over window of an abandoned store. He was combing his hair with a plastic deli fork, performing his morning ablutions with the little white fork, a paper cup of water, and the looking glass of that ruined temple of commerce.

"Manhattan had many more homeless the last time I was here," my friend Y. mused. "Where did they all go?"

"Shelters in the outer boroughs, mostly," I answered, describing the official effort to "clean up" the streets of New York. "Relatives, jails, subway tunnels, probably. Elsewhere, nowhere," I finished lamely, realizing that, except for vague statements from politicians about shooing people in the direction of the South Bronx, I really didn't have any idea.

Back at my apartment, we scoured the newspapers for

clues, and before the morning was out we found an article
about the dismal conditions in Camp LaGuardia, a thousand-
bed shelter located seventy miles northwest of the city in the
small town of Chester. When block associations in Manhattan
demand that the police and social service workers "sweep" the
streets of the homeless, this is where at least some of them end
up. Tensions were high in Chester, apparently because, as
one middle-class resident put it, "there's a lot of lowlifes walking the road when you come off the exit. We moved here to
get away from people like them." While at one point the men
in the shelter were confined to the grounds of the camp, they
were not any longer, thanks to a lawsuit reminding officials
that the men were homeless, not criminals. While there have
been some instances of petty shoplifting and drinking from
open containers, police in Chester reported that no serious
crime has been committed by any shelter resident. Nevertheless, as one neighbor put it, "there's a level of uncomfortabil-
ity because a lot of these men are a different race." Indeed, the
shelter residents were the object of such resentment that some
local residents had taken to swerving at the men when they
were walking the three miles of shoulderless highway between
the shelter and the nearest shopping center. "My older daughter's friends, I've heard them talking," said one attentive father. "It's a game they play, like smash the mailboxes—you
know, bored country kids."

My friends and I discussed the genealogy of the word
"lowlife." The British tend to hear the question of high and
low status with a literalism that is remarkable to my American ear. There is still a strong Edwardian ethic of Upstairs-
Downstairs built into their syntax. My friend Y., for example,
always goes "up" to London even if she's proceeding south
from Birmingham. When she comes to the United States, she
always confuses me by saying she's coming "up to New York,"
even when she's coming down from Canada. "New York is

your cultural capital," Y. once offered by way of weak explanation. But no, I told her, our cultural capital is a degree of freedom from that kind of ingrained linguistic ranking.

British cultural imagination, it would seem, places the seat of the empire very high on an imaginary hill. It puts the peasants below, down in the country, prostrating themselves so that the king can always gaze in a full 360-degree arc upon their lowliness. The scientific currency—and equality—of the compass rose is completely displaced by anxious superstitions about where the king's head rests.

"What about Booker T. Washington's *Up from Slavery?*" asked Y. "Or when slaves were sold down the river even when the river ran west? African Americans always talk about freedom as up, bondage as down."

"The river was the Mississippi," I informed her. "It runs south, down from the North. The free states were up north. Slavery was down south. Even the habit of referring to the uppermost state of Maine as 'down east' refers to the practical enterprise of having to sail downwind to get up there. The United States," I blustered on, "was built upon the solid foundation of geographic good sense. New York City is laid out on a nice, tidy, rectangular grid; Washington, DC, is one big metaphor, what with the notion of equality built right into its radial urban symmetry."

I carried on for quite a while, hypothesizing that straight thinking about the lay of the land is what makes us such a mobile society, this clear correlation between our political geography and the points of the compass. It has freed us from the superstitious status constraints that keep some people from traveling across social lines because they can't tell if they're going up to a down place or down to an up place. So they get stuck in one place, "their" place.

"Americans aren't mobile," snapped Y. "They're in a constant state of flight."

I had to think about that one for a minute.

I had a final question for her, though. What happens, I asked, when you're in a middling kind of place, like Indianapolis or Buffalo? In other words, is it a planed upward progress between thither and yon, or is it just a lowland slough of despond in all directions but for the pinnacular destination?

"Have you never heard the nursery rhyme?" she asked. And then she recited what I suddenly realized was all along the anthem of the anxiously sycophantic bourgeoisie or, in American terms, the rapidly vanishing middle class: "And when you're up you're up, and when you're down you're down, but when you're only halfway up, you're neither up nor down . . . "

The most indisputably "down" place in the city of New York is the emergency room of any given hospital on a cold, slushy night during the winter season of holiday cheer. Which is exactly where I found myself one wretched December evening, sitting on a gurney in a large examining room filled with misery. The room was partitioned into small rectangles of faux privacy by a series of shower curtains that suggested rather than provided separation of one patient from another. You could hear everyone discussing his or her most intimate bodily secrets, you just couldn't see them. It was an odd disjointed cacophony. There were lots of sad, elderly people who couldn't remember what medication they were on, or the names of their doctors. There were lonely people who were eager and polite, enjoying the minimal human contact with harried, worn-out doctors, making small imperious requests, demanding to see the dinner menu, expressing genuine pleasure at the prospect of being held overnight.

I was there because I had abandoned the universal parental proscription always to wear warm, thick-soled bunny slippers when walking about the interior of one's home. I had been padding about in my bare feet and had stepped on a piece of glass that lodged itself high in my heel, well beyond the reach of tweezers. As I considered the lessons of my situation, my reveries were interrupted by a tableau of new voices on the other side of the curtain.

"He's an animal," said a man.

"I thought he was going to kill me," said a young woman, apparently his daughter. "The way he was staring at me."

"He's on drugs," said a nurse. "He's sedated, he's harmless. He's gonna stare."

"He *looks* like a drug addict," rejoined the father. "You can tell the guy doesn't like white people."

"It's not that," said the nurse impatiently. "He doesn't like white people, he doesn't like black people. He's crazy! He doesn't like anyone!"

"Well," groused the father, "that's why I resent those NAACP cases. These guys are trouble."

It turns out that the young woman had come in to have herself checked out after being rear-ended riding in a taxicab. While she had been sitting in the waiting room, a homeless black man began staring at her with some measure of un-pleasant glassy-eyed fixedness that the woman interpreted as menace. Her father was furious, and the more he thought about it the louder he got. A hospital administrator showed up eventually and apologized for "the incident" with smoothly professional aplomb.

"It just really upset me," said the girl, appeased. "I feel, like, bad for him, but . . ." Her "but" hung in the air, drifting through the room like a strange, magic cloud.

Many hours later, when I was safely back in the warmth of my own home sipping tea and wearing slippers, my British house-guests reminded me of a meeting of human rights activists to which we had once gone. A woman in attendance had spoken eloquently of her recollections of the so-called Cable Street Riots. In the 1930s, a group of brown-shirted Fascists led by Oswald Mosely tried to march through the streets of London. The residents of Cable Street were determined to prevent the march from proceeding in front of their houses. They were too poor to procure wood or other materials with which to build a proper blockade, so they pulled the furniture from their houses and blocked the marchers with heaps of house-hold goods, with beds, tables, chairs, and even pianos.

It is an arresting thought, this turning inside out of one's home to press a political point. The image makes me think of its visual converse, perhaps: those pictures in so many urban American newspapers over the last few years of the heaped possessions of homeless people routed from their hidden en-campments in abandoned buildings, subway tunnels, high-way underpasses, and underground cable passages. There has been no lack of public gloating over the supposed bounty torn from those underground lives. They were pirating electricity from the taxpayers' lampposts! They had toaster ovens! They had boom boxes! They had brand-new Nike sneakers under there! It is haunting, this image of lives turned inside out, so repeatedly, so cyclically, the bulldozers crushing, trashing, pushing aside the scavenged scraps of scavenged lives as though it were a victory . . . but for whom?

In many places these days, one hears politicians and citizens alike speaking of "cleaning up" and "getting rid of" that part of the population whose only fault is their poverty. By what authority, we must insist on knowing, comes this pur-chase of state force? "We" (as in "the people") "got rid of" whom, and how?

I think of the young people of Chester taking potshots at mailboxes, veering their cars at the homeless. If someone gets hit, I wonder how the narrative of bored country kids will mesh with an ethic of citizenship, how the narrative of blind consumption with that of burning hunger.

My father and his cousin Bill are both so close to ninety that they are no longer secretive about their age. They both stand tall—over six feet—and straight. They have great eyesight, their own teeth, and the hearing of good hunters. Their bodies are strong, their faces unlined. Best of all, they both have long memories and what you might call perspective. Whenever they sit down together over Thanksgiving dinner, the stories are of another era.

"The horse!" they were recalling. "That horse!"

The horse had rubber shoes and a drunken night rider.

"You can't hear a horse that's been shod with rubber," said my father.

"And it would barrel through town doing thirty-five in the dark," said his cousin Bill.

"With no lights," said my father.

"You couldn't see it coming," said his cousin Bill.

"It could kill you and you wouldn't hear a thing."

My father comes from strong, resourceful people. What I know of his side of the family begins with my great-great-grandfather. Born sometime in the early 1800s, he was the son of an African woman and a man remembered only as "an Englishman." I don't know much more about him, other than that he died in Florida in 1894 at what one source says was the age of seventy, although other family lore says he must have been close to a hundred. The latter age would be more consistent with the fact that his wife died at the age of 104 in 1913, also in Florida. According to a 1920 edition of *The History of the American Negro*, she, like his mother, had come "directly from Africa."

Their son, my great-grandfather, was always referred to as Old Pete. We also called him the Walkaway Slave. He was reportedly well along in years the day he got up and started walking away from the swamps of north Florida, up the road toward the promise of freedom. Family legend has it that he walked slowly, very slowly, so slowly that no one noticed. He was always described as being old when he took off, but the calculation is so imprecise that he could well have been only in his thirties. The calculation is imprecise because it had to be kept secret. Unlike Frederick Douglass or those who ran rather than walked, he didn't make it all the way to a free state, just as far as a missionary camp in South Carolina run by the abolitionist-minded American Missionary Association. There he seems to have invented his own personal freedom of status, perhaps with their help, by saying that his father was Cherokee, his mother Creek, that they were married in a white church, and that therefore he was free. My father says, "They were no more Indian than this table. They were slaves." (Of course my great-grandfather's parents could have been both. People forget how dark-skinned Eastern coastal indigenous people were, or that many of them were enslaved as black. But the bulk of the evidence seems to indicate that most of my great-grandfather's father's family were, or were descended from, African slaves.)

As best I can piece together, Old Pete ended up in a so-called maroon colony near the Pee Dee River in Marion County, South Carolina, one of a number of places where missionaries from New England provided secret shelter to runaway slaves and Native Americans driven from their land. There they lived "marooned" in these small safe places but surrounded by the dangers of the larger world. I don't know precisely when he got there, or if he was to have been spirited north at some point, but he was still there when the Civil War ended, and there he stayed for the rest of his life.

By all accounts, he enjoyed his later years, during which

some measure of briskness returned to his step. He married a woman who was much younger than he was, a good-natured "lively" woman whom my father and Uncle Bill remember fondly for her ability to flatten a galloping goat with one well-placed backhand wallop. Her name was Mariah Currie, and she was also born a slave, the daughter of her white master and a woman variously described as "Gullah" and "pure African." Old Pete lived into his late eighties; Mariah lived into her nineties. Together they had eight strong and long-lived children.

Old Pete was what my neo-Bostonian, no-longer-of-the-South maternal grandmother called, with unbecoming haughtiness, a "stump-knocker" preacher. He'd preach upon request, under less than formal circumstances. "He wasn't part of an organized church," says my father. "He came from the older traditions, the underground slave way that blended all sorts of things, pulled out all the stops to provide the sustenance you needed to get through the tribulations. He was a fine, fine speaker." In a letter from the 1950s, my grandfather describes going back to visit "the old Friendship Church which Mother and Dad talked about so much and of which our parents and grandparents were once members. It is still an old style church without an organ or piano and the songs are supplemented with the clapping of the hands and the patting of the feet. But"—and here my grandfather is signaling a change from older practices—"they have individual drinking glasses for the communion." Today there is a Friendship African Methodist Episcopal Zion Church in between Gresham and Pee Dee, South Carolina. I don't know if it's related to the one in which my ancestors may have worshipped.

Old Pete also ran a sawmill. At some much later point he purchased land near the Georgia border—forestland with pine trees from which he tapped sap and made turpentine by distilling it. "It was a very decent living," says my father. "You could make all kinds of things from turpentine, from medicine to Bakelite."

Old Pete and Mariah's first child was my grandfather, born in Gresham, South Carolina, October 4, 1879. They named him "I.D." No name, just the letters "I" and "D." My grandfather was by all accounts a brilliant man, with his father's initiative for traveling distances to get what he wanted. Sometime around the age of ten or eleven, he left South Carolina by himself (his parents did not have the means to accompany him) and walked—in my mind he is barefoot, but my father says I have a romantic imagination—all the way to Dorchester Academy, a Congregationalist boarding school set up in 1868 for newly freed slaves. The school was in Liberty County, Georgia, a distance of about two hundred miles from his home. (Indeed, in 2001, a group of citizens trying to establish a museum on the site raised $34,000 by sponsoring a Walk to Dorchester of nine miles, to symbolize the extraordinary migrations made by so many of the earliest students. One ninety-one-year-old woman walked all but the last thousand yards.)

My grandfather attended Dorchester from the fourth grade through high school, paying his way by working in mills and on riverboats, to graduate with first honors in 1903. He went on to then-all-black Meharry Medical College, from which he received his MD in 1907. In 1908, he married Blanche Evans Clark, daughter of Dorchester Academy's chaplain, the Reverend William Armstead Clark. Reverend Clark was a "college-educated Northerner," a white man from Worcester, Massachusetts, who'd come to the South to be a missionary to those few Cherokee who'd fled and remained hidden from the Trail of Tears. He'd stayed on, and married Margaret Davis, the mixed-race (i.e., illegitimate) daughter of a white landowner and a Cherokee woman, near Walhalla, South Carolina. Their daughter Blanche, my grandmother, had also graduated as a first-honors student from Dorchester Academy and later taught there.

It is interesting to contemplate what might have led my great-grandfather to name his son with only the letters of the alphabet. (Both of Old Pete's other sons' names also began with "I.") Old Pete could not have been educated—it was against the law during slavery. But he was an exceptionally curious and clever person, and apparently set out to teach himself to read. My father remembers helping him when he struggled to read the newspaper as quite an old man. So it could be that my great-grandfather was learning the alphabet at the time his son was born. Just the letters themselves must have seemed a great gift to him, as to so many ex-slaves. The alphabet represented the code, the key to all knowledge.

That's one theory.

Another, simpler explanation might be that in many parts of the South, referring to men by their first and middle initials is a common tradition, often conveying a certain status. The devious, corrupt-to-the-core character J.R. in the old television show *Dallas* is a good example. My great-grandfather just might have been trying to give his son a name with a ring of power to it.

I like the complicated theories, though. Old Pete was a preacher, after all, at least some of whose thoughts were influenced by New England missionaries. It is conceivable that he became acquainted with what scholars might more loftily call the tetragrammaton—that Jehovah (or Yahweh) is a transliteration of four letters, YHWH, the Hebrew consonants signifying God. Early Hebrew had no vowels, but the mystery of its ancient pronunciation has complemented, in some cultures, the belief that the name of the divine is indeed unpronounceable. Certainly many mystical traditions, from Middle Eastern to Irish to West African to Native American, believe that calling someone "by name" or "calling someone out"—that is, revealing a true, or a secret, identity—incurs great and sometimes terrible power.

In that spirit, many African Americans gave their children

complexly coded names during the first years after the aboli-
tion of slavery. Sometimes the names were to disguise their
origins so that their old masters could not find them. Often
they were from the Hebrew Bible, drawing heavily from the
times of exile. Sometimes they were made-up names, frequently having traceable African roots, but so fractured from
their origin by that era that they were just rationalized as
sounding "nice" to the ear. Some gave their children "official," written names for interface with the white world, as well
as another, more intimate, "spoken" name within the family.

And so it was, when my very young grandfather walked
those many miles from South Carolina and presented himself
for enrollment at Dorchester Academy, he was met at the
door by a well-starched, no-nonsense schoolmarm.

"What is your name?" she asked.

"I," replied my grandfather.

It's a lovely bit of play, that. Imagine, in those volatile
post–Civil War days, the dilemma confronted by this white
teacher: the not-insignificant social drama of having to introduce him around the school by saying, "This is I."

Perhaps it's apocryphal, but I like to think that this was not
accidental. In those days, white people almost never referred
to black people by anything but their first names. It is a significant feature of the family dynamic that even my father remembers his black grandfather as "Old Pete" and his white
grandfather as "Reverend Clark." Moreover, whites often re-
tained the power of naming blacks, like pets. My grandfather
used to tell us about the white doctor in one small Georgia
town who, while "kindly" enough to have delivered many of
the black children in the area, had named all of them after
medical procedures, as in "Appendectomy Jones" or "Hy-
dropsy Smith." It was very moving as my grandfather described it: The illiteracy of the parents meant that they were
actually grateful for the grand-sounding names.

It took a while for the bitterness to set in.

Perhaps in response to such experiences, after the Civil War many ex-slaves began a tradition of outfitting their children with aggressively honorific first names, like Prince or Countess or King or Precious or Duke. One of my grandfather's cousins bore the moniker of Commodore. Naming became a desperate art of self-creation.

And so I wonder if my grandfather's name might have been a syntactical calculation: He was able to say, "I am I." After all, not only did slaves not get to name themselves, in no other sphere did they get to be agents or authors or, quite literally, subjects. For all the debate about the sloppiness of ebonics, much of black vernacular has that unfortunate but logical consistency—one does not refer to oneself in the subjective case—coded into it. In older black dialect, the objective case is frequently substituted in the subject position, as in "Me want . . ." That positioning places the self as the object of a verb, as acted upon, rather than a self-directed "I." Alternatively, and in more modern black idiom, the "I" will be used, but the verb will disagree, as in "I is . . ." That third-person verb signals an alienation from the self, a disconnect from the boldly active—and impermissible—first person.

In any event, the principal gave my grandfather a good, safe biblical name before the end of that first day at Dorchester Academy. His "proper" name became Isaiah, although I suppose it didn't matter in the end. Unlike his father, no one remembers him as "Old Isaiah." For the great length of my grandfather's adult life—he died in the early 1970s when I was in college—he was known as and responded exclusively to the name of Doctor Williams.

Having the title of doctor was a social lubricant even in the Jim Crow era—the odds of survival adjusted somewhat more in your favor in those dangerous times. "Doctor," after all, has talismanic power in the best of circumstances. If you have a

"Doctor" in front of your name when ordering catalog merchandise, for example, Mrs. Wilcox, the computer, upgrades your profile and you end up with much nicer solicitations in your mailbox the next time around—more polite wording, classy layouts, good heavy vellum, quality stuff. It's still stuff you don't need, but the fantasies enabled thereby are of a much higher aesthetic order than those promised by Odd Job. I should know. Whenever I get a break from singing in the Mormon Tabernacle Choir of Missouri, I tend to my duties as a cardiovascular surgeon in Ontario.

I know, this is a supremely irrational game—the glib snatching up of false masks as protection, as refutation of stereotypes about my worth, even when the stereotypes are computer generated. But the blind mechanical knowledge of me sometimes feels like the modern equivalent of always being called by your first name. It assumes too much. It deadens human curiosity—they have your stats, they know it all.

I'm a traditionalist, I suppose. I bristle every time some teenaged salesperson hands me back my credit card and says, "Thanks, Pat." My gills start to bloat when they say, "Thanks, Patty." And I dream of levitating up over the counter to have at them when they call me Patsy. Never a Mizzus Williams, not even so much as Patricia. It's like they've all been trained to do this at salesperson school, like little machines. They staple the receipts, look for your name on the card, then hand it back to you with robotic gratitude, with a sing and a song, as though someone at corporate headquarters were grading them on the most obnoxiously efficient abbreviation of your first name they can come up with.

But I realize that my bad attitude might be construed as a drag on the otherwise frictionless wheels of free enterprise. So I've decided to go legit. I'm changing my official name to She-Whom-You-Really-Do-Not-Know.

. . .

If our personal data has become more fungible, our money seems to have gotten less so. I'm thinking of what happened when my son and I showed up at the bank recently to cash in the contents of his piggy bank. My son collects my change. I give him the random coins that come from little daily transactions, the pennies, nickels, and dimes that build up in my coat pocket. Every so often, when his piggy bank is full, we take it to a real bank and run it through the coin counter so it can be changed into bills. Most goes into his school savings account; some of it he spends on foolish pleasures like Yu-gi-oh cards.

This has been a ritual since he's been old enough to count—until last Wednesday. This time, when we showed up at the bank with a quart freezer bag of coins, the clerk refused to change it into bills. She said I was not a client of the bank, which was true: My own bank is a very small local branch and doesn't have a coin counter. "But I've been changing coins here for years," I protested. "Could you check on that? They usually just charge me a service fee for use of the machine . . ."

"Homeland Security," was the response. "It's a new policy to prevent money laundering."

"You think we're laundering thirty-six dollars and eighty-nine cents?"

"Would you like to open an account?"

In fact, I don't think the Homeland Security Act demands anything of the sort. (And ultimately, we changed the coins at another bank farther down the street that had no such policy.) But before I let it go, I quizzed half the clerks in the bank as well as the manager. Weren't they obligated to accept the coin of the realm? Didn't their policy violate the very notion of currency? Since when has cash exchange been dependent upon the identity of the bearer? What about the duty to honor negotiable instruments? What happens to the homeless, the gleaners, the can collectors with no home telephone number, no fixed address, when they are not permitted to own unaccounted-for currency? When credit is the credential for possessing currency?

The bank's policy, they explained, was based on fear of drug money and transactions with "transients." But the shape of their fear was somewhat idiosyncratic. For example, if I had presented them with a hundred-dollar bill, they said, they would have given me change, no questions asked. It was interesting, this: Their suspicion trickled down but not up. A small transaction with a sack of coins seemed to have gotten me lumped with petty thieves who steal from parking meters, Coke machines, and children's piggy banks. The shifty sort who travels from bank to bank laundering ill-gotten millions, thirty-six dollars and eighty-nine cents at a time. The patient, long-suffering kind of evildoer.

But if I'd have come in loaded with hundred-dollar bills, the bank's logic would have distinguished me as less transient, more substantial. Just making change to tip the valet—might that have been what they assumed? And how does race play into this? I don't look like my stereotype of a transient. But I suppose I could have looked like the clerk's: suspiciously well-dressed brown person floats in, a strange, dandelion-puffy quality about her, with a sack of coins and lots of questions about just what sort of cash the bank *would* take. I know, fear clearly drove the policy, fear generated by the war on drugs and the war on terror. But the implementation of fear-driven policies could hardly be less rational.

"Small change" has always been, I suppose, a metaphor for the uncharted migratory miscreant, the asylum seeker with no credentials. There was some amusement when, while confessing her drug addiction on national television, singer Whitney Houston declared, "Crack is cheap. I make too much for me ever to smoke crack. Let's get that straight, okay?" But crack is not just cheap, it's also a cipher for race.

Similarly (if ever so differently), National Security Adviser

Condoleezza Rice once got very angry at a jewelry store sales-person who showed her only the costume jewelry. Rice was quoted in a *New Yorker* article by Nicholas Lemann as snap-ping, "Let's get one thing straight. You're behind the counter because you have to work for six dollars an hour. I'm on this side asking to see the good jewelry because I make consider-ably more." Lemann's interpretation was that "Rice responds to an insult based on her membership in a group by angrily proclaiming her personal, individual superiority to the deliv-erer of the insult: she doesn't offer the counterargument . . . that the assumption that black people don't have money is a stereotype; she says that the slur on the race is disproved by her achievements."

I would interpret it differently. Yes, the assumption that black people don't have money is a stereotype. But sneering at the salesperson's wages is not a necessary component of pro-claiming one's achievement. I think what the encounter demonstrates is less about Rice's vaunting her accomplishment than about class bias in black society. In other words, it is not merely a story in which individual identity is pitted against group identity, but rather one in which those two great group identities—race and class—sometimes battle each other in complex and unconscious ways. It will be interesting to see how racism and class bias reconfigure themselves—if some-times behind the front of "individual superiority"—as we enter a time when Homeland Security is profiling us back to the class stasis of feudalism. For all the talk of global market-place, we are fast retreating to precapitalist immobility—not serf, burgher, and noble, but ghetto, soccer mom, and Bill Gates. Red, orange, and green, in the new parlance of Home-land Security. What will happen to us when everything is pri-vatized, including the scrip, when all transactions are conducted within tight circles of preordination, in which we become to one another You Who Must Be Known—in which

one's status is fixed, not negotiable, not malleable but as-
signed?

The first cup of cappuccino I ever had was at the home of my
godmother Marguerite and her husband Carl. They had lived
in New York since their marriage in the late 1920s, and so
they knew about all things exotic, which is what cappuccino
was before it became a cliché. Between the time they had
moved there and the time I was old enough to drop in for coffee, their neighborhood had changed from poor, ethnic, and
artsy to pure yuppie. "From Automat to autocrat," Uncle Carl
would say. (All the adults on my mother's side of the family
were called uncles and aunts, even when they were cousins or
in-laws.) Given the course of his life, however, it might better
have been described as proceeding from Automat to fast-food
feast.

Uncle Carl was a chemist, you see. He made many contributions to the betterment of humanity, like the softness in
most American toilet papers, which required actual study of
the fibrosity of wood pulp. He developed a process that ultimately allowed powdered sugar to be made in a commercially
efficient manner, and he spent years seeking a way to cheaply
desalinate water. But perhaps his most enduring gift to humankind was in the field of food preservatives. If you see any
comestible with a shelf life of twenty-five years, you can just
bet Uncle Carl had a hand in it. He was a good man, and a
brilliant one, with many honors and awards. His only flaw and
greatest conceit was that he fancied himself a cook.

One often hears it said that cooking is just chemistry. Perhaps. But Uncle Carl was living proof that chemistry is not
cooking. Growing up with him meant having to sample a
range of molecularly sustaining but horrifically unappetizing
recipes made by reviving things normal people would bury.

Or had buried but that Uncle Carl had dug up. (I shouldn't overstate—really, he only skimmed from the top of the compost heap.) When he volunteered to make dinner, we knew he'd been lurking behind the grocery store again, collecting discards. My sister and I were sometimes dispatched to accompany him, to help carry back the trove of mashed melons and rotting peaches. Uncle Carl was extremely ethical about the enterprise—he would never take anything that could be recycled; he wouldn't take things that were only slightly bruised or that could be used at the local nursing home or homeless shelter. He took only those fruits and vegetables whose resuscitation lay at the frontiers of science.

Once home, Uncle Carl would lay out the bounty on a marble slab, hack out the worst of the rot, and begin a process he thought of as resurrection but to the rational observer more closely resembled embalming. By the time they made it to the table, his concoctions always lay on the plate in a state of unnatural polish, their color a bit too bright, like excessively rouged corpses. I have French friends whose parents taught them to taste along a meticulous and nuanced spectrum of flavors, aromas, and freshness. Uncle Carl taught us the same thing, if you drop out the concept of freshness. I have a nose for alpha-tocopherol. I am the rare individual who can distinguish a monosodium glutamate from a disodium guanylate.

It is destiny, I suppose, that my life is fueled by flash-frozen, reconstituted, and ready-made food, although that is not what I anticipated for myself whenever my sister and I played house, which is what we played whenever we weren't busy reconstructing the adventures of the Jackson Twins. If the twinning allowed us to test our similarities, it was in the game of house that we explored the differences of mind and spirit that divide our worldviews even to this day. She dreamed of minimalist interiors, uncluttered floors, and no housework. Her dolls spent very little time hanging around the dollhouse. They had actual savings accounts of carefully accumulated play money that they applied toward traveling the seven seas in shoe box rafts they made themselves. I, on the other hand, envisioned enormous Victorian houses, filled with books and creaky staircases, lace curtains and linen tablecloths, with dinner settings for twenty-four. My dolls could not imagine a better world than life within the dollhouse, and they used shoe boxes to expand the bounty of inner space—my dolls had shoe box gymnasiums, shoe box ballrooms, shoe box libraries, and dozens of extra guest shoe box bedrooms.

Now that we are grown, we live each other's dreams. My sister abides in a pleasant suburb in a sprawling old house which, while not boasting a gymnasium, does have a very nicely appointed guest bedroom. She married, quit her job as an attorney, and stayed at home to raise her children as our mother had. She reigns over a garden full of lavender, irises, and peonies. As she rolls out the crust for perfect apple pies in her perfect sunny kitchen, there is a buzzing of bees, a chorus of songbirds. The blissful essence of sliced apples and new-mown grass encircles her. She says she sometimes pines for my globe-trotting life, but I don't believe her for a moment. I think she's trying to make me feel better for having switched dollhouses when I wasn't looking.

And so I live in a minimalist urban shoe box that I rarely see because I spend most of my waking hours rocketing from place to place, trying to pay the bills. My only child came to me late in life, if not full grown from the brow of Zeus, then miraculously and wonderfully full-blown from the pages of a casebook on adoption law I had been reviewing. Never married, I sometimes long for the time to plan a menu, for an oven large enough to bake long loaves of bread, and for sufficient culinary skills to host intimate dinner parties for no fewer than thirty-six. When I was younger I thought of this dream as my literal destiny—surely I would end up little wife, genteel helpmeet, artful homemaker, the kind who writes thank-you notes with calligraphy pens and perfumed ink.

Practicing law changed all that for me; it left me cranky, liti-
gious, and way too tired to figure out what wallpaper goes
with which rug.

Now, in middle age, I understand that perhaps the domestic yearning functions more as an inherited hunger. My family, like so many black middle-class families, raised girls for
one of two and only two destinies. You went to college, got
married, and settled down, or you went to college, got a job,
and stayed single so as to fulfill your lot as Providing Aunt, the
backup parent, the fairy godmother, supplying a little money
when times were thin, raising the orphans in times of catastrophe. My sister and I lead exceptional lives, having come of
age in a time when we had more opportunities than any previous generation to savor a bit of both worlds. But revolutions
don't happen overnight. And as the state of the economy
(even more than the women's movement) slowly pushed the
majority of American women, black and white, into a workplace that is not yet always accommodating of parental concerns, most women of my generation remain conflicted about
the tension between career and caring for children. Things
fall between the cracks.

In so many ways, my life is as fortunate a one as you get on
this planet, and so when the angst about domesticity curls into
my dreams like a small, smoky warning, I've come to see it as
more of a metaphor, a way of ordering my thoughts, a kind of
personal reinvention, a visitation from my unconscious.
When I wake up in the middle of the night exhilarated by the
thought of knocking out walls, I know it's time to change jobs.
If the dream is only about hanging wallpaper, it's time to re-
examine my personal relationships. At the threshold of each
passage from one stage of life to another, I always find that I
am renovating the big old Victorian house in my head.

When I was a student, each graduation—from high school,

college, law school—triggered three a.m. revelations of a new beginning: I would wake up triumphant, having discovered hidden staircases, corners of the attic I'd never visited. When I moved to California to assume my first job as a lawyer, I actually camped for a while in a very small caravan. I never felt as cramped as most people might, partly because that fanciful little-girl part of myself had gone to work and taken over: The actual cabinets in that caravan were so small one couldn't even store full-sized plates, and as I chased my suppers of boiled chicken and toaster-ovened potatoes around on a five-inch saucer, in my mind I was having a tea party. My life was reduced to a few essentials of clothing and food, because there were no closets and the refrigerator was the size of a hatbox. But I became very orderly in that economy of space, because my home economics were practiced in the limitless realm of pretend.

In my twenties and thirties, I gardened in my mind. At first I tried to make it literal again and used my little strip of sky-rise balcony to grow what my sister called "gallows tomatoes"—every season I would reap but one small cherry tomato drooping from a spindly stalk that looked for all the world like a noose. Eventually, I learned to garden metaphorically. I bought my first word processor in those years and began to write in earnest. I harvested essays that filled me with satisfaction, and before long my apartment bloomed with bright bouquets of reprints of the articles I had published. I loosened up and treated myself to big buckets of silk and paper flowers. I went to Fairway for tomatoes.

In my forties, the ruthless New York real estate market filled me with great and unhealthy yearning for not just inner space. I no longer just imagined, I coveted. I would dream I'd purchased the apartment next door and knocked out the wall between. I'd evicted the frail old widow lady who lived there and expanded the kitchen to vulgar immensity. Double ovens, Traulsen fridge, the works. I'd get a long trestle table for the imaginary dining hall, with a hand-embroidered runner to grace its great length. The bookcases would be so high you'd need ladders to reach the upper shelves, which would mean I'd have to dream that my ceilings were twice as high as they were in real life—very bad news for the elderly gentleman on a fixed income who lived upstairs with his quivering, half-blind dog. Those were greedy, resentful years, years in which I actually thought all my problems would be solved if only I had a little extra disposable income with which to buy stock in the telecommunications industry.

Now, in my fifties, I am wiser and more settled. I don't have a ballroom, but I do have a hat. Not just any hat, mind you, but one I almost didn't notice in the store because at first I thought it was a vine growing up the wall behind the cash register. It was so big it had a name, kind of like a ship: "Wild Hawaiian Lunch." It has an Audrey Hepburn–esque brim a little wider than my shoulders and a broad tunnel of orchids on steroids encircling the crown. It's the sort of thing that would never make it through airport security and so I wear it only around the house.

Actually, my real house isn't as minimalist as it used to be. These days it's filled with my son's little action figures, sheet music, cockatiel feathers, Lego bits, Monopoly money, soccer balls, and abandoned bowls of popcorn. In fact, my house is so stuffed to the gills that I joined an informal support group of overworked single mothers, divorcées, and widows. We e-mail each other or chat on the phone about how we are all about to be carried away on a tidal wave of clutter and guilt. When I confess that my son is so slovenly it makes me feel as though I have failed as a mother, I get a flutter of comforting messages, tales of mythically proportioned mess, soothing little psalms of maternal endurance:

> Pat, dear—If it makes you feel any better, I went into my
> son's room last week and found an almost full bowl of mac

and cheese that he had left on his windowsill. It wasn't completely full because he had dropped some beside the bowl. The ants were swarming under the window frame and had covered everything. I'm sure I was screaming as I picked up the bowl, scraped the clump back in, and ran down the stairs with the Million Ant March crawling up my arms in protesting waves. They were almost at my shoulders by the time I made it to the kitchen sink. My daughter's suggestion? That her friend Nadia had told her that chocolate kills animals, so we should try leaving chocolate under the bed as a way of killing the ants.

There's always somebody worse off than I am, and misery truly does love company. (And company there is. Even as this book was going to press, one of the editors paused to write me notes in the margin about the dinner plate of decayed food she had found in her son's desk drawer.)

I also subscribe to a virtual housecleaning service. You get fifteen e-mail messages a day from a woman who calls herself the Fly Lady and sounds exactly like your mother (if not mine). "Shine your sink!" she orders. "Eat lunch!" she directs. "Do you know where your shoes are? Are they laced to your feet or are they under your bed, in your closet, or hiding under your computer desk? . . . Shoes tell your head that it is time to go to work."

It helps in a rudimentary sort of way. Of course, my problem is that shoes are laced to my feet all right, but more pairs are to be found under the bed, in the closet, under the computer desk, beside the piano, and in the hallway beside the front door. There are a few pairs under the dining-room table, some sneakers in the washing machine, a pair in each of the five different-sized suitcases I carry when I travel, and more in my car and in my office, and that's not counting the ones my son hurled onto the balcony when driving away the squirrels that were trying to chew their way in through the vents.

The Fly Lady recommends the "27 Fling Boogie" for my sort. That involves taking a garbage bag and running through the house, throwing away twenty-seven items. "Then close the garbage bag and pitch it. DO NOT LOOK IN IT!!! Just do it." I pitch and run, boogie and fling.

But like every mortal commanded by the gods not to peek, I cannot resist looking back into the bag. I see an old *New York Times Magazine* with pictures of refugee camps from around the world. The camps are filled with huddled masses, dispossessed by myriad wars. The idea that I have twenty-seven random items that can be rapidly pitched to the pulse of a disco beat . . . It is the kind of information that in sane moments spurs me to passionate political involvement. But I am not sane just now. Instead I stand paralyzed by the realization that I could survive for a week in the wilderness with the contents of my sack. The wilderness—or some state of chaos—feels so close at hand. I take out the warped Tupperware salad storage bowl and envision the day when it would be the perfect vessel in which to collect rainwater—you know, after Rome is flattened by barbarians. I'd be grateful then, wouldn't I, for a burrow filled with bits of warm cloth and scraps of tinfoil and brightly colored plastic forks with only a few missing tines, and an old roll of Life Savers furry with lint that would wash right off in case of emergency.

This is the musing of panicked pack rats everywhere, clinging to our many odd, unused possessions. It is a state of mind that exceeds mere consumerism, I think. This kind of hoarding is the survival instinct of small hibernating mammals in fearful overdrive. If we do not possess obscene multiples of twenty-seven random items, we feel less-than, and threatened.

While all this has lent me salvation from the sin of overweening house pride, it has left me with a mild but chronic case of house shame. The few dinner parties I've ever thrown always involve some innocent but significant mishap, like discovering I had five mismatched forks in the whole house just as eight friends rang the doorbell. (I made a quick call to my local Japanese restaurant for a large delivery of sushi appetizers. "And don't forget the chopsticks, please." I do so love New York.)

The most memorable of my dinners, unless you count the small but messy saga of the exploding eggs—I was trying to boil them in the microwave—occurred about two months after I moved into my present home. Never having had occasion to use the oven, I invited ten people for Thanksgiving dinner. The oven had never been installed; it was just leaning against the wall looking good, a fact I didn't discover until three hours after I'd put the turkey in to roast. I spent the rest of the day in a frenzy of creativity, hacking up the bird and committing its parts to emergency committees of my guests. One-third was barbecued on the hibachi on the balcony. One-third was grilled in the toaster oven. One-third was boiled into a surprisingly pleasing hash.

But then, it was Uncle Carl whose experiments with holiday turkeys dominated my formative years. Of course not everything can be blamed on Uncle Carl. My principal role model, my kind and intelligent mother, had little in common with Martha Stewart. I have no fresh-from-the-oven mother-daughter recollections—only the daily creaking of cans being opened and the sucking sound of gelatinous vegetables splurting from their tin-encased vacuums. Her kitchen was filled with smoke and impatience. How deeply my mother believed in the conveniences of the 1950s as almost a kind of political freedom; how grateful she was for boxed mixes, canned soups, Jiffy Pop, instant rice, and homemade ice cream you didn't have to make at home. My mother was as happy to have been born in a time of TV dinners and washing machines as I am to have come along in time for cell phones and laptop computers. And so I grew up finding my own path, frying what could not be boiled, winging my way through life without recipes.

I do suffer a certain degree of culinary culture clash whenever I visit with the mothers of my more skillet-skilled contemporaries. Mme M. is the mother of one of my best friends. When I visited the family in France one summer, I found her in the kitchen. She had leaned her cane against the sink and was scaling fish that the children had just caught in the little river that flowed through the village. There was a lovely smell of woodsmoke, the ringing of church bells, ticking of clocks, the muted rustling of human movement in all the rooms of the very big house . . .

"So," she said gently, "you want to cook some fish." Not "would you like," and in this there was something of a command. But it was also an anointing. Not just anyone gets to help Mme M. prepare a meal. What's more, it was a kind of blessing, a prayer, a gift especially for me, in that Mme M. has spent years predicting, with the hushed intonations of a soothsayer, that learning how to cook might help me settle down and find a man.

I was an eager pupil, but with my acid personality, finding a man is hard work, and to have to achieve it culinarily, given the weird maelstrom of my upbringing, diminishes the prospects considerably. Besides, I was too intimidated by Mme M. to ask what I did not know. For starters, the stove was old and German and unfriendly. The temperature markings were in Celsius. The cookbook said centigrade. The measuring cup was in grams. My brain was panicked in ounces and Fahrenheit. When I let the sauce overheat—I don't think the word "burn" was quite fair—Mme M.'s inventive daughter told her that I had spent my life working for the betterment of humankind.

"Oh, well, then," snapped Mme M., "she's smart enough to buy her own food ready-made."

These days, I run to the deli when asked to potlucks. I dial for Chinese when I invite people home to dinner. But prêt-àporter has its limits. One Independence Day not long ago, I was invited to a party to celebrate pluralism and the great diversity of us, the American people. "Bring an hors d'oeuvre representing your ethnic heritage," said the hostess innocently enough. It caught me off guard, and I was stumped. It was hard sorting my ethnic from my racial heritage. What were the flavors, accents, and linguistic trills that were passed down to me over the ages? What were the habits, customs, and common traits of my social group by which I had been guided in life—and how did I cook it?

I made a list of ingredients:

A British plantation owner left us his—our, my—last name. My mother chose my first name from a dictionary of girls' names. "It didn't sound like Edna or Myrtle," she says, as though that explained anything. I have two almost-full-blooded-Cherokee ancestors, one on my mother's side, one on my father's—in addition to the imaginary ones. There's a Scottish great-grandfather and a French-Canadian one and a bunch of other things no one ever talks about. Not one of them left recipes.

Of course, the ancestors whose contribution most touched my fate in the world were the nameless West African grandmothers, and I can tell you right off that I haven't the faintest idea what they do for hors d'oeuvres in West Africa, although I have a Senegalese friend who always serves the loveliest, pouffiest little fish mousse things in puff pastries that look, well, totally French. Perhaps there is something of my African ancestors in my father's cooking, which is distinctly inflected by his having grown up in Georgia, but I suspect it's probably more marked by what foods were available in the rural South. His specialties are fried fish and rice, pork chops and pies, as well as the black-eyed peas on New Year's. His recipes are definitely black in a regional sense in that, until relatively recently, most blacks in the United States lived in the Southeast. He loves pig. He loves lard. (You don't see lard in stores much these days. That's because my father used it all up.)

In retrospect it occurs to me that I might have gone with a regional theme as a cipher for my background, but I was raised in Boston, a city whose gastronomical pedigree is rarely touted as anything but uninspired. There's good reason they call the place Beantown.

Then too, I suppose I could have served myself up as something like Tragic Mulatta Soufflé, except that I've never gotten the hang of soufflés. Too much fussing, too little reward. So as far as this world's concerned, I've always thought of myself as Just Plain Black. Let's face it, however much my categories get jumbled when I hang out at my favorite kosher sushi spot, it's the little black core of me that moves through our brave new world as I hail a cab, rent an apartment, and apply for jobs. Although it's true, I never have tried hailing a cab as an ethnic . . .

To make a long story short, I ended up bringing that old perennial favorite:

CHICKEN WITH SPANISH RICE AND NOT-JUST-BLACK BEANS
Boil the chicken.
Boil the rice.
Boil the beans.

Throw in as many exotic-sounding spices and mysterious roots as you can lay your hands on—go on, use your imagination!—and garnish with those fashionable little wedges of lime that make everything look vaguely Thai. Watch those taxis screech to a halt! A guaranteed crowd pleaser that can be reheated or rehashed generation after generation.

Coffee? Tea?

For years, my mother's father worked as the solemn, brown-faced maître d'hôtel at the Parker House, one of Boston's finer eating establishments. From all accounts, my grandfather was a gentle steward and tireless "race" man, as W.E.B. DuBois put it, quietly devoted to the cause of social equality.

Long after he died, the civil rights movement swept the nation and my family set out to dine at places whose thresholds we had never quite dared to imagine crossing before. Dressed up and slicked down, we were a determined little band of gastronomical integrationists. Our favorite place to go on special occasions was a wonderful seafood restaurant. The clam chowder was what the critics always praised, but the restaurant's real draw as far as I was concerned was its lobster—baked or steamed, the best anywhere. My parents took my sister and me there to celebrate birthdays if we had been very good, and, some years later, for our graduations from high school, college, and law school.

Eating lobster, I think in retrospect, was a kind of class sabotage in Boston. It was hard not to be inclined to some notion of human equality in seeing the devastation generally wrought by the arduousness of the endeavor. This particular restaurant was quite formal, yet the lobsters were served whole, gloriously encumbered by those pretty red shells, so impenetrable, so resistant, so hard—the sweet lobster meat quivering within. The restaurant would arm Boston's finest citizens with all the implements of attack: linen napkins, starched bibs, slender forks with cruel little tines, elegant silver tongs, exquisitely wrought nutcrackery things designed to snap and twist and crush. That this was a sloppy endeavor made it no less noble a struggle.

I have always envied the ladder-backed calm of the "proper Bostonian," so imperturbably self-confident amid even his own self-induced turmoil of flying lobster bits—the splashing butter, the badly spotted bibs, the impossible heap of crustacean parts sliding from the plate, the public struggle like some wet salty version of mud wrestling—all while resting on the prerogative of being unflappably highborn.

I have never been able to relax eating lobster publicly. I am afraid that the world will see me as the sort who is always soiled after a good meal, it being my nature to roll in the trough. This anxiety about propriety and place, race and class, marks me as hopelessly bourgeois, I suppose. The quest for acceptance is a kind of escape, the borders of oneself patrolled so closely that one is eternally looking outward, looking toward a home beyond where one is. I wonder always what it must be like to know freedom from such anxiety.

Even with her penchant for three-minute concoctions, my mother's cooking was relentlessly steeped in New England traditions of hard-winter cuisine. One of the earliest memories my sister and I share is that of my mother borrowing my father's screwdriver so she could pry open a box of salt cod. In those days, cod came in wooden boxes, nailed shut, and you really had to hack about the edges to loosen the lid. Cod from a box had to be soaked overnight. The next day you mixed it with boiled potatoes and fried it out in Crisco. (That's how my mother described it, with those unconscious, telling little prepositions. She'd always be frying something "up" or "out.") Then you served it with baked beans on the side in a little brown pot, with salt pork and molasses. There was usually some shredded cabbage, with carrots for color. Oh, and of course there was piccalilli; every good homemaker of the 1950s had piccalilli relish on hand. And there'd be hot rolls served with my grandmother's Concord grape jelly. Or maybe just brown bread and butter.

We'd have baked chicken on Sundays, otherwise boiled. My mother has actual recipes for boiling chicken. A whole range of them, with and without bay leaf, onions, potatoes, carrots, or not. Life can never be dull with boiled chicken.

These were the staples of my mother's home cooking.

The truth is we also liked watermelon in our family. All of

us. But the only times we ate it—well, those were secret moments, private moments, guilty, even shameful moments,
never unburdened by the thought of what would happen if
our white neighbors saw us enjoying the primevally, stereotyp-
ically "black" fruit. We were always on display when it came
to things stereotypical. Fortunately, my mother was never
handier in the kitchen than when under political pressure.
She would take that odd, thin-necked implement known
as a melon baller and gouge out innocent pink circlets and
serve them to us, like little mounds of faux sorbet, in fluted crystal goblets. The only time we used those goblets—wedding
gifts—was to disguise watermelon, in case someone was peer-
ing through the windows, lurking about in racial judgment,
albeit for lack of better things to do.

I suppose it's unusual: Virtually none of the women in my
family truly invested themselves in the kitchen. I don't remember my mother baking a cake even once, although we
certainly kept the local bakery busy. Perhaps I'm romanticizing again, but I think it was because my mother grew up
among a lot of determined African-American women who
were just plain tired of cooking. She was among the first generation in any kind of position to break out of the mold of
cook and nanny, and she took that mold breaking as an urgent
mission. To both my parents, education was the path to freedom; they and all their determined siblings and cousins were
college graduates. The women among them were liberated in
a way that most other groups of American women were not
able to realize until the 1960s. They became professionals
and never fully counted on marriage to protect them from
life's vicissitudes.

And so my mother was gently, quietly independent at a
time when certain things just weren't done. There is a wonderful picture of her that my father took on the day she received her master's degree from Emerson College. She was
seven months pregnant, with me, and her graduation gown

ballooned before her in a most unsubtle way. It was the early
1950s, after all, and pregnant women, married or not, simply
didn't display themselves in those days. But she was not going
to let anything stand in the way of her "marching up that
aisle." My grandmother, she says, supported her completely
and invited all her friends and neighbors to the graduation,
even though her being hugely pregnant scandalized a number
of them.

The women's liberation movement of the 1960s did inspire
my mother in one particular way, however. She was of a generation that did not generally learn to drive; ladies relied on
their husbands. One day, at the age of fiftysomething, she
got tired of asking my father to drive her here or there. There
was no angst, no fighting, no overcoming self-defeat or con-
fronting the symbolism of it all. (It helped, of course, that my
father simply wasn't the sort to dream of fighting about such a
thing. They fought about the big things. Like whether the
thermostat should be turned up or down.) So under the quirk-
ily combined sway of Betty Friedan and Erma Bombeck, my
mother just signed up for lessons, passed on the first try, drove
till her seventies, when she recognized that age and arthritis
were beginning to affect her mobility and reflexes—no one
had to tell her—and then went back to relying on my father
and public transportation.

As a parent, I suppose I am very much my mother's daughter—well educated, independent, and a halfhearted, intermit-
tent boiler-up of chickens. Luckily, my kitchen has a phone in
it, with a million little menus from places like the Fast Macro-
biotic Wok stacked next to it. I have a few cans of peas and a
couple of frozen dinners for home cooking's sake, but the
unfortunate truth is that a globalized, "redi-serve" version of
Uncle Carl's legacy has already shaped my son's childish
imagination. One day when he was two, he volunteered to

help me make dinner. "By all means," I said in grateful wonderment. He ran to the phone and picked it up. "Room service, pleez," he demanded. Now that he is a bit older, my son dreams of his own future house, a vision heavily inflected by lifestyles of rich and famous superheroes: He longs for a paintball range, a basketball court, dogs he is wildly allergic to, and a kitchen full of vending machines that dispense eel sushi and Orangina.

In real life, my son and I sit having a snack of cinnamon toast with lovely big mugs of steamed milk. (The froth nozzle on the cappuccino machine is working at long last.) I am explaining to him that Chippendale is a very finely crafted line of furniture. He is just as earnestly explaining to me that Chip 'n' Dale are a couple of chipmunks who rescue creatures larger than they through clever detective work. We argue until it's time for him to go to bed. I tuck him in. "Sweet dreams," I say.

We are playing house. We make ourselves at home.

IV

The Boudoir

I have friends who live in rural France. They reside in a lovely old farmhouse, a labyrinthine stone dwelling, built by hand and according to no standardized plan, with ceilings that generations of bats have called home, staircases that sprout at right angles to other staircases in order to wend over the kitchen and into the hayloft that is now a music room, sufficient bedrooms for hordes of guests, and a nice large kitchen to make up for there being only one bathroom.

They live a romantic life, suspended between the small duties of daily life and great notions of human enlightenment, and some years ago, when they became concerned about the stereotyped Prince Charming fantasies their eight-year-old daughter was acting out with her dolls, they sat the little girl down and told her that it didn't matter whether one's husband was tall or had lots of money or lived in a modest house or came from the "wrong" class.

"The only thing that matters is that he have a good heart," said my friends. The next day, their daughter came to breakfast with her little brother in tow. He was dressed up as a cat.

"Mummy, I want you to meet my new husband."

"Meow," said the little boy.

"But . . . he's a cat," said the mother.

"I love him," said the daughter.

"He's a cat—" said the father.

"A good cat," insisted the girl. "And Mummy? There's one more thing."

"Oh?"

"I'd like to introduce you to our baby, panda bear . . ."

Last summer when I visited these friends, there were six adults and seven children visiting at the same time—a loose network of friends and godchildren, British, French, Caribbean, American, all having dropped in on our way to someplace else. I would always get up at dawn in order to take a long uninterrupted shower, in my leisurely, would-rather-be-swimming, excessive American way. When I was dressed, I made strong coffee and sat in the kitchen, reading the papers and enjoying the early morning sounds. A few villagers greeted each other in the street, their voices falling and rising like those of the settling owls, the roosting pigeons, the kestrel's call, the slowly gathering busy-about-nothing sounds of the twittering sparrows. The occasional farmer rode a rumbling tractor down the road and into the fields.

By eight o'clock, a few of the children were up and sprawled about, some reading comic books, some—the boys—wrestling, some in the sitting room playing computer games. The house was filled with creaking and flushing sounds as the rest of the adults got up one by one. I went off to the bakery and purchased five baguettes, twenty-four croissants, and some postcards.

It was interesting staying in that household, a jumble of families, our every meal reflecting the odd diasporic mix of who we were. Our breakfasts were French, our lunches very English, and our dinners a mélange of African, European, and American cuisine. We ate brioche and Marmite, *pain au chocolat* and Heinz baked bean pizza, boiled eggs and herbed omelettes, curried lamb and *croques-monsieurs*, new potatoes with rosemary, red-peppered yams, poached lot, sardines fried with cornmeal, *tarte aux fraises*, bread pudding with coconut, prunes in Armagnac, and twenty kinds of cheese. We drank hot Ribena, Coca-Cola, Orangina, fresh ginger mash, gin and tonic, fizzy lemon, and twenty kinds of wine. Every time I looked in the cupboard, I thought: We creatures survive by adjusting and mutating on a daily basis. My heart swelled with the warm, encompassing nobility of it all.

That particular morning, the children had to be repeatedly summoned to the table. All seven of them had converged on the computer at some point. They were crowded around it, engrossed in a game they found in the Microsoft puzzle pack among the desktop goodies. Mixed Genetics, it was called. While the game was an otherwise inoffensive and amusing little sorting race, the narrative and images were . . . let's just say loaded: After a spaceship landed in a cyberplanetary Garden of Eden, discharging an alien monster among the fluffy innocents below, the world became populated with horrid little hybrids sporting random monster body parts. The object was to unjumble the parts so you end up with a recognizable elephant, a normatively configured crab, etc. To this end, the instructions told players to "[b]reed pure offspring from the mutant animals. Then rescue the pure offspring by putting them in the glass dome at the bottom of the screen . . . Use the Unmixed Genetics Guide in the bottom left corner to see what pure offspring should look like . . . Offspring inherit any body parts that two or more parents have. Animals can breed three times before they disappear."

In keeping with this three-strikes-and-you're-out mind-set, animals that had been bred twice were marked with a big palpitating black heart that expanded, popped messily, and consumed them when they did the hoo-ha that third time. "Your game is over when there are too many animals in the waiting room."

"Fear of the natives," concluded my British friend.

"Fear of immigration," countered my French friend.

"Fear of miscegenation," said I, the American.

Ah, miscegenation. The widespread, unofficial, nonconsensual use of black women to "let off" white men's "steam" in the Old South is still a sore spot in the American psyche. To be sure, there has been quite a bit of revisionist history in the wake of the popularization of Sally Hemings's relationship with Thomas Jefferson, much of it casting master-slave affairs as "love." Perhaps. But even assuming the very best of individual intentions, such unions occurred against a violent social backdrop in which blacks were not legally human, in which the children could be sold for income, and in which miscegenation was considered a form of bestiality, a violation of the species barrier.

I think that this has left a hole in our collective imagination. The most openly segregated sectors of American society are the personals columns of any given newspaper or magazine. "Straight white female . . ." "Gay, Jewish man . . ." "Athletic, blue-eyed music lover . . ." "Tall, blond, European . . ." Always looking for mirrors of themselves, always searching for "the same." To the extent that black-white intermarriage ever occurs in the United States, despite the much-vaunted "growth" rate, it is still only 2.5 percent, compared to Britain, for example, where it's 40 percent. Furthermore, it usually occurs between relatively economically well-off black men and white women. But if women marry men with an eye toward financial stability, men tend to marry women in part for their looks. Thus, black women have a much harder time in the face of many white men's reluctance based on contemporary Western beauty standards. But it is huge, the aesthetic value placed on looks and the envy of others. Then there's the role of the model, if not trophy, wife in advancement up the cor-

porate ladder. A black wife isn't likely to bring money or con-
nections into a marriage. She isn't likely to be an asset at the
country club. And there's the little matter of hair in a culture
of relentlessly billowing tresses . . .

The United States has very little transracial folk literature
of the sort that has, during our long immigrant history, usually
cropped up as a way of romanticizing other boundary trans-
gressions, like class or religion or ethnicity. We have very few
Cinderella stories in which the handsome white prince or
lord of the manor is smitten by the poor-but-beautiful black
servant and then they get married and next thing you know
they've created a dynasty. Even after all the effort expended
during the 1960s in trying to create a culture of black as beautiful, Hollywood is only now, in the twenty-first century, testing timorous pap like Jennifer Lopez in *Maid in Manhattan*.

"Chattel" slavery in the United States so completely dehu-
manized those of African descent that even today a substantial
swath of American society opposes black-white intermarriage
on deeply felt, even religious grounds. Senator John Mc-
Cain's bid for president ran aground in South Carolina when
pictures of his adopted Bangladeshi daughter were circulated.
The politically powerful Bob Jones University abandoned its
official antimiscegenist stance only in the year 2000, and then
only out of concern that it might harm George W. Bush's
chances of being elected president. (Bush had kicked off his
campaign at Bob Jones and was photographed seated in front
of a giant mural of Jesus Christ, all but wrapped in the sym-
bols of the Confederacy, a pose suspiciously like the closing
scene in D. W. Griffith's film *Birth of a Nation*. And people
wonder why 92 percent of blacks voted for the Democratic
ticket.) In the mass media, moreover, radio hosts like Rush
Limbaugh get away with telling black callers to "take that
bone out of your nose," while Boston disc jockey John Dennis
is given a short suspension for describing a gorilla that had escaped from Franklin Park Zoo as probably heading for "the

Metco bus"—Metco being a program that transports children
from Boston's mostly black neighborhoods to schools in its
largely white suburbs.

But this is only the tip of a much larger iceberg—that is,
the great historical power of the so-called Christian Identity
movement in this country. We must take seriously the legacy
of Jim Crow's theology no less than its laws. It is no accident,
after all, that a burning cross became the calling card for the
Klan's deadly visitations. It is no accident that the Klan's robes
and hoods look so similar to those of the Inquisition. Polygen-
esis—the theory that God made blacks and whites in separate,
unmixable batches—is at the root of Bob Jones University's
antimiscegenist beliefs. It is also at the heart of many (certainly not all) creationists' resistance to scientific conclusions
that man and "the lower orders" are related. God's supremacy
and white supremacy are still very much confused in many
people's minds, and even if the crudest and most violent
forms of racism have subsided, there still exists a large measure of taboo about physical intimacy, or even neighborly
proximity, across the color line.

In a letter dated May 4, 1955, my paternal grandfather,
Dr. I. D. Williams, wrote the following to my father:

> Dear Son,
> Doris, Ella, Sarah, Clara, and I spent the weekend at the
> old home site up in South Carolina where we were born.
> You are a Georgian but we still think South Carolina is
> better.
>
> We had a wonderful time and hope you will someday
> find time to visit this spot on one of your vacations. There
> are many close relatives still living around this spot. We
> saw at least 30 relatives (immediate) and we saw one of
> Mother's mother's half-brothers (white) who is 96 years old

who came strutting to the door of his palatial mansion without the aid of a cane or glasses and said that he can read fine print . . . I called on him and he received me very courteously. He walks up straight and his mind and memory are very good . . .

It would be nice to have a letter from you anytime.

As ever yours,
Dad

This letter is interesting on many levels. To me, the most striking thing is the casual mention of my great-grandmother's half brother. The "strutting" man in the "palatial mansion" upon whom my grandfather came calling was J. H. Davis, the legitimate white son of the plantation owner who had impregnated my great-great-grandmother, a Gullah or African slave woman who spoke very little English.

What is remarkable about it is that he wrote of the relationship at all. We all knew of it, but speaking of it always took place behind closed doors. To write it down was kind of a brave thing in those days. "Hush-hush" was the lesson we all practiced. My grandfather's locutions seem terribly tame by today's standards, I know. But it must not be forgotten that he was writing in the post-Reconstruction, pre–civil rights era South. He had lived through the violent times so romanticized in *Birth of a Nation*. These were years when the very word "strutting" was reserved almost exclusively for black people who had accumulated more power than the Klan could stand and "had" therefore to be "taken out" — out of the proverbial barnyard, that is, like troublesome roosters. He may have gone calling upon J. H. Davis, but it is unlikely he called at the front door.

My grandfather's son, rather overly giddy with the oxygen of relative Northern freedoms, would translate all this for us in no uncertain terms.

I was four years old in the May of 1955 when that letter was written. The holding in *Brown v. Board of Education* was less than a year old; whatever that decision implied—or yet implies—for the long-term future, the dismantling of Jim Crow had not yet happened on the ground. The media was celebrating a general warming of race relations, largely premised on the year 1953 having been declared "the nation's first lynch-less year." At the same time, civil rights leaders were anxious about the rise of new forms of violence directed against blacks. My godmother Marguerite, writing in *The Crisis*, worried that the decline in lynchings did not necessarily signal "greater reverence for human life." She counseled against complacency in the face of what she feared was "a shift in the plane of violence" away from lynching and toward that "modern instrument of terror—the hate bomb."

These were still dangerous times, in other words. Everyone knew that as long as you kept your mouth shut, as long as you lied through your strong, smiling white teeth, you just might stand a chance of being received very courteously indeed. It was better for everyone that way.

But, as I said, my grandfather was a courageous man. He spoke his mind to the end. No doubt thanks to his very fine gene pool, he, like my great-grandmother's white half brother, lived on into his midnineties, standing straight, reading all the fine print, outlasting two good wives. He died at the height of the civil rights era, on vacation, frolicking on a beach to which blacks had been denied access in his younger years, in a stylish terry wrap, apparently in the company of a sprightly younger woman. Everyone agrees he lived a rich, full life.

Among the collection of little wiglets, false ponytails, and clip-on chignons crammed on the back shelf of one of my late godmother Marguerite's closets was a yellowed collection of "Progress Reports" submitted to her by her Hunter College students in the spring of 1955. "What is the best way of letting a person know through a letter that you are not a negro?" asked one young woman, titling the question "A Problem That I Would Like To See Discussed In Class."

The author was at pains to explain that the question was a strategic one presented by the necessity of doing sociological fieldwork as part of the class: "I know that the above question may seem very jouvenile [*sic*] when you first read it, but if you observe it closer, you will notice that the matter is not as simple as it first appears. During this course, I am sure that I will have several occasions when I will write letters to negroes. I want to show my sincere interest in the negro and yet I am afraid that they may resent the fact that I may consider it necessary to specify in my letter that I am white. [C]ould you let me know the best way in which I can let a person know that I am not a negro and at the same time avoid any hard feelings? I want to let the negro person know that I am sincerely interested in him and that I am not showing an interest only because it happens to be a school assignment . . ."

Among the great challenges facing your average Negro person in the modern world is trying hard to act naturally around your average white person when the white person in question is trying *this hard* to act naturally in the presence of the aforementioned Negro. Although I suppose a little extra effort never hurts. Once the white person has struggled through the revelation that she is Not a Negro, the cordially inclined Negro person could likewise break the ice by revealing that he is Not of the Caucasian Persuasion.

One of the many challenges Anna Deavere Smith put out for discussion during those vibrant summers at the Institute on the Arts and Civic Dialogue was asking us to think long and hard about the one person we could never be. In some ways this whole book began as an effort to answer that question.

There are glib answers to it, I suppose. I could never be a singer. I could never be George Bush. But the matter is not as simple as it first appears. I think the person I could really never be is something closer, more intimate; the question suggests a more complex dimension to my sister's and my juvenile game of twinning, of role playing two sides of the same coin—the ideal we wanted to be and the anathema we avoided. At the most instructive level of that game—although we certainly didn't see it back then—we ended up having to tackle the question of being what we denied, or of not being what we thought. Perhaps it's why, even today, I try so hard to unlock the puzzle at the center of my great-aunt Mary's life passage from indentured child servant to elderly grande dame. Passing requires the purposeful abandonment of the problem of race as political; it substitutes a calculated and loveless escapism for civic commitment to the notion of transformation through equality. Somewhere at her core Aunt Mary was always in exile. As a linguist friend points out, it's the kind of inner searching that links the etymology of the words "host," "hostile," and "hostage": All three derive from the same root, embracing simultaneously the concepts of guest and stranger, as well as a body for sacrifice.

When my son was very young, he had enormous difficulty with what people meant when they referred to our being black. I'd given him all the best literature, the uplifting material about struggle and triumph, with ennobling pictures and stirring stories. He knew about Martin Luther King Jr. and had read books about the necessity for black self-esteem and education and economic power and how beautiful we all were. I underscored the great crudeness of race as category, the complexity and imprecision of its meaning. Yet . . .

"Grandma's white," he would say.

"No, she's not," I would say. "She's lighter-skinned than we are. But she's black."

"But she's lighter-skinned than Don. Isn't Don white?"

"True. But the interesting thing is that he's Italian, and Italians sometimes weren't always considered white a hundred years ago; darker-skinned southern European immigrants have their own history of having been discriminated against in many ways."

"So if Don's family was once black and now they're white, why isn't Grandma white?"

"Well"—I wasn't doing well with this—"it's not just about color. Blackness is and isn't a color. It's kind of political, it changes. Sometimes it's what the law says it is; sometimes it's what other people think it is; sometimes it's whatever you say it is."

"Political?" he asked, looking a little lost.

"Look," I said. "We called ourselves black to really emphasize the importance of color at a certain moment in time. But perhaps it's easier for you to use the term 'African American.' It's more precise in many ways. It tells you that blackness is not just about legal or social status or 'one drop of blood,' but also has something to do with acknowledging where your great-great-grandmother came from and being proud of that in a world that frequently tells you to be ashamed of it."

"*National Geographic* says that every human being has ancestors who came from Africa."

"Umm, yes, well, I mean those who came from Africa within the last few hundred years as opposed to tens of thousands of years ago. Recent African ancestors."

"So why isn't everyone with an Italian ancestor called Italian? Why does Don keep saying he's white?"

I found it very hard to explain the arbitrariness of race and color to a very young child, or how it trumps ethnicity. It's hard enough explaining it to myself. Its power—both visible and invisible—is so pervasive and systemic, so ordered and ordering. This totalism is at such seeming odds with its whimsy, its irrationality.

After many such conversations, I finally hit upon something that brought the point home with somewhat better success. We were having dinner one night, a nice salmon fillet. My son found some small bones in it and proceeded to complain, in terms for which I had no patience, "It's disgusting!"

"Fish have bones, young man," I snapped. "Don't be so spoiled, eat your dinner. We are so lucky to have food at all . . ." On and on I went.

"It's still disgusting," he said sulkily.

I looked closely at his plate and said, "Well, you're in luck. Those don't appear to be fish bones after all. I think they're big old spider legs." Now I freely admit that this was not a high point in the history of my mothering. He thought fish bones were disgusting? I'd give him disgusting. Unfortunately, that's precisely what I did. My highly suggestible child put down his fork and looked utterly stricken.

"I was just kidding," I said contritely. "They're not really!"

"I know," he said miserably. "But it's in my head now and I can't get the spider legs out."

I saw in this the perfect opening for a very edifying discussion about the power of imagining compared to knowledge of physical reality. Sometimes, I told him, imagination is much more powerful than our rational knowledge. Sometimes the "truth" of things is very hard to grasp if it's obscured by the associations, the images, that are put in our heads—by the lessons we learn at home or in school, by the messages drilled into us by the media.

I am an ambitious mother, and by the time I moved on to the definition of ontology, I had ground him down completely. "Mummy, you're lecturing," he said with the weariness of someone who had suffered enough. "Here. I'll eat my fish."

Racial categories are a lot like those spider legs—they don't exist in the rational world in any coherent, consistent, or scientific sense, but nevertheless they have great power over us. It is an imaginary force but one that constantly embellishes what our five senses tell us, constantly filters our experiences of taste, touch, smell, fear, beauty, humor, dignity. In this way, race does affect intelligence as well as knowledge, albeit not in the way social Darwinists think. Whiteness is a kind of cultural canvas upon which American existence is depicted in myriad artful visions of the possible. Whiteness is the site of privileged imagining, the invisible standard. It is whatever it wants to be. And blackness has been for too many generations whatever was left over. If our children struggle with race's lack of unifying theme or crisp clear edges, it is because its history has been just that: mercurial and contingent. Race is a careless, deeply unconscious, and highly aesthetic phenomenon, even if that aesthetic ultimately deprives us of greater vision.

How do we unimagine, or envision differently, the spider legs of race in our national melting pot? Facile pronouncements of "color blindness" are about as helpful as my telling my son just to pretend I never said a word about arachnids, you know, the big creepy ones, with the fuzzy legs that crunch when you bite into them. Don't give it another thought, my cherub . . .

But beyond metaphor, there is a very specific history that gave rise to all this confusion, amnesia, and sloshily reimagined boundary. As the institutions of slavery and slave breeding evolved in America, there grew whole populations of Aunt Marys: people whose descent was ambiguous or questionable and whose status thereby confounded the clear color distinctions that had marked Africans from Europeans in earlier times. This group included indentured servants of Irish, Portuguese, or German lineage; Native Americans who were dark skinned but presumed free; a growing number of mulattoes trying to pass as white; freed blacks; and those presumptively dissolute white men and women who were mistaken for black, usually because they had "taken up" with black sexual partners.

In her book *Double Character*, legal historian Ariela Gross documents the degree to which racial identity was the frequent subject of litigation during the nineteenth century and was determined by a wide variety of measures. Since the litigation of whiteness dealt with inherently "deceptive" racial subjects, color was not the only evidentiary standard. Of course, appearance counted for a great deal, particularly straightness of hair, width of nose, and thickness of lips—the dimensions of which were sometimes measured "scientifically" by such devices as calipers. But other evidence of whiteness included ancestry of "blood" (the famous "one drop" rule, among other formulations); exercise of citizenship and voting rights; self-presentation or claimed identity; reputation and acceptance among others, both white and black; and "white conduct and character," or, as Gross puts it, the "performing" of whiteness.

"A white man's honor resided in the public sphere," explains Gross, "in his statesmanlike behavior towards superiors and inferiors, his adherence to the gentleman's code of conduct, his mastery of slaves, and his exercise of citizenship . . . For a woman, performing whiteness meant acting out purity and moral virtue." In the 1835 South Carolina case of *State v. Cantey*, the judge observed that, despite an ambiguous appearance, "it may be well and proper, that a man of worth, honesty, industry and respectability, should have the rank of a white man, while a vagabond of the same degree of blood should be confined to the inferior caste."

And in an 1845 Louisiana trial litigating the whiteness of one Sally Miller, her lawyer cited Miller's "moral power, and weight, and influence. An influence, which I contend no one but a white woman could possibly raise up and control—an influence as inconsistent with the nature of an African, as it would be with the nature of a Yahoo." In courts throughout the South, the borderline statuses of the "enslaved white" and the "passing black" were methodically examined, defined, and reduced to stereotypes that endure to this day. Putatively enslaved whites came mostly from the ranks of "poor whites," whom the common law generally disparaged as those with coarse features and bad manners; in contrast, "passing" blacks were those with "fine" features and deceptively good manners. Poor whites were altogether uninspired by the civilizing arts; uppity blacks were those with pretensions of being inspired by the finer things of life yet who revealed themselves by an amusing propensity for malapropisms and a telltale affection for gaudiness. Sally Miller's lawyer argued in her "defense" against blackness that "the Quatronne is idle, reckless and extravagant, this woman is industrious, careful and prudent—the Quatronne is fond of dress, of finery and display—this woman is neat in her person, simple in her array, and with no ornament upon her, not even a ring on her fingers."

One must wonder if this history is not echoed in the chilling belief structures that linger with us still. Today, "real" blacks are not just those who are dark skinned or impoverished or politically disenfranchised, but those who supposedly exhibit that malleable cipher for black character, the "culture of pathology." (I will never forget hearing a white friend's son describing a fraternity brother as a "nigger." By that, he explained, he meant not to smear all blacks. That would be bad. It's just that "some blacks *are* niggers. It's up to them; it's how they act.") "Real" whites, meanwhile, remain known by the mobility of their hair in a spring breeze, by lips so thin they need collagen implants before the calipers can get a read, and by adherence to a moral code so pure they need neither abortion nor birth control, just a good clean petri dish into which to scrape select genetic characteristics for culturing, reproduction, and sale.

In between these two conceptual extremes remains the legacy of enslaved whites and passing blacks who, in today's world, seem to occupy a limbo of prewhiteness and postblackness. Prewhites include downsized poor white factory workers but also those whom the mainstream media always mark as aspirational immigrants—those who don't yet look like "real"

Americans but who, with hard work at two or more jobs and lots of intermarriage, should be white in no time. A postblack, on the other hand, is that light-skinned, ubiquitous pretender to victimhood who malaprops his way through the one professional job that should have been divided among ten better-qualified whites and who is known less for the content than the contentiousness of his character. Postblacks exist in the realm of that utterly paradoxical category of social projection: the "new black middle class," which includes anyone—from security guards to Oprah Winfrey—deemed not a member of the "real" black underclass.

Not a bit of this history is in any standard American textbook of which I am aware. Yet the degree to which these portrayals still hold such uninformed and unquestioned sway—"But it's true!"—is the degree to which we Americans may find our best work still ahead.

Some years ago I wrote a parodic little story for the then-infamous Women's Issue of *The New Yorker*. That would be the one for which Tina Brown brought comedienne Roseanne Barr on board, causing great writers to bolt from the staff, like first-class passengers from the *Titanic*. (Never having been that close to the A-, B-, or even C-list before or since, I was only too happy to leap aboard in their stead.) The story was titled "My Best White Friend." After it was published, some of my younger students visited me in a heated little knot, accusing me of racism. "How would you like it if I wrote something titled 'My Best Black Friend'?" one young woman demanded. I explained that I was parodying what I had thought was a cultural cliché—as represented by the well-meaning defender of segregation who used to deny being a racist because "some of my best friends are black" but who still doesn't want his sister to marry one.

The students went away looking dubious, unconvinced. I

don't know. Maybe we have reached the happy time when all this history is beyond the reach of a general audience. Maybe I've grown curmudgeonly by filtering out of my life the communal oblivion of cable TV. Maybe they're too young—a flyer circulated by the student life committee of a campus I visited recently notes that to today's college students, Michael Jackson has always been white. But my sense is that there are a lot of young people who spend too much time watching the Fox Network, and it's turning their brains into a thin, acidy gruel.

Anyway, a little background as to the specifics: I've called my best white friend my best white friend ever since she started calling me her best black friend. I am her only black friend, as far as I know, a circumstance for which she blames "the class thing." In fact, at her end of the social ladder, I am *my* only black friend, a circumstance for which I blame "the race thing." We have known each other since our late teens and we spar about everything. Maybe we even fight about everything. But it's safe, somehow, as though the habit of it reassures us. For almost thirty years we have engaged in edgier-than-average girl talk as a means to the nirvana of greater self-understanding.

It always begins with my best white friend asking some innocuous but annoying question that pitches me over a meditative edge. Something like, "What's a radical black intellectual like you doing reading O magazine?"

"I subscribe," I told her evenly.

"Why?" she asked, making a face that suggested disdain.

Why, indeed, I thought, as I glowered past her to look at the clock. Twelve more minutes of the dark brown suds prickling my scalp. She had convinced me to dye my rapidly graying hair, and I was waiting for the color to "develop."

"It's comforting," I replied, and settled into an article about
the mathematically unlimited ways to accessorize the same
blouse and skirt over the course of a week. Hadn't I read this
someplace before? And what had it to do with the national
crises about which I usually write—suspect profiling, the death
penalty, eugenics, human rights? What comfort was it I wanted
so much, what hope of belonging did it awaken in me?

The truth is that I buy O for an accumulation of little
reasons, not one of which is very earthshaking but all of
which are related to finding a peculiar solace in Oprah's self-
presentation as normative. I am seduced by the illusion of banality she proffers, of just-folks colloquial encounter. You have
to bear with me here and forget that the real Oprah is a cover
girl for the likes of *Fortune* magazine, and there's nothing banal about it. But more on that later.

Compared to almost any other women's magazine on the
market, O presents an image of black women as comfortably
integrated, pleasantly mundane. I suppose it says more about
me than it does about the world that I find that such an attractive concept.

If the world were a different place, I might join those who
have sniffed that O is just another yearning-for-a-middle-class-
lifestyle mag like *Martha Stewart Living*. But O, for all of its
aromatherapeutic take on life, is the most integrated magazine on the American market. This musing is probably driven
by my age. You see, it is a kind of nice confusion to wake up,
as from a dream, and find oneself in the Age of Oprah. When
I was growing up in the 1950s and '60s, the only black women
in the national eye were Marian Anderson, the opera singer
whose attempt to integrate Constitution Hall was one of the
galvanizing moments of the civil rights movement, and Hattie
McDaniel, the film actress who played Mammy in *Gone With
the Wind*. They, in their very polarity, symbolized the rock
and the hard place of African-American womanhood: the

martyr and the mammy, the hyperarticulated classicist and the folksy frump, the chin held high and the ample, encompassing bosom—with the occasional tragic mulatta, always in tears.

These were the most visible models. There were also cartoonish renderings of Jezebels, and Sapphires, exotic hoodoo root women in skirts of bananas; insurrectionary half-white witches whose supposed "gift" of half a white brain was always undone by the curse of a really bad black attitude. Suppressed but haunting us too were the archetypes of Pansy and Prissy— the silly trollops in *Gone With the Wind*, the ones with squeaky voices who knew nothing about birthing babies and who made terrible servants but very fine comics. White people would wink and laugh about certain little black girls having "grown like Topsy," in the parlance of that time, when they mysteriously turned up pregnant. The babies would always be light skinned and fatherless. "The night has no eyes," my grandmother would sigh.

We live in a great memory-gobbling global marketplace now. Our sense of racial history has expanded and contracted in marvelously complicated ways. "Growing like Topsy," insists conservative columnist William Safire, now means nothing to people beyond Harriet Beecher Stowe's original reference in *Uncle Tom's Cabin*, to wit, a young slave "untutored in religion." If the array of black women in the national imagination still ranges from welfare queen to rap queen to quota queen, it now also includes Toni Morrison, Marion Wright Edelman, Barbara Jordan, Barbara Lee, Cynthia McKinney, and even a few archconservatives like Condoleezza Rice. And while almost all the aforementioned women have been controversial, I guess none of us really ever expected any of this to come easily.

Progress is a complicated phenomenon. My mother would think it amazingly progressive just that I was sitting with a headful of inky, squishy mud as applied by my best white friend's personal stylist. A generation ago, she would say, no white hairdresser would even think of touching a black person's hair other than to rub a black man's head for good luck. I darted a look at the mirror for a moment to see what me was there. (I see myself differently every time I look in a mirror. The malleability related to confidence, I suppose, and mood. But there are a lot of selves, like little clowns in a toy car, compressed inside the outer me.) Then I buried my face farther into my magazine while my thoughts drifted back through the decades.

September 12, 1966

Dear Aunt Margaret,

Thank you so much for the birthday money. It is fun being fifteen. I promise to use it for a socially responsible purpose. It will probably end up in my college savings account, although I almost spent it on a haircut. I am trying to do my bit for the integration effort, and so I made an appointment at Jordan Marsh's hair salon. I was very frightened, but when I showed up the hairdresser was even more afraid. She said she had no idea how to cut my hair, and she called the manager and the supervisor and the vice executive in charge of everything. They stood around my chair and panicked. They kept saying to each other: "What are we going to do?" And "Any ideas?" And "Such a nice face!" And "Isn't it a shame!"

I don't think I had such a nice face. I was sweating too much. They were too. They all touched my hair tragically, as though it were dead, and cautiously, as though it were alive, but they didn't charge me anything, so that's how I still have the money. Then I went home and cut it off myself. That's when my troubles really began, because I cut it really short, in an Afro, and my father is furious. He says I look like a boiled egg or a man or a billiard ball or a pompom. Every time he opens his mouth he gets more inven-

tive. A pinecone, a cantaloupe, a cabbage, a tumbleweed.
But I can't stand it. A helium balloon! You are the only one
he'll listen to. Would you mind calling him and telling him
to stop? I would be eternally grateful.

> Your loving niece and miserable grapefruit-head,
> Patricia

Aunt Margaret was my father's very successful younger sister. She and her husband were both doctors. They never had
children but gave themselves entirely to public interest medicine and charity work. To my eyes they were not just noble
but also glamorous. They traveled to the most remote parts of
the world. My aunt wore saris. She was bitten by tsetse flies.
She survived encephalitis. She sent us packages with sandal-
wood incense and African textiles for Christmas. She wore
a small diamond in her nose back in the 1960s. And most
thrilling of all, she had cut off almost all her hair and dyed
what was left platinum blond. To many in the black middle
class of that era—and certainly to my mother's desperately
conformist family—Aunt Margaret was scandalous beyond all
measure. Those clothes! That hair! Given all the unkind
things people said about her, I thought she was marvelous,
courageous, heroic. I envied that she really didn't seem to
care what people thought. By contrast, my father was trained
as a lawyer, but he'd not found a place in the Boston law firm
world of those times. He became a technical editor instead
and spent his hours writing manuals for COBOL and FOR-
TRAN and other early computer languages. He and my
mother cared very much what other people thought.

My best white friend and her very fashionable hairdresser
were sparring in Italian. I looked inside myself for the courage
to command him to cut my hair to a carefree length of a quar-
ter of an inch. I did not find that courage. It is good to be liv-

ing in these times, I suppose, part of this rarified moment, the
beneficiary, however indirect, of a royal lifestyle, with a myriad of personal choices. I've come a long way, baby, and I am
happy. But the effort of self-presentation is still a complicated
enterprise.

A few years ago, I appeared as part of an evening discussion at Sotheby's auction house in New York. (It was at the invitation of Inger Elliott, the socialite whose unfortunate
encounter with a black con artist pretending to be Sidney
Poitier's son inspired John Guare's play *Six Degrees of Separation*. It was a lovely event and she was very gracious despite
the fact that I was trying much too hard to be myself, my
whole self, and nothing but myself. Of course this little tidbit
is neither here nor there; I mention it nevertheless . . . well,
because it's just too irresistible. Little encounters like that are
an exotic treat to a black person like me; I think it must be a
vague sort of inverse of the experience of my best white friend,
the little frisson that makes her smile so when she drops my
name over and over and over again, introducing me like a
newly procured Ming vase, this acquisition of a finely
wrought best black friend. No, heavens no, really, nothing
about this should be read to imply that I harbor a secret desire
to strangle her. But back to my story.)

At some point during the evening, I joked, as I assumed
countless others have, about finding myself on such a gilded
auction block. After the discussion, a very well tailored Englishman scolded me for having dared make such a joke, but
not because it might have been a little obvious. Rather, he
was upset because "you should have been grateful to be up
there at all." He spoke to me as though I were a naughty pet. I
was there to lick the figurative hand, not bite it. And it didn't
take much of a nip for him to slap my nose. His was perhaps a
particularly British take on things: I had spoken, acted, beyond my place, above my station, "station" being that assignment of class stasis as well as racial status that traps you, pins

you like a butterfly, up, down, higher, lower, upon the social ladder.

My aunt, the bohemian black female doctor, was such an unusual character for her generation, always a first in everything she did, always considered "theatrical" precisely because she did not feel the need to act. It's a little disconcerting sometimes to find myself described in those terms—always bohemian, always a first. Yet I am not my aunt. I am much more anxious about my role in the world. I try much harder to conform, I feel much more acutely the precariousness of my place. Despite all the bestowed privilege of this global moment, despite all the progress, I worry that there is still a great deal of public ambivalence about African-American successes, from above and below, that renders prior generations' achievements invisible or idiosyncratic. There is an out-of-placeness to the success, an edgy resentment that lurks in the shadows. It is a post–civil rights hybrid of a resentment, part class, part race, akin to the structure of anti-Semitism in its conceits about who should have power, who deserves wealth.

Each battle to carve out some social zone where race is not a factor seems not to have built on the last. The public image of all of us seems on the line each time one of us is on the line. This makes for a sense of precariousness in the world—a fragility, a vulnerability, a political resonance to the erstwhile romantic fluffiness of Terry McMillan's term "waiting to exhale."

Indeed, I thought, still musing behind the pages of my magazine, O is perhaps the nonfiction equivalent of McMillan's books, which created a genre of black bodice rippers. I'm not a particular fan of this sort of light romantic literature, but I confess also to a certain gratitude that Oprah reigns as fairy princess in the dreamworld O creates. No other magazine has ever left me fantasizing about what it would mean to do yoga on the deck of my yacht in red silk lounging pajamas. But then, what other magazine before it has ever featured a black woman who owns a yacht?

I don't posit this as anything I aspire to in a material sense; this sort of fantasy serves psychic longings, not physical needs. But the image of a less stressed, more escapist me with tropical breezes rippling over my bare shoulders, my dark eyes flashing in the moonlight, is oddly attractive, a kind of little-girl dream, like that of being the perfect bride. "Like" because Oprah herself seems to have grown past the perfect-bride phase and gone on to envisioning the perfect life. And since I, like Oprah and many of my generation, was never a bride but was nevertheless socialized to want something like that, the Oprah fantasy of happiness ever after with personal trainer and spoiled-rotten little dogs is a peculiarly satisfying substitute.

When I was growing up, fairy-tale contentment was always the property of very specific kinds of white girls and women. In my mostly white high school, teen life was driven entirely by the promise of such fairy tales, and there was always a singular golden girl whose looks captured that promise at the expense of everyone else. At my school, the Golden Girl—I'll call her G.G. for short, but she could have been Melissa or Muffy or Blythe or Alexandra—served to remind all of us what we did not look like. In her younger days, Martha Stewart looked a lot like G.G. (My theory is that it was this exuded adolescent quality not just of being too perfect, but of not having suffered enough in high school, that contributed to the disproportionate public gloating at Stewart's financial downfall, as compared to the relative complacency of response to far larger crimes committed by the dull, suited personalities at Enron and WorldCom.)

I confess I resented G.G. because she was so, well, golden, although I do not mean to imply that I didn't have an amicable enough relationship with G.G. It's just that G.G. had boyfriends and I didn't. G.G. was also the blondest girl in the whole school, and that had a currency that had no relation to how nice she was. She was destined for bliss in Connecticut and everyone knew it. No one cared whether she was nice or not; she was just so perfect. I always tried to be very, very nice to everyone, not just blonds, but no one ever looked at me the way they did at G.G., because apparently being seen as nice always seemed to depend on being seen to begin with.

I was pretty invisible in high school, or at least I felt it. Most people did, I suppose. Perhaps that's the great integrating sentiment upon which Oprah Winfrey capitalizes. Maybe G.G. felt invisible too, but somehow I doubt it. In fact, I think she might have felt too visible, or at least she gave off the kind of vulnerability that made you bet some prince would come along and protect her from the rest of us by sticking her behind high palace walls, or at least in a nice gated community. And sure enough, these days she's on her third prince, third palace. Some people have all the luck.

So here I am, at that glorious life intersection called middle age, still with this ghostly sense that being nice is not enough. My ghosts are small and petty, for which I maintain a consistent stance of gratitude and for which I hope the entire category of good people who just happen to be blond will pardon me. Some of my best friends are blond.

But . . . such thoughts were a diversion from more important matters at hand.

My best white friend didn't like *O* magazine because it's not *Vogue*, and she was trying very hard to give me advice on how to get myself up like a trophy wife in waiting. This particular day, she and I were obliged to attend a gala fund-raiser for an organization on whose board we both sat. I've never been a wife, and she was saying she knew why: I'm prickly as all get-out. I dress down instead of up, and my hair is "a complete disaster." MBWF, who is herself a trophy wife of considerable social and philanthropic standing, was pressing me to borrow one of her real designer gowns and a couple of those heavy gold bracelets that are definitely not something you can buy on the street.

I told her she was missing the obvious stumbling block here. Cinderella wasn't a middle-aged black professional with an attitude. What sort of master of the universe would go for that?

"You're not a racist, are you?" she asked.

"How could I be?" I replied, with wounded indignation. "What, being the American dream personified and all."

"Then let's get busy and make you up," she said soothingly, breaking out the little pots of powder, paint, and polish.

From the first exfoliant to the last of the cucumber rinse, we fought about my man troubles. From powder base through lip varnish, we fought about hers. You see, part of the problem is that white knights just don't play the same part in my mythical landscape of desire. If poor Cinderella had been black, it would have been a whole different story. I told my best white friend the kind of stories my mother raised me on: about slave girls who worked their fingers to the bone for their evil half sisters, the "legitimate" daughters of their mutual father, the master of the manse, the owner of them all; about scullery maids whose oil-and-ashes complexions would not wash clean even after multiple waves of the wand. These were the ones who harbored impossible dreams of love for lost mates who had been sold down rivers of tears to oblivion. These were the ones who became runaways.

"Just think about it," I said. "The human drama is compact enough that when my mother was little she knew women who had been slaves, including a couple of runaways. Cinderellas who had revolted against their tense, self-involved stepsisters, burned their master/father/lover's beds and then fled for their lives. It doesn't take too much to read between those lines. I didn't play with Barbie dolls growing up; my mother was busy telling me cautionary tales about women who invented their own endings, even when they didn't get to live happily or very long thereafter."

I told her the kind of fairy tale I grew up chewing on:

Once upon a time, in a magical kingdom not so far away, there lived a king and queen who ruled over a gentle, ambitious, and profit-seeking populace with an almost invisible hand. The king was wealthy and the queen was beautiful, but to their great sorrow they were unable to conceive the child of their dreams. Time and again, they had tried but produced only average products, never more than three-fifths of their dream; time and again they were obliged to discard these defective components and renew the process of selecting only the most fit and perfect heir.

One day, a confident young man clad in the resplendent raiments of a gentleman and a scholar entered the realm. "I am a dream factor," said the self-assured young dandy. "If I may have patent and royalty rights, I will grant your true heart's desire."

Nine months later, a beautiful baby princess was born to the great joy of all. She was named Beauty. At her christening, nine fairies dressed in pouffy gold evening gowns appeared and blessed her with nine gifts. The first fairy blessed her with the gene for superb testing skills. The second fairy blessed her with a gene protecting against the five most deadly forms of cancer, the third with the gene for low cholesterol, the fourth for height, the fifth for physical grace and cotillion skills, the sixth for resistance to obesity, the seventh for antiwrinkling emollients, the eighth for long blond tresses with no split ends, the ninth for perpetual mood enhancement.

Bliss reigned. Life hummed along. By the time Beauty reached adolescence, she was the envy of every girl in the court. She was willowy, graceful, and the kingdom's undisputed champion at the game of bobolink. She was a flawless musician, had translated all known volumes of Etruscan poetry into

Middle French and Old Croatian, had devised a spell for de-salinizing seawater cheaply, and of course her test scores were off the charts.

One day when Beauty was fifteen, she was sitting at her loom embroidering her signature quadratic equations into the silken woof. Suddenly she pricked her finger on a needle that the Blue Fairy had fashioned from the thorn of a bramble bush bred for its toxicity to pesky insects and corn blight alike. Unfortunately, since Beauty's gossamer good looks were cloned from a bio-enhanced brew that included butterfly wings, the prick of the insecticidal thorn was nothing short of poisonous to her cancer-resistant but otherwise quite delicate constitution.

Beauty fell instantly into a deep, unshakable slumber.

A shadow fell across the land, and the people began to weep. In the sky, the constellations re-formed themselves into long il-legible sentences with question marks at their ends. The fairies held out their arms and small sparks of light scattered beneath their touch, but that was all. Storms encircled the land. The days became gray with falling snow, the sun no brighter than the moon. A gauzy luminescence settled over the land like bandaged fireflies, or as though the sky were hung with a strange veil of glowworms trapped in cotton.

The king and queen offered a chest of gold to anyone who could awaken Beauty, but to no avail despite the efforts of wiz-ards who had gone to the very best schools. A fog blew in and a long season of freezing drizzle began.

It was still drizzling a year later when a handsome prince with rippling muscles, a natural immunity to the tragic afflic-tion of erectile dysfunction, and a cleft in his chin happened to pass through the realm. He had been riding for many miles and was tired and thirsty. He presented himself at the castle, where the king and queen laid out a sumptuous repast with fine wines, strolling musicians, and a silver-tongued public intellec-tual seated upon every guest's right.

Late that evening, as the prince was guided to his elegantly appointed sleeping quarters, a door mysteriously blew open just as he passed before it. It was the door to the room where Beauty, a little waxen perhaps but still stunning, lay reclining on a tastefully backlit golden bier.

The princess made quite an arresting vision and the prince was instantly smitten. To make a long story short, Beauty awoke from her trance and locked eyes with the prince, there was a splendid wedding, and the whole kingdom dined on candied hummingbirds' wings and danced for days.

If they had just left well enough alone, Beauty and the prince probably would have lived happily ever after. As it was, however, the prince fancied himself a scientist and engaged the services of a knowledgeable astrologer and a rather grand alchemist just to make sure that they and their children lived in eternal rapture.

Over the next year, the astrologer and the alchemist made their lives a marvel of clockwork precision. Up in the tower, the astrologer mapped out their royal destinies to the nanosecond: when it was time to deliver proclamations to the masses, when it was time to send prisoners to the salt mines, when it was time to eat soup. Down in the dank nether rooms of the dungeons, the alchemist made evil-smelling potions in his fiery furnace, things that fortified the blood and made the pineal gland supple and rendered the liver effusive.

Over time, the prime minister (whose advice had been ignored in deference to the astrologer's) began to feel slighted. The head cook (whose delicate creations were generally overwhelmed—shall we say?—by the alchemist's sulfurously sizzling, metallic-green predinner cocktails) began to serve boiled turnips and dry toast. Everyone in the castle was thoroughly miserable, and the princess grew sullen and wan. But the prince remained determined to apply the most up-to-date advances toward the maximization of his chances for the perfect heir.

One day the alchemist mixed up a conception-inducing po-

tion of mercury, wolf bane, and tree sap, and the astrologer de-
termined that Beauty must imbibe it beneath a full moon with
Venus in perigee. And so Beauty grew great with child. There
was rejoicing in every corner of the realm. Nine months later
the princess gave birth to a bright-eyed, healthy little werewolf.

"Oops," said the alchemist. But such large acts of enchant-
ment, once done, can rarely be undone, and the astrologer, the
cook, and the alchemist all went into early retirement, never
again to dabble in the magical arts. Meanwhile, the new
princeling's plushly dark physique was widely understood to be
an omen of misfortune. The little werewolf was banished to the
forest, where some very kind chimpanzees took him in, raised
him up, and ultimately condescended to allow him to marry
one of their sisters. Beauty and the prince remained childless
and bereft for the rest of their days. Some years later, when the
barbarian horde swept down from the east, the populace sur-
rendered gratefully.

My best white friend said, "Get a grip. It's just a party."

If the truth be told, I had been looking forward to the make-
over. MBWF has a masseuse and a manicurist and colors in
her palette like Après Sun and Burnt Straw, which she swears
will match my skin tones more or less.

"Why don't they just call it Racial Envy?" I asked, holding
up a tube of Deep Copper Kiss.

"People should stop putting so much emphasis on color. It
doesn't matter whether you're black or white or blue or
green," she said from beneath an avocado mask.

"Lucky for you," I pointed out, even as my own pores were
expanding or contracting—I forget which—beneath a cool
neon-green sheath.

"Now, now, we're all sisters under the makeup," she said
cheerfully.

"When will we be sisters without?" I grumbled.

I'd come this far because she'd convinced me that my usual slapdash routine was the equivalent of being "unmade," and being unmade, she underscored, is a most exclamatory form of unsophistication. "Even Strom Thurmond wears a little pancake when he's in public."

MBWF is somewhat given to hyperbole, but it was awfully hard to bear, the thought of making less of a fashion statement than old Strom. I did draw the line, though. She has a long history of nips, tucks, and liposuction. Once I tried to suggest how appalled I was, but I'm not good at being graceful when I have a really strong opinion roiling up inside. She dismissed me sweetly: "You can afford to disapprove. You're aging so very nicely."

There was the slightest pause as I tried to suppress the anxious rise in my voice. "You think I'm aging?"

Gently and a bit too pleasantly, she proceeded to point out the flawed and falling features that give me away to the carefully trained eye, the insistent voyeur. There were the pores. And those puffs beneath my eyes. No, not there—those are bags. The bags aren't so bad, according to her, no deep wrinkling just yet. But the puffs are just below the bags. Therein lies the facial decay that gives away my age.

I got over this particular anxiety the day we were standing in line by a news rack at the Food Emporium. Gazing at a photo of Princess Diana looking radiantly, elegantly melancholic on the cover of some women's magazine, MBWF snapped, "God! Bulimia must work!"

This was not the first time MBWF has shepherded me to social doom. The last time, it was a very glitzy cocktail party where husband material supposedly abounded. I had a long, businesslike conversation with a man she introduced me to, who, I realized as we talked, grew more and more fascinated by me. At first, I was conscious only of winning him over; then

I remember becoming aware that there was something funny about his fierce infatuation. I was surprising him, I slowly realized. Finally he came clean; he said that he had never before had a conversation like this with a black person. "I think I'm in love," he blurted in a voice bubbling with fear.

"I think not, " I consoled him. "It's just the power of your undone expectations, in combination with my being a basically likable person. It's throwing you for a loop. That and the scotch, which, as you ought to know, is inherently depoliticizing."

I remember telling MBWF about him afterward. She had always thought of him as "that perfect Southern gentleman." The flip side of the Southern gentleman is the kind master, I pointed out. "Bad luck," she said. "It's true, though, he's the one man I wouldn't want to be owned by if I were you."

My best white friend doesn't believe that race is a big social problem anymore. "It's all economics," she has always insisted. "It's how you came to be my friend"—for once she didn't qualify me as black—"the fact that we were both in school together." I felt compelled to remind her that affirmative action is how both of us ended up in the formerly all-male bastions whose walls we have transgressed.

The odd thing is, we took most of the same classes. She ended up musically proficient, gifted in the art of interior design, fluent in the mother tongue, whatever it might be, of the honored visiting diplomat of the moment. She actively aspired, she says, to be a "cunning little meringue of a male prize."

"You," she says to me, "were always more like Gladys Knight."

"Come again?" I say.

"Ethnic woman warrior, always on that midnight train to someplace else, intent on becoming the highest-paid Aunt Jemima in history."

"Garrackh," I cough, a sudden strangulation of unmade thoughts fluttering in my windpipe. She meant it to be funny, but she just had no idea.

The night after that husband-hunting cocktail party, I told MBWF, I had a dream:

I was in a bedroom with a tall faceless man. I was his breeding slave. I was trying to be very, very good so that I might one day earn my freedom. He did not trust me. I was always trying to hide some essential part of myself from him, which I would preserve and take with me on that promised day when I was permitted to leave; he felt it as an innate wickedness in me, a darkness that he could not penetrate, a dangerous secret that must be wrested from me. I tried everything I knew to please him; I walked a tightrope of anxious servitude and survivalist withholding. But it was not good enough. One morning, he just reached for a sword and sliced me in half, to see for himself what was inside. A casual flick, and I lay dead on the floor in two dark, unyielding parts; in exasperated disgust, he stepped over my remains and rushed from the room, already late for other business, leaving the cleanup for another slave.

"You didn't dream that!" MBWF said in disbelief.

"I did so!"

"You're making it up. People don't really have dreams like that."

"I do. Aren't I a people too?"

"That's amazing! Tell me another."

"Okay," I said. "Here's a fairy-tale dream." I was being held by Sam Malone, the silly, womanizing bartender on the old television sitcom *Cheers*. He was tall, good-looking, and strong. My head, my face, were pressed against his broad, muscled chest. We were whispering our love for each other. I was moved deeply, my heart was banging, he held me tight and told me that he loved me. I told him that I loved him too.

We kissed so that heaven and earth moved in my heart; I wanted to make love to him fiercely. He put a simple thick gold band on my finger. I turned and, my voice cracking with emotion and barely audible, said, "What's this?" He asked me to marry him. I told him yes, I loved him, yes, yes, I loved him. He told me he loved me too. I held out my hand and admired the ring in awe. I was the luckiest woman on earth.

Suddenly Diane Chambers, Sam's paramour on *Cheers*, burst through the door. She was her perky, petulant self, bouncing blond hair and black-green eyes, like tarnished copper beads, like lumps of melted metal, eyes that looked carved yet soft, almost brimming. She turned those soft-hard eyes on me and said, "Oh, no, Sam, not tonight—you promised!"

And with that I realized that I was to be consigned to a small room on the other side of the house. Diane followed me as I left, profusely apologetic with explanations: She was sorry, and she didn't mind him being with me once or twice a month, but this was getting ridiculous. I realized that I was Sam's part-time mistress, a member of the household somehow, but having no rights.

Then Diane went back into the master bedroom and Sam came in to apologize, to say that there had been a mix-up, that it was just this once, that he'd make it up to me, that he was sorry. And, of course, I forgave him, for there was nothing I wanted more than to relive the moment when he held me tight and our love was a miracle and I was the only woman he wanted in the world, forever.

"Have you thought of going into therapy?" frowned MBWF.

"As a matter of fact, I have," I said, sighing and rubbing my temples. "On average, we black women have bigger, better problems than any other women alive. We bear the burden of being seen as pretenders to the thrones of both femininity and masculinity, endlessly mocked by the ambiguously gendered crown-of-thorns imagery of 'queen.' Madame queen, snap queen, welfare queen, quota queen, queenie queen, queen queen queen. We black women are figured more as stand-ins for men, sort of like reverse drag queens: women pretending to be women but more male than men—bare breasted, sweat glistened, plow pulling, sole supporters of their families. Arnold Schwarzenegger and Sylvester Stallone meet Sojourner Truth, the real real thing, the ace-of-spades gender card herself, Thelma and Louise knocked up by Wesley Snipes, the ultimate hard-drinking, tobacco-growing-and-a-spitting, nut-crushing ballbuster of all time . . . I mean, think about it—how'd you like to go to the ball dressed like a walking cultural pathology? Wouldn't it make you just a wee bit tense?"

"But," she sputtered, "but you always seem so strong!"

When I was in school living in those postadolescent pressure cookers called dormitories, I remember marveling that most of my white friends struggled with the fear of looking like everyone else. My best black friend and I, on the other hand, struggled to fit in, tending to find the middle ground of "ordinary" something of a relief—even a luxury. This is a purely anecdotal observation, I admit, but let me posit it provisionally, as something that makes me wonder about the source of such hypothetical social forces and how they might shape us. For me, the general paradox of African Americans' attempts to render ourselves mainstream is that the very rituals of proving that we are "just like" the girl next door are themselves the proof of our marginality.

Back in college, we worried about women's magazines selling fewer copies every time they put a black model on the cover. Hopeful little sisterhoods all over the country would run out to buy the occasional copy of *Glamour* or *Mademoiselle* just because a black face had been sighted on the supermarket news rack—always in the tenacious belief that our pumping up sales would "show them" that black beauty is no less than white. Thirty years later little has changed at those magazines; the sisterhoods grew tired long ago, many abandoning the quest for integration with the advent of *Essence*.

For me the distinguishing feature of *O* is its visualization of a mixed society as "normal." I don't mean that it's color-blind. Rather, it purposefully arranges people like bouquets of wildflowers. People with differing looks, opinions, tastes, and ages are put side by side to ruminate about random things—marriage, money, books, etc. It's equalizing in a very quiet sense, this pictorial impression that the soap opera of life's little issues touches everyone.

Of course, I still read Bulgarian deconstructionism and *Jet* and the kinds of New York–based political journals that keep me testy and sarcastic. And yes, *O* serves up calculated fantasy, is studiously apolitical, and is rather long on fluff. But where else can you find images of women who are black, white, Asian, large and small, mothers, wives, singles and sisters, braided, dreadlocked, and hot-combed, on a budget or with Oprah's money to spare—all just girlfriends together?

The only way I can explain it is perhaps by way of contrast. I remember running out to buy the October 1998 issue of *Vogue*, just after the debut of the movie *Beloved*. Oprah Winfrey was on the cover, and all of us determined middle-aged, middle-class black women made the pilgrimage to the newsstand to show our support. There she was, wasp-waisted no less, reclining on a hammock, looking positively sultry in a little black nothing of an evening gown. So, I thought. Here I am, almost thirty years out of high school, and when I see Oprah Winfrey gracing the cover of *Vogue*—a black woman literally in vogue—I cannot help thinking what a very good thing! This thought was immediately followed by another, as I remarked upon the debutante cotillion–style evening gown that she was wearing: what an unsettling thing!

The cover of *Vogue* is so complicated as a cultural symbol.

It's the province of Helmut Lang's spiky, emaciated teenagers in white lipstick, cashmere underwear, and shoes designed for those who have little occasion to ride the subway. In that space, Oprah appeared so . . . unusual.

She was thin all right, that one saw first and foremost. But she was also too substantial in a way that had nothing to do with weight. It wasn't even a visual thing; perhaps part of it was that her television persona allowed me to feel as though I know her even when I don't.

Oprah, after all, has made her career on the friendly reve-lation, the girlfriendly tell-all, the presumption of being on a first-name basis. Like a sweet kitten that rolls over and shows its belly as a sign of concession, she loads a wagon full of the equivalent of her lost belly fat and rolls it across the stage. Who could fail to find that endearing, if in a weird kind of way?

But I also feel as though I know Oprah because she likes potato salad made the Southern way, my grandmother's way. I like her because I know she runs marathons and sweats as much as I surely would were I ever to run anywhere. Then there was that pedicurist on her show talking about corn re-moval. That chat with Jada Pinkett about depilatory practices. The weepy confessions about the sorts of biological shortcom-ings generally covered by that handy blanket of a word, "funk."

So when I looked at the cover of *Vogue*, I could only mar-vel at how completely embodied Oprah was, how completely enfleshed, indeed, all black women tend to be seen, at least on some imagistic level. We are known by our aches, pains, and appetites. We have ashy legs, rusty elbows, big butts, and "bad" hair that does not flow or swing. Flat, as though in un-grateful opposition to Barbie, feet. Hard to be a ballerina look-ing like you do. We little girls of a certain era grew up in freshly pressed sausage curls and fluffy tutus, looking like hope and feeling like failure. The front maintained in a world

that did not love, desire, or romanticize you. You could not
trust, and so you maintained an edited self, a well-groomed
self, a commercial, compressed, and well-oiled self—eternally
prepared for display in a world that invents you, projects upon
you, mixes you up, makes cyborgs with your parts. Your best
bet was to try to rationalize the relentless self-scrutiny as artful rather than secret, choice rather than deference, comportment rather than disguise.

All said, we've had to claw our way through so many stereotypes that "getting real" has become our meta-stereotype, our
very own archetype.

Perhaps part of Oprah's great genius is the ability to take a
cultural history of being owned and turn it around. She has
taken a personal history of being known too intimately, too vi-
olently—a history of invasion and rape—and instead of letting
her molesters own, as secrets kept, her deepest scars, she's
made a business of their revelation and remediation. She's not
only gotten title to and mastery of the fine art of suspenseful
self-exposure, she's also made it a mirror—a social mirror, reflecting the biggest audience share this sort of offering will
ever have.

Again, I think of how completely embodied Oprah appeared in *Vogue*. I look at past issues of *Vogue* and think how
completely disembodied everyone else who's ever been on the
cover has been—a long procession of icons to the illusory, the
airbrushed, and the unattainable. It wasn't as though Oprah
didn't have all the right moves for *Vogue*; she reclined like an
odalisque, so fey, so vulnerable, so . . . unlike herself, somehow. I think of the literal meaning of "odalisque"—not a pose
in a painting, but "female slave or concubine"—and a certain
discomfort befalls me.

What happens when the very substantial Oprah Winfrey
enters the space of this particular kind of romantic mirage?
What happens, indeed, when any living, breathing person,
white or black, blond or Jheri-curled, becomes the malleable,

reclining odalisque? Will she actually be able to expand the symbolic territory of anxious anorexics? Will the general "desirability" of African-American women be maximized by Oprah in *Vogue*, or will we be drawn into the neurotically self-conscious world of the anemically seductive G.G.? (Oh, did I mention that G.G. was completely body obsessed? She was acutely aware of how much her place in the world depended on the approving gaze of others.) I wonder: If, in these interesting times, President Bill Clinton sparked debates about whether he was our first black president, then could the *Vogue*-ish Oprah vamp her way into becoming our nation's premiere icon of white womanhood?

I don't mean to imply that Oprah was "acting white" in the way some people use that term when they want to describe a black person who is hoping no one will notice that she's black. Rather, my interest is focused on the iconic nature of whiteness and womanhood. I'm trying to place her—and myself—in a culture where white womanhood has always embodied the essence of femininity, and black womanhood has too long been seen as its opposite. While white women have fought for sexual liberation and recognition of their strength in the workplace, black women have sought liberation from stereotypes of being strong, overly sexualized workhorses. While many white women have struggled to liberate themselves from femininity as constraining destiny, most black women have never stopped hunting for the perfect adornment, that little bit of fabulous frippery that will render the wearer "pretty."

So it was that Oprah's appearance in *Vogue* represented an odd intersection of these two incongruent cultures within the women's movement. Who was Oprah in that moment? The collective projection of best girlfriend? That rock-solid confidante to us all . . . yet primping like a coltish debutante and dressed like a Southern belle, complete with gardenias in her hair and diamonds at her throat. There she was, resting on one elbow, knocking back champagne while all the rest of us were still stuck at home in that same old terry bathrobe, eating Mallomars, longing for the days when she was on a diet too, because then you could both languish in the camaraderie of mutual self-loathing turned safely outward and aimed at the silky person of G.G.

I am, of course, not condoning this small-minded behavior. I make the observation not only because I own a terry bathrobe and several boxes of Mallomars, but also because my life has been characterized by this kind of nagging doubt—by a sense of limit and not belonging, by a sense of being sur-veilled and measured and always being inadequate. I am al-ways caught up in the question of self-presentation. I am always listening to myself, always watching myself through others' eyes. This was the precise anxiety that seeing Oprah, airbrushed in *Vogue*, stimulated in me.

Oprah in *O*, in contrast, comes closer to negotiating a resolution between the common longing to see oneself in idealized terms and the tyrannically perfectionist images modeled in most women's magazines. It's a subtle distinction, I suppose. Although Oprah Winfrey is exceptional by every measure—extraordinary wealth, extraordinary power—she nev-ertheless projects an image of Every Black Middle-Class Woman. No, that's not quite right: She projects an image of Every Black White Yellow and Red Working-, Middle-, and Upper-Class Woman for All Seasons Castes and Creeds. My point is that despite the fact that there are few human beings on the planet as well situated as she, the most endearing part of the Oprah myth is that you out there—Me? Yes, you!—can be all that she can be.

Oprah Winfrey's talent for what is called "crossover appeal" has the potential for forcing the culture to rethink other cate-gories of desire, particularly romantic and associational desire. But I say "potential" because others before her, like Bill Cosby, have achieved crossover appeal on television without as deep or lasting an impact as might have been hoped. Oprah Winfrey has risen to powerful heights because she has been so savvy in shaping her role as communal friend and helpmeet.

After all, what really is there not to like about her? Toughened New Yorker that I am, I actually find some of her programs mildly annoying because she is almost too nice, too accommodating. She stands for nothing if not shared values—moderation in eating and drinking, getting lots of exercise, clean living, self-motivation. She's no threat to capitalism—every girl should have such a knack with the checkbook. She stands for team spirit as well as radical individualism, down-home as well as high fashion. She loves all hues and views of humanity. She is kind to fools and Klan members, and publicly encourages reading, reading, and more reading.

I don't want to be understood as overstating Oprah's significance in a world as encumbered as ours. In particular, I do not wish to style my thoughts about her as any kind of political analysis. But given a history in which certain bodies have been ruthlessly deromanticized as a first step in that process of dehumanization that has imagined some of us as "suspect profiles," "undesirables," and "trash," I wonder if Oprah's romantic humanitarianism isn't such a bad thing. The mass media have become our most important font of collective imagination. While Oprah has been charged with inventing the kind of confessional TV that has led to the end of all things highbrow, it's probably a teensy bit unfair to charge her, rather than Jerry Springer, with the worst excesses of the genre. Oprah takes the stories of confused, abused, generally less-than-normative people and meticulously tracks the misfortunes and bad choices that have brought them to their lot. Then, like some kindly force of Anti-Fate, she unravels the mess, shakes it out, sets *les misérables* on the path toward Happy Ending and gives them a friendly shove.

It's an art, this treading of thin lines through emotional quagmires that perhaps risk exploding in passionate polarization but that also harbor opportunities for personal reflection and deep empathy. It is magic, the ability to control and broadcast information, a test of whether that seductive power will be used for narcissism or goodwill.

Again, Oprah is hardly the revolution. But as a tiny turning point in a culture that has not easily opened doors to those who don't conform, she beats Martha Stewart any day. And in a world where appearances matter so much to so many, the control of images on TV, video, and film is an inevitable concern to people of color. Hollywood, of course, is the engine of this dream machine, and in the film industry one hears the same questions asked over and over: What is the long-term significance of the most visible African-American stars—Sidney Poitier, Denzel Washington, Chris Rock, Will Smith, Halle Berry? Will they be remembered as black actors, or will their reputations rest on recognition of their artistry in a more general, unraced sense? I would like to think it will be both, but the very fact of such a debate underscores the distance we have to travel before we achieve anything so sunny as an "unraced" competition involving black people.

Only time will reveal whether the African-American stars of today are fluke or trend in the ultimate transformation of the unhappy history that Spike Lee's film *Bamboozled* parodied so sharply. Does Halle Berry command the same salaries as Reese Witherspoon, for example? Did *Monster's Ball*, for which Berry won an Oscar, make as much money as other award-winning films? Are films with black stars distributed internationally as widely as, say, Arnold Schwarzenegger's? (And what if Arnold Schwarzenegger were black? Would the transgressive behavior of his Terminator alter ego more readily be condemned as outlaw rather than heroic?)

It is interesting to consider the subtle configurations of racial imagery that permeate the American landscape of great, if idiosyncratic, celebrity. Not long ago, I was thumbing through my "archives" of very old magazines (I like not to admit that I have trouble disposing of things) piled haphazardly on my bed stand. I found first a copy of *People* brimming with photos of Liza Minnelli's remarkable ill-fated potlatch of a wedding to David Gest. Serving as his best men were the odd couple of Michael and Tito Jackson. Michael, milky faced as a corpse and sporting a coiffure somewhere between Little Richard and Little Lord Fauntleroy, wore a satin Peter Pan collar blouse, velvet breeches, and a diamond brooch that outdid anything even Elizabeth Taylor had mustered.

Tito was a startling apparition next to his science-fiction marvel of a brother, an odd shadow of what the little boy Michael might have grown up to be. Tito, who wears his hair in a modified Afro, is apparently the only member of that family who has not undergone extensive plastic surgery. It was like looking at the passing of an era—Tito, the face of Motown at its height, the music of the early seventies, so infused with the victories of the civil rights movement, and of protest movements, a time of big hair, fists in the air, hope, anger, and promise. Tito mirrored a moment in history when black was beautiful, a moment that magically dissolves in the sad countenance of Michael Jackson's literal transmogrification of that Man in the Mirror.

I suppose there's no law against Michael Jackson's carving up his face like a paper doily, laws against the rest of his alleged activities notwithstanding. If only as to his own body, he is free to be as eccentric as he wants to be. But what's fascinating is how staunchly and for how long he was put forward as a model of male virtue. He was well past the point of highly unusual when, in the late 1980s, President George Bush the First invited him to the White House and extolled him as a role model for inner-city youth. Since then, questions about his alleged molestation of and certain "overinvolvement" with young boys have rightly compromised that part of his symbolic niche, but I wonder that the extreme degree of his own self-effacement should be less troubling. And I wonder that more people did not until very recently find extremely alarming his financed fathering of that procession of sad, faceless children, so eternally veiled as to resemble the widow's weeds. Certainly Jackson's physical transformation has been the subject of much detached media bemusement, and I suppose one shouldn't hope for much more in an environment where movie stars inject Botox into their armpits so as not to leave sweat circles on their designer gowns. But Jackson has performed a kind of self-mutilating reverse minstrelsy of white-face. As he pantomimes his own molestation with each bodily invasion he orchestrates upon himself, one senses the personal pathology at work—a kind of racial anorexia?—but it is also a culturally symbolic, public act of scarification.

Michael Jackson is surely at the extreme end of those who employ plastic surgery for greater social acceptance. But if Geraldo Rivera, Greta Van Susteren, and other visible media figures use surgery to make themselves look younger—or all the way to shrink-wrapped, in Van Susteren's case—it is a great big elephant of a public secret that more and more people of Asian and African descent are using it to look "whiter." There is a lot to be said about this as a form of high-tech passing, but my concern here is more with the external social pressures that encourage this behavior to begin with. I can only hypothesize, but just as anorexia is said to bear some relation to the pervasiveness of stick-thin images of femininity in magazines, I suspect racially motivated surgery is related to the ubiquitous visual aesthetic of whiteness as body ideal. To some extent this may be stating the obvious, but I do think it's worth repeatedly disaggregating the beauty standard as more than political or economic choice; the ongoing entrenchedness of racialized ideals is very connected to the subtly tyrannical power of what is often felt as a wholly internal aesthetic preference. I think there is a connection, in other words, between the public lauding of black castrati figures like Michael Jackson, perpetual boy singer, and the public fear of fully grown black men.

I remember reading an account of the life of J. M. Barrie, author of *Peter Pan*. I found it helpful in comprehending the little echo of sadness in that book (obliterated in the Disney version) to learn that Barrie's elder brother had died when he was only twelve years old. Barrie cited the odd, terrible feeling of watching himself grow older than his dead brother, whose youth was frozen forever in time. I think of that background to the creation of Peter Pan when I look at the corpselike demeanor of Michael Jackson. To me, and maybe to himself, he died around the age of twelve; certainly he went about burying himself alive in Neverland. And therein lies the link, perhaps, between Michael Jackson's fate and that of too many poor young black kids who are scared to death of what the real world holds.

The journalist Jill Nelson tells a rich little story in her book *Straight, No Chaser*. She's sitting in a bar, chatting with a man who suddenly tells her that he would never consider dating a black woman.

"Why?" she asks as nondefensively as possible. Too bossy, too strong, a host of other stereotypes fall from this man's lips.

"Well, here's my date," says he. Jill turns her head and sees "a woman approximately the color of milk chocolate with shoulder-length straightened hair" walking toward them.

"What about not dating black women?" asks Jill.

"She's not black. She's West Indian," says the man.

I like this story because it illustrates the complicated way ethnicity traditionally has been used by some African Americans as a bulwark against the terrifying psychic messages of stereotypes about one's blackness. It's a much too familiar script to many blacks, if not to many whites: *I'm not really black—I'm Moorish, with a touch of Choctaw. Well, okay, let's put it this way, I'm not only just black—before the slave master, my family was descended from an uninterrupted line of Egyptian priestesses and Asian warriors. Okay, okay, so I'm kind of black—but if you tilt your head and squint your eyes and gimme some credit for the red in those skin tones, I could be Something More . . .*

But the degree to which racial yearning among nonwhites is viewed casually, or as comprehensible, makes me wonder what if the situation were reversed. What if we pushed through the looking glass to a world where young white people didn't just "dress black" or try to "speak black," but took to applying all kinds of caustic carcinogenic skin-darkening agents—anything to achieve the deep 'n' lovely charred-brown look of the true fairy princess? What if whites were lining up for collagen implants in their upper lips as well as their lower, or if people started pumping silicone into their rhinal cavities because *Vogue* featured only those impossibly gorgeous models who had no flesh other than in their large-blooming, beautifully bulbous noses? What if young girls were earnestly, desperately trying to floof up their woefully slick hair with little stick-on polyester dreadlocks—not as a sign of protest or countercultural cool, but because blacks, not blonds, were universally known to have more fun?

In such a world I suppose I would be distantly bemused, as I wallowed in the protective grace of attractive black normativity. I suppose I would be vaguely flattered by such industries of effort, albeit secretly a little repelled by the obviousness of the artifice, what with the glue always visible at their hairlines. I suppose too that I might worry a little about those who wore their hair defiantly lank or, worse, tried to undo the aesthetic order of things. It wouldn't necessarily be racism that might rise in my bosom—I'd be a liberal!—but rather, perhaps, an offended vanity too profound to admit. In such a world, I might indeed find the blackfaced, Afro-wigged version of Michael Bolton, shall we say, to be an awfully sensible young fellow. And that he would pay huge sums to a succession of black women to bear him a line of cosmetically upgraded children? Well, who could blame him, poor thing . . .

But this social pressure toward racial assimilationism is not only about color. Color is intimately linked to images of threat and danger. Black people who flirt with images of danger or threat, even if only in their music, sport, or acting careers, do not end up as romantic outlaw heroes—whether as cowboy presidents or as chairs of the National Rifle Association or as governors of major states. The closest African-American equivalent I can think of to the improbable political ascent of a Ronald Reagan or a Charlton Heston or a Jesse Ventura or an Arnold Schwarzenegger is perhaps the complicated political presence of Muhammad Ali. But consider his trajectory from edgy threat to all-American hero: As a young man, Ali was politically unpopular yet magnetically attractive, so stinging and unrepentant. He was fast and funny then, supremely confident and outrageous at a time when it was dangerous to be so. He was a symbol of both black defiance and white resentment, a thoroughly transgressive swashbuckler.

Today, Ali is reportedly the same inside, but outwardly he's sluggish and tattered, puffy and docile. His wife hovers protectively; his daughter does the fighting in the family. These days, Ali is loved, even adored, by most Americans, belatedly an icon. Perhaps it is no more than his due finally delivered, but this Ali seems so distantly connected to his former self that I can't help wondering if he would be so loved were he the smart-mouthed, backtalking, middle-aged bad boy leading a noisy call-and-response in support of Jesse Jackson or Al Sharpton. I wonder that it is only in this present form that he became the poster boy for pride summoned in the face of the body's betrayals, his perpetual tremble figured as Olympian struggle, as fortitude rather than lack of control. I marvel that this is the Ali chosen by President George Bush the Second to help plead for *Wall Street Journal* reporter Daniel Pearl's release in Pakistan—as though someone in the administration thought the kidnappers might relate better to a Muslim, any Muslim, and Ali was the only Muslim they knew. I do think there was probably unfortunately little that would have changed the tragic outcome in Pearl's case, but I also think that using Ali as hostage negotiator was as grave a symbolic misstep as proposing Michael Jackson as a role model for young black boys.

Somewhere in between is the image of Ali as depicted in the movie of the same name. There, Ali was played by Will Smith, otherwise known as the Fresh Prince of Bel-Air, and the more stylish half of the Men in Black. Smith is a fine actor but is nevertheless a tamed exemplar of an outlaw genre—a "nice" rap singer and thoroughly exportable version of the American dream. Will Smith is undeniably charismatic and nimble tongued, but he also has no prickles; try as he might, he is not threatening. To cast him, of all actors, in this role practically guaranteed the muting of the dangerous edginess that made Ali seem so brilliant behind the barely controlled craziness of his bravery.

If black men have had to be nonthreatening as a price for their iconic status—whether neutered like Michael Jackson, or sexy but extra, extra "nice" like Will Smith, or dangerous but forgiven by virtue of disability or age like Muhammad Ali—black women have had an inverse problem. Black women have been archetyped not so much for their sex appeal as their overproductive sex drive, usually thought to exceed that of any ten men. Alternatively, we are known for our overbearing physical strength, which is also rumored to exceed that of ten men. Halle Berry defies such stereotyping to a certain extent, and even though some have worried about her being overly sexualized, I attribute her particular exploitation less to race than to what Hollywood does to women generally.

(Let's face it, we live in an era when Gwyneth Paltrow's bare bosoms are everywhere.) Perhaps the savvy Whoopie Goldberg defies the stereotype more consistently. But for my money, the most complex female figure in entertainment today remains Oprah Winfrey.

Much was made of how some newspapers and magazines chose not to place Halle Berry prominently on their covers when she won her Oscar, for fear that sales would diminish. Yet I was just as intrigued by how few zeroed in on the remarkable and contemporaneous fact that a woman, indeed a black woman, was on the cover of *Fortune*. (No one seemed worried about whether *Fortune*'s sales would diminish. It's the liberating thing about capital. Big balance sheets are always beautiful.) Winfrey had certainly been on covers before. And, since the founding of *O*, she has graced each and every one of its covers with her glowing, unconventional good looks. I suppose she's just playing the print version of her role as welcoming hostess, but in the process she has turned herself into the most consistently employed cover girl in the world.

But now this, the cover of *Fortune* . . . Halle Berry's Oscar was a milestone, all right, but the cover of *Fortune*? Now, that's remarkable.

If the world were a different place, I might join those who have sniffed that the Oprah show is just a girlfriendly gabfest. But besides the fact that *Oprah* is vastly more civil than most programming, there is a kind of relaxation in visualizing oneself as banal, beset by the common afflictions of life. Black people are always stereotyped as rattling their cages from the margins of top or bottom, far right or left fringe. As with Bill Cosby before her, I find a certain relief in her purveyed images of black people safely within the normative range of good and evil, of suffering and sublimity.

Of course, the quiet egalitarianism of this sort of idealized representation can do only so much in a world where poverty and imprisonment are the more important political forces.

The significance of either the Oscars or Oprah should not be confused with concern about political crises whose roots touch on but reach far beyond any analysis of the entertainment industry. Nevertheless, the fact that Oprah Winfrey has managed to construct this little alternative niche of black femininity in a magazine read by Americans of all stripes and races is quite remarkable when you think about it. I don't know of a media vehicle that does the same for black men, that depicts them so routinely, in integrated settings, radiating such quiet, confident power. I think we need one. While the Oscars were symbolically important, Winfrey's business success is really the better measure of general progress in the entertainment media. It's probably not good to place all our hopes on an award ceremony that is essentially a popularity contest. The real trick is to continue building the sorts of media structures and influence that are not so subject to the vagaries of chance and to invest instead in the kind of long-term human regard that is more than just skin deep.

My best white friend and I had just about completed our toilette. She looked at my hair as though it were a rude construction of mud and twigs, bright glass beads, and flashy bits of tinfoil. I looked at hers for what it was—the high-tech product of many hours of steam rollers, shine enhancers, body spritzers, perms, and about eighteen hundred watts of blow-dried effort. We gazed at each other with the deep disapproval of one gazing into a mirror. It was inconceivable to both of us that we had been friends for as long as we have. We shook our heads in sympathetic unison and sighed.

One last thing: It seemed we had forgotten about shoes. It turns out that my feet were much too big to fit into any of her sequined little evening slippers, so I wore my own sensible square-soled pumps. My prosaic feet, like overgrown roots, peeked out from beneath the satiny folds of the perfect dress.

She looked radiant; I felt dubious. Our chariot and her husband awaited. As we climbed into the limousine, her husband lit up a cigar and held forth on the reemerging popularity of the same. My friend responded charmingly with a remarkably detailed production history of the Biedermeier humidor.

I do not envy her. I do not resent her. I do not hold my breath.

V

The Music Room

I love my mother—she is fifty years old, by the way— very much." This remarkably High German–inflected message was written by my nine-year-old son in an e-mail he sent to a friend. His friend's mother e-mailed it back to me so that we adults could laugh together about the odd locution. So she laughed with me and I laughed with her and no one "laughed at"—as we always tell the children—although at a mere thirty-seven she did laugh longer.

My son, on the other hand, rarely misses an opportunity to rub it in. I am the oldest of the mothers among my son's classmates, and this has turned me into some sort of weird perpetual math problem. "If you add my age and Byron's age and Callan's age and Alex's age and Sam's age, you *still* wouldn't have fifty." Or: "If years were liters and you subtracted Mona's mother's age from my mother's age, you could fill two ten-liter buckets." Or: "Fifty years is half a century. Can you figure out how many centuries fifty times forty times thirty times twenty times ten is?" My age even made it into a school composition about "Why Fishing Is My Favorite Hobby." (As it turns out, my life span exceeds that of the oldest known salmon or even

that of the saw-toothed barracuda.) At last I understand why
women of my mother's generation kept their ages to themselves. It wasn't vanity; it was self-defense.

I've been lucky, I suppose. Until recently, I'd never been
saddled with angst about the milestones that worry many baby
boomers. At thirty, when many have their first crisis over age,
I was an up-and-coming career woman and so well established that I stopped worrying about not being married. At
forty, when women get anxious about their biological clock, I
was so happy and confident about life that I decided to spread
my good fortune by adopting a child as a single parent. And at
forty-nine and three-quarters, I was a passionate civil rights advocate, productive in my career as teacher, lawyer, writer, and
mother to a child whose every tic and gesture filled me with
delight.

On the morning of my fiftieth birthday, however, I woke up
feeling odd. My thoughts did not turn to the lark on the wing
or the dew upon the cowslip. Instead I woke up considering a
future in which my son will hit his teens at the precise moment I start having hot flashes. I did not leap out of bed with
a glad spring to my step that morning, because my heart was
fluttering, my bones ached, and my back hurt as though I had
run a marathon—which I had not done, but which I keep
meaning to do, maybe one day after I finish making dinner
and doing the laundry.

Before noon of my fiftieth birthday, I had suffered what I
thought was a massive coronary occlusion but what my doctor
classified as a mild panic attack. She recommended green tea
and yoga, an idea I have every intention of exploring right after I run that marathon.

By midafternoon, I discovered that my hair had turned gray
since last I looked. I had to comfort myself at once with a
large box of birthday éclairs, and by the end of the day,
mirabile dictu, I had put on twenty pounds. Just like that.

The point is, at fifty, I realized I had to get my life in order.

So I drew up a protocol for eating right and getting plenty of exercise. I made lists and goals and used up a whole pad of paper that had come with "Room for Improvement" printed across the top of each and every page. I bought a box of red pencils for drawing arrows and checking things off, I bought jogging shorts with a drawstring waist, imagining that I will have occasion to draw it steadily inward over time. I stocked up on flaxseed oil and red miso, and promised myself to consume them in quantities equal to my intake of chocolate éclairs.

But ten months later, the only real change in my life, aside from passionate list making, was that I decided to take piano lessons. Don't ask me why. Perhaps because I could do it sitting down. But maybe it's also that, even more than whipping myself into shape, I realized I needed just one activity in my life that involved no whipping at all.

Music was not a predictable outcome of my midlife crisis, although I had, at least, learned to read notes in my childhood. My mother was a very good cellist in her younger years and played with the Civic Symphony in Boston. She was an ambitious mother, to say the least, so I began music lessons when very young. To no avail. Complete waste. I have pictures of me holding my quarter-sized cello, looking quite pint-sized and precocious, but I never came close to living up to the image. I remember playing at a nursing home when I was nine—no Carnegie Hall for me—and a little old lady came up afterward, shook her head, and said, "Keep practicing, dear, do just keep on practicing." I haven't touched a cello since my last year in high school. Even my mother gave up at that point; indeed, I believe it was a music teacher who first suggested that my playing indicated great promise as a lawyer.

I did buy a piano when my son was born, not for me but as some remnant of my mother's ambition—a conviction that my child shouldn't grow up without one in the house. When he was four, I enrolled him in Suzuki piano classes, where he spent a great deal of time rolling on the floor underneath the piano, groaning loudly. Luckily for him, a friend gave him a trombone two years ago, an instrument he loved and with which he bargained his release from the hated piano. But it was at that point I realized that if I'd never liked cello, I'd always loved the piano.

As it turns out, studying music in middle age is a lot easier than when you're a child. No one expects anything of you other than that you will be dreadful. No one wants to show you off in recitals. It was very liberating, this. So I found a great and patient teacher and I practice every day before dinner, even though I don't have to. And lo and behold, I'm good at the piano! Let me rephrase that: I'm much less dreadful than anyone expected. To my surprise, I love music theory! I even enjoy scales now that I'm middle-aged! Playing the piano is the most wonderful form of meditation. I have never been the world's most relaxed person, but these days I kick back by learning a new piece. I get lost in the deciphering of notes. And while my teacher has accused me of thinking that the metronome is there only to swat flies, I am thrilled that I'm actually good enough to butcher Chopin and Debussy, however slow the butchering, however much it brings to mind large animals being dragged to slaughter.

My son's friends' young mothers all congratulate me for taking piano "at my age." They cite studies about how mental activity keeps you spry, and I thank them sweetly for their thoughtful research. It keeps my idle hands from the devil's workshop too, I suppose. But for me, the most comforting thing about piano lessons is that no one's going to flunk me. For those of us who have spent our entire lives plagued with a fear of failure, there is nothing so refreshing as stumbling upon a pursuit in which absolutely nothing is at stake. Don't get me wrong—I think personal best is a fine idea. But in the relentlessly competitive, high-stakes world that most of us inhabit these days, I think there is a very similar redemption in taking the time to chart one's personal worst.

Recently, my teacher taped a little American flag to the metronome, to "give that waving arm a sense of purpose." He was trying to get me to pay more attention to meter, but I apparently charged through that Beethoven rondo on my own internal funky-chicken time. When I finished playing he said, "You know, I feel great sympathy for your mother."

Oh?

"Yes, and particularly when you were a teenager."

My playing inspired this?

"Well, you are the most persistent human being I have ever met, and I suspect that this trait was at its peak during your adolescence . . ." He held forth about how sheer determination has brought me a long way since I began lessons but that I needed to loosen up in the elbows and wrists so as to feel the music rather than approaching it like *The New York Times* crossword puzzle. He's like that. A great teacher but a little tart. He meant it as a compliment, he really did. Not at all like that time he compared my playing to Napoleon's troops marching through the Russian winter. ("Has he made you cry yet?" asked another of his students whom I met recently. "No," I replied. "But I have made him cry. For mercy. Every single lesson.")

I told my mother what he said about my adolescence, and she just laughed and laughed. And then she laughed some more, which I thought a bit beyond what was necessary for a woman of her dignified liters.

Anyway, I'm getting myself together in other ways too, if through the back door. I drink green tea these days because it goes so well with D minor. I've signed up for a yoga class because it might help with that chopping-wood thing I do to the keyboard when my shoulders tense up. I've taken to lifting a few small weights, just enough to give me stamina for all those scales. And a friend invited me to run a 5K race next weekend, which is actually kind of tempting since it takes a lot of aerobic ability to be able to hold my breath when I try trills with my left hand. Who knows, maybe I'll run that marathon sooner than I thought: After all, my ultimate goal is to set Rachmaninoff a-spinning in his grave.

Actually, my fear of performing goes back a long way. When I was about five, my teacher at the Boston Conservatory put me in a trio with the only two other black children in the entire school—we were of very disparate ages and abilities—and had us playing hoedown music rather than the classical repertoire all the other children were presenting. They thought it would be "cute" to have a black violinist, a black pianist, and a black cellist playing "Jimmy Cracked Corn." My father didn't see the artistic advantages at all, and so he took me out of the school and my mother took over my instruction with somewhat halfhearted resolve.

"You could have been a cellist in a symphony," huffs my mother, who to this day works herself into a froth at the very sound of country music. "It's an incident like that that makes you lose your appetite."

I think my mother is wrong about my musical promise. I also think I ended up in the best of all possible careers. But it is true that "Jimmy Cracked Corn" is such a bitter memory that, years later, when a friend very innocently suggested that my son might enjoy folk fiddling more than Suzuki piano, I snapped at her. From the look on her face, there is a good chance she chalked it up to pure snobbery.

Maybe snobbery is always rooted in such anxiety, always a cover for shame. Up until about the 1930s there used to be a flourishing American tradition of black fiddlers. I suspect that at least some of the reason it died out has to do with collective embarrassment. Like the popularity of the banjo or tap dancing, some significant measure of pleasure in performance was driven underground by association of the art form with the cruelly racialized mockery of minstrelsy.

I really hate performing.

Yet these days I do a lot of it; I support myself by walking onto a stage or standing behind a podium, speaking, lecturing, always breathing deeply to try to keep my composure. I write about race and gender, law and politics—topics about which people become easily unhinged. It's hard work trying to find precisely the words that will wend their way through the turmoil of preconceptions, the walls of resentment. I work so hard at performing.

Sometimes I dream that I can make music effortlessly. I dream that I am singing rather than speaking, and emotion pours forth, like exhaled silk.

A few years ago I heard Anna Deavere Smith, in her role as impresario, interview opera singer Jessye Norman. It was a remarkable combination, those two. Norman revealed that singing was like language to her, an emotional currency in her family and in the community where she grew up. When people were sad or exhilarated, they had a song to express it. What a wonder, I thought, to have that flowing, liquid, electric form of language. To be able to breathe out what's inside. No need for the clanking stones of words like "I am depressed." No groans or whines or shouts. The mood is music; others join and harmonize. I think this human capacity to harmonize with one another is one of the most magical properties of the species, the essence of sympathy. I do wish I had a better voice, but in grammar school concerts, teachers would always put me in the last row with firm instructions just to move my lips.

My grandmother and her sisters were never subject to such inhibitions. They were legendary for making a joyful noise in praise of the Lord, always trying to outsing one another in church. They seemed to share a belief that God would hear them better if they literally raised their voices up to Him. And so they shouted their praise, they conveyed their hymns to the heavens, in a competitive cacophony that few who heard ever forgot. The generations after my great-aunts were necessarily quieter. None of us ever raise our voices in song or anger or glee. We yearn to harmonize, but then think of Aunt Mary trying to beat Aunt Rose to the end of the Hallelujah Chorus, and we whisper apologetically instead. We clear our throats by way of announcement.

Anyway, Jessye Norman ended the interview with an aria. Back in the very last row, I closed my eyes and ever so imperceptibly dared to move my lips.

The matter of audience is such a funny thing. One day not so long ago when I was crashing about on the piano, my son observed that my lessons might give me an edge were they ever looking for a new national security adviser. I suppose it's well known that Condoleezza Rice plays the piano, but I was surprised that he would have kept such close track of her hobbies. As it turns out, his school had recommended her as a role model on Martin Luther King Day. I had to stop and think about that. Unlike Dr. King, Dr. Rice is said to have claimed that she has not really faced discrimination because she speaks French and Russian and plays Chopin.

Rice is fortunate indeed if she has never experienced the baggage of race. But to implicitly claim that black classical musicians or multilingual black people don't face bias in the workplace simply isn't supported by data. It is as old a piece of the problem as Thomas Jefferson having allowed some of his slaves to learn to speak French and to play the violin. There has always been a complicated interrelationship among access to education, notions of culture as inherent, and racialized presumptions of social worth.

A few years ago, a friend cast my son, who was about six at

the time, in a Christmas pageant. He was to read a passage from the New Testament heralding the advent of Christ's birth. He rehearsed his lines brilliantly and I was extremely proud of my handsome angel. Then we got to the theater—actually a drawing room in a beautiful old mansion on the Upper East Side of Manhattan. It was quite a lovely room, glimmering in soft candlelight, smelling of holly, waxed wood, and established wealth. What a classic tableau, I was thinking, as my son peeked into the hall, took one look at the assembled hordes, and—oh, dear Lord!—there was that groan he had heretofore reserved exclusively for his piano teacher.

To make a long story short, it took quite a bit of wheedling, begging, and bribing to get him on that stage. In the end, I went out with him, and together we delivered alternating verses to great effect. Old ladies wept.

Later, in the taxi hurtling homeward, my still-unhappy son grumbled, "You black-guyed me! That's not fair."

"I did what?" I asked, not sure what he'd said but sensing irony.

"You black-guyed me."

"What does that mean?" I said, still not comprehending.

"It's when someone wants to force you to do something so they threaten to tell all your secrets," he said.

"I think you mean blackmail."

"Oh yeah, you black maled me."

"Angel boy, I think we need to talk . . ."

The conversation that ensued wandered from nefariously extortive uses of the postal service to the metaphorical meanings of male, man, gentleman, and mailman; to the question of racial scapegoating as distinguished from sacrificial lambing; why goats and lambs make terrible pets; and finally to a lengthy discussion of the concept of homophones (to be distinguished from homophobes).

They say that performance anxiety is caused by fear of failure. Sometimes fear of failure is bred by a quest for perfection. There's certainly a lot of that in the world today, particularly as applied to children. Infantile precocity is very much in vogue, driven by the pressure of ever-dwindling and ever-more-competitive access to good education. But I also think fear of failure occurs when the actual risk of failure is pervasive, like a moat full of alligators encircling you, waiting for you to fall in, whether you're perfect or not. When the unkind judgments of others are palpable and you can never be quite sure, upon walking out of your inner sanctum and onto the public stage of life, whether you will have been cast as a happy hoedowning hillbilly, a solemn credit to your otherwise unlucky race, or perhaps just a sad little minstrel, it's hard. And so you stay in the wings.

In fact, I don't really stay in the wings. I do try to get out there and soar, feel the wind beneath, and all that. I resigned myself years ago to a career entwined with questions of race and gender; it was wholly predictable that I would be assured my measure of controversy.

Actually, I began my career as a trial lawyer, then as a consumer advocate, these days as an academic and a journalist. "You epitomize liberal bias," an unhappy student once told me, and I guess it's true that my professional life has touched on all the hot-button spots at one time or another. That student also grumped that I followed this path for the sake of sheer self-aggrandizement, that being part of the civil rights– civil liberties "establishment" won me kudos and fortune I did not otherwise deserve. Sigh. Perhaps he's right. Sometimes I do wonder how different my life would have been if I'd been more principled, if I'd been more self-sacrificing, less power hungry, and just taken that plunge into investment banking.

But every now and then the pendulum swings, and I get plenty of what that unhappy student thought that I deserved. In January of 1997, I went to London to do a series of broadcasts for the BBC and stepped off the plane to find myself described as "slave stock." That's the epithet that was hurled at me by the British tabloid *The Daily Mail*. The BBC had chosen, it said, a "militant black feminist of slave stock" as the forty-ninth Reith lecturer. The war on diplomacy had the likes of me in its sights?! To someone who in high school was always voted "most ladylike," this was not good news.

The Reith lectures are a yearly radio series of considerable preeminence in Great Britain, allowing chosen academics an unusual amount of air time (six half-hour presentations) on Radio Four. While earlier broadcasts I had done for the BBC (about immigration, race, prisons, gender, American legal issues, even utopia) had been well received and uncontroversial, the Reiths are a major event. I was the fourth woman ever to have done them (each of my predecessors having been attacked vociferously as the tragic end of Great Tradition), the second black person (although I was repeatedly hailed as the first), and the first American (if you don't count John Kenneth Galbraith, who's one of those Canadian kind of Americans). I guess I should have been prepared, but we all live in our own little worlds and I think I went expecting to dine with the queen.

I hadn't a name in the first sentence of *The Daily Mail*'s first parry. Just She. So in the second before I realized that I was the stock in question—the stock-in-trade, livestock, fat stock, peasant stock, blood of a certain sort—I must say that I had a vision of someone else entirely. That distance from the description in the papers later became a kind of haven; as the public furor grew, there was shelter in the disconnection from that person wreaking havoc in my name.

A few days later, there was a second article in *The Mail*, a big one this time, whose headline alone read: "She's a militant black feminist who hates all white people and doesn't believe in the family. She's reviled in her own country so why in the name of Lord Reith is the BBC giving her so much promi-

nence?" This "she," the article continued, is famous in the
United States for her completely indefensible defense of pre-
posterous moral positions, and there followed a dizzying list of
things the alien Patricia Williams supposedly supported, like
favoritism, tribalism, liberalism, literalism, and the degrada-
tion of civilization as we know it.

It got worse before it got better. In the two months before
the lectures were broadcast, and therefore in the absence of
any substance, every major British newspaper had a turn discussing my status in the most contradictory and stereotyped
extremes—my single status, my American accent, my ver-
bosity, my diction, my "blood." There was no mention of any
professional qualification, no books I had written, no articles—even my prior work with the BBC became invisible. I
was described as "striding" among my followers as I hypno-
tized them with "sarky sing song," "magnetic eloquence," and
plain old "gobbledy-gook."

In a steady stream of such commentary, I was buried beneath the projected titillations of a press corps seemingly glee-
ful that someone had come along to fill columns at that
particularly humdrum, scandal-free moment in the lives of
the royal family. According to BBC protocol, I was not allowed to respond, for to do so would "lower" me. Besides,
even I could see that this controversy was not entirely about
me but was rather part of a larger attack on the publicly
funded independence and presumed "political correctness" of
the BBC itself.

In her book *Lift Every Voice*, Lani Guinier describes how
she felt in the wake of the rabid battering that derailed her
nomination as head of the Justice Department's Civil Rights
Division during the Clinton administration: "I was simply re-
made. An elite group of opinion molders depersonalized and
demonized me. With access to my real ideas withheld, my
words and most especially my voice were suppressed . . . 'She,'
this media construction, spoke for me . . . 'She' talked for me;

'she' thought for me. 'I' had disappeared." Indeed, at one point I called Lani from London and sobbed, "Help! I'm being Lani Guiniered!"

Like Lani, I found myself alienated more and more from my own image. It was hard to see myself in the alarming apparition whose every frequent stumble came to symbolize the BBC's foolish capitulation to "racialist hate-mongers," hysterical feminists, and the incoherence of American media culture. One of the more memorable moments occurred at a reception in my honor: Nervous BBC press officers thought they spotted a reporter from *The Daily Star*, a tabloid of even greater than usual bad taste. They shut me in the bathroom for the rest of the party for fear that I might appear in the next issue with enormous, computer-enhanced breasts. I don't know if it was easier that I remained an ignorant, malapropping mass of mediocrity distinguished only by what even BBC presenter Melvin Bragg called my "violent" proclivities. It might have been better with big breasts.

In any event, Fleet Street earned its reputation with my battered remains. At the height of it, the BBC was getting close to a thousand calls a week about me. At one point, my son, who was three then, picked up one of the newspapers featuring a grim, startled-deer-in-the-headlights photo of me. Not yet able to understand all the invective with which it was captioned, he simply said "Mummy!" with great satisfaction and kissed it. That was the moment at which I realized there were officially two mes in the world. I was struggling with the competing forces of two entirely different bodies.

A friend once shared an experience she had of sitting next to a mentally ill woman who reached out and touched her inquiringly. "Is that you or is that me?" she pleaded. When I was suffering through the Reiths, there was an invented me, a me that had nothing to do with me but to which people responded when my body came lumbering toward them. It was a fictional me, but the power was real. I had to walk out from behind her, make a lot of noise to be seen and heard. And even then it was confusing. London taxi drivers would say, "I know you!" When I insisted that I was not really the me they had read about in the tabloids, the uncertainty of that unbalanced woman transferred to them. Is that you or is that you? Or, as one particularly insightful cabbie put it, "Ah. You must be Irish."

In the long run, what's enduringly worrisome is that this second me—the evil one, that is—still enjoys a wild life that is much more mediagenic than my own: Monsterization, like pornography, always sells, I suppose. Back in the United States, *The Atlanta Journal-Constitution* published a commentary by Michael Skube attacking theorists, including me, as "intellectual imposters who once were a lunatic fringe but now lay siege to the most basic tenets of the Western Enlightenment . . . [and who] retail absurdities that haven't the remotest connection to jurisprudence . . . The Holocaust matters because it did happen, not because someone imagined it. Yet there are those who deny anything unusual was going on in those ovens. Would Patricia Williams say it isn't so important? You wonder."

Somewhere, perhaps only in the privacy of my own home, I'm a kind of boring liberal Democrat, surely not yet the automatic equivalent of hatemonger. I didn't do anything to warrant this kind of attack—I'm not even famous enough to have been as roundly "reviled in my own country" as was made out. I view what happened as the work of a few powerful, very far-right propagandists who counted on no one's ever having read any of the we-are-one-worldish things I've written and who wanted to make sure no one ever did.

These sorts of rabidly polarizing, take-no-prisoners attacks have become all too common in the last decade. If a student doesn't like something you say, it doesn't simply become a matter for dispute within the classroom. The student notifies his congressman or calls up the kinds of reporters for whom car crashes are not enough or puts your name on a hate mail list or circulates rumors about the purported hair under your arms on national Listservs. What ensues has little to do with ideology and everything to do with raw sensation. Scholars like Deborah Merritt, Regina Austin, and Lani Guinier have compiled data documenting the frequency of both harassment and discrimination directed against women law students and faculty—particularly women of color.

Those of us in teaching are particularly aware of the impact among our students of forces like Rush Limbaugh and the culture wars. We are always aware of being in the sights of the hundreds of young missionaries of the right who have been trained at such places as the Heritage Foundation, the American Enterprise Institute, and the Manhattan Institute. A recent article in the *Los Angeles Times* described the kind of journalism ethics received at the Jesse Helms Center, in North Carolina, where college students are trained and funded to "seed" the media with conservatives in an effort to "alter the basic makeup" of the nation's campus and professional media. " 'What do you want professors to feel when you call them up?' asked Owen Rounds, a former speechwriter for New York mayor Rudolph Giuliani.

" 'Threatened,' replied Duncan Wilson, a tousle-haired 19-year-old from the University of North Carolina, Charlotte."

After leaving fifteen years of corporate law practice, my friend E. now teaches business associations, property, trusts, wills, and estates. She finds teaching somewhat easier than I do, because "I'm not trying to talk about difficult subjects like race and gender." Nevertheless, it surprised her to find herself, after all that time, returning to a law school environment in which she was "still the only black faculty member. I was having to overcome the presumptions all over again. All new faculty members have to prove themselves, but we have to overcome all these negative stereotypes before we can even get to zero."

Some time ago, someone vandalized the faculty mailboxes at her school, leaving dead fish in only certain mailboxes. The man who did immigration law got a fish wrapped in a tortilla, the person who did anti–death penalty work had wires protruding from his fish, and E. received a black fish. "Many students have never had anything like a black intellectual role model before," she observed, "and it's hard for some of them to see anything but the color." Still, she loves teaching and her school: "It's one of the most supportive, collegial environments I've ever experienced. It's just that until we have some counterbalancing of the stereotypes, bias will rear its head anyplace you are."

My friend G., on the other hand, was somewhat less sanguine. G., who enjoys a national reputation as a civil rights litigator, started out at the Equal Employment Opportunity Commission and then argued voting rights and employment discrimination cases for the NAACP Legal Defense and Education Fund, where she "absorbed the legacy of Thurgood" and "basked" in the company of great litigators. After that, for a while she taught law. Teaching, she observed, "requires kamikaze energy if you're a black woman." (Not only for black women, one might add. It is hard to be anyone but Professor Kingsfield in the traditionalist environments of most American law schools.) But "to litigate all these really important cases all over the country and build a reputation—then to go into this experience where I needed representation!" G. was referring to the overheated responses to critical race theory (the school of thought with which I am often associated), those neoconservative concerns about whether feminist and minority scholars are tyrannical antischolars, silencing the young and impressionable with exotic courses in "victimology" that represent dangerous flights from reason and logic. The prevalence of such impressions has had real consequences. "To give you just a small example," G. said, "I was called 'the best-dressed bitch on campus.' They constantly challenged me as an intellectual authority of any sort."

I reminded her of a larger example, an incident she had told me about when it happened: A student, a police officer going to law school to further his career, had engraved her name on the side of a bullet and was showing it off to his classmates as a kind of joke. "I had forgotten that," she said quietly. "Sometimes there are things that are just so . . . It was so devastating. It just knocks you off your feet. You don't know what to do with it."

VI

The Pool Room

One rainy afternoon, I sat shelling peas. It had been a long, hard day. One by one, I scraped the little round heads loose from the pods, then tilted my palm so they rolled down my fingers into a water-blue glass bowl. It was soothing, repetitive work, with a pleasant green smell, a moist green feel, a calming sensation that almost made me forget the playdate I'd just survived.

My son had had a friend visiting earlier, a modest little one who proclaimed, more than once, that he had been genetically engineered for perfection. Living in New York does that to some children. They just pop out of the womb with a giddy overconfidence that makes you want to wallop their unrestrained ids with a broom. Soft end, of course.

He was gone now and calm had returned to our dwelling. He had to be sent home for terrorizing the cat. This is the kind of perfect child who corners an animal, stunned and mewling, with a strobe light, in order to see its pupils contract and expand.

"I'm the Grim Reaper," explained this spawn of high expectation when I demanded to know what in tarnation.

"It's worse," whispered my son urgently. "He's the *happy* Grim Reaper."

His addled mother proved a classic case. "Did he kill it?" she asked when I called to have him picked up. "Of course, I'll replace . . ."

The house was peaceful now, the cat shut away in my bedroom to recover, my son cleaning his room, the peas rolling off the conveyor belt of my hands.

For a brief period in my life, I had seven cats. They were given to me, like consolation prizes, to replace my mottled little Siamese, Greycat. I had entrusted her to the custody of an airline whose cheery agent assured me not to worry about a thing. Greycat was lost somewhere in the bowels of Kennedy International Airport and never found. Various friends brought new cats to make me feel better—three cats, really, but one was pregnant and promptly gave birth to four more. They were amiable little creatures in their own right, but I hadn't really been seeking replacements as a way of not missing Greycat.

My son came in to start his homework. "Was I generically engine-eared when you got me?" he asked, clueless and anxious. My son, like many adopted children, sometimes worries about the mystery of where he came from.

"Your ears were always the most perfect little engines," I assured him.

As my son settled into his books, my mind ambled in the direction of sheep. It was the fungibility of felines, perhaps, that reminded me of that cloned sheep, so prosaically baptized Dolly. You remember Dolly—for weeks, her forlorn, floppy-eared image graced the pages of *The New York Times*, with teasing legends hinting that the technology might "conceivably" be used to clone humans. Ah, the conceivable conception. It was sobering, gazing into Dolly's large, sad eyes as the dewy mirror of one's own.

Theologians and politicians worried aloud that we would

all soon be reproduced in sesquicentuplicate. The public discussion was startling for its weird mix of theology and psy-
chobabble. "What of Dolly's soul?" came the question. It's
been a long time since *The New York Times* inquired about
the status of anyone's soul, never mind that of a sheep in Scot-
land. But not to worry, a Jesuit priest was quoted—on page
one—assuring the fold that each clone had a distinct and separate soul. This was good news, surely, even if the greater miracle was its being greeted as newsworthy.

If some were a-tremble with the fevered contemplation of
notions grown mossy since the Middle Ages, geneticists, in
contrast, seemed to be suffering from an odd case of muffle
mouth. On TV, they shrugged their shoulders blankly. Use in
humans? Nope. Can't imagine much point in that. No need
to regulate at all. Yup and yessiree, it'll be ever so handy in animal husbandry, but absolutely no one we know is interested
in the industrial potential of human replication. It was all so
blatantly disingenuous, you just knew that the financial stakes
in medical research and reprotech had to be very high indeed.
Sure enough, within no time at all, doctors across the globe
began announcing their intentions to clone a human being,
the lion's share of publicity captured by a company called
Clonaid. Clonaid is funded privately—some say secretly—
and is associated with a creationist religious cult that claims
humans did not take hundreds of millions of years to evolve
from protists, frogs, and chimpanzees but enjoyed a celestial
genesis, having been cloned from Rael, an extraterrestrial
Yahweh-prototype about twenty-five thousand years ago. For a
mere $200,000 a shot, Clonaid promises to advance us a little
closer to the phylum of the sponge, which has the unregu-
lated option of reproducing either sexually or asexually. "And
no one can stop us," the Clonaid executives have chortled,
referring to the higher powers of Rael as well as the dearth of
anticloning laws but sounding an awful lot like Dr. Franken-
stein.

When my son had finished his homework, I entertained him with the kinds of cautionary tales all good lawyers tell their children:

Once upon a time, there was a young couple who resided at the very tippy-top of New York's most swank society. All of Manhattan had closely followed the details of their fairy-tale wedding at The Plaza hotel, as recorded in the Style section of The New York Times. The young woman was named Bella, and, as her name implied, she was very beautiful. The daughter of a poor but noble woodcutter, she had been discovered by a top modeling agency during a shoot in the Black Forest. Her looks won her a contract that took her to New York, where she learned English and met Sebastian, her husband and heir apparent to a corporate empire upon which the sun never set.

Sebastian and Bella were now planning their family. Sebastian, however, was worried about what sort of future any biological child of his would have. Sebastian had the heart of a prince but he was also just a bit of a literal beast—with paws, claws, fur, and fangs. Actually, he'd tried to have the fangs capped, but there is only so much cosmetic dentistry can do. Some generations back, there had been some dillydallying across the species barrier, resulting in a pioneering form of genetic enchantment that had marked the family DNA with a recessive little touch of the red-meat eater. Thus, he had been very badly teased as a boy; besides, it was hard to find a collar size that fit.

Determined to spare their offspring a lifetime of struggle, Sebastian and Bella paid a visit to Babybee, Inc., a pharmaceutical operation specializing in designer genetic enhancement. Sebastian had heard that Babybee was close to perfecting a pill that would allow them to pass along only those traits of their choice. They asked Babybee to whip them up a batch by which they might pass on to their little ones Sebastian's brains and about half of his brawn. Inasmuch as Babybee was still in the process of conducting long-term clinical trials and had not yet received FDA *approval for mass distribution, Babybee asked them if they would mind being part of a test group.*

"We can guarantee its general effectiveness," assured Babybee's authorized representative. "It's just that we haven't worked out all the side effects. We think there might be a degree of hair loss and some loss of energy. That's why it would be great to have you help us by trying it out."

"I'll do whatever I can," said Sebastian. "If it works as promised, I'd be very interested in making sure this stuff is distributed to a mass market. It would be a comfort to know I'm helping future generations of those in my position."

Sebastian's celebrity patronage and the potential of his marketing capabilities were very attractive to Babybee. Sebastian's vast family fortune included state-of-the-art pharmaceutical production facilities, advertising agencies, and a chain of twenty-five hundred drugstores. Over a power lunch of vodka martinis and salmon tartare, Sebastian and Babybee's CEO and head bioengineer entered into an oral agreement whereby Babybee agreed to develop the drug and administer it to Sebastian at their own cost. Sebastian, for his part, agreed to pay a king's ransom for the privilege of marketing the drug. (A king's ransom is officially one chest of gold and two sacks of rubies. Sebastian happened to have that and more. Most people do not.) Sebastian signed a consent form and they shook hands over espresso and biscuity little chocolate things.

After some boiling and toiling, Babybee gave Sebastian and Bella each a tiny golden pill with the promise that their child was assured the unalloyed inheritance of Sebastian's great wealth and Bella's great genes. They each swallowed it with the tremendous ceremony of their station and settled back to wait. Bella soon swelled with child, although it did induce in her an unexpected case of acne and significant lethargy, costing her the cover of Mothers in Bloom *magazine as well as that of* Esquire. *Sebastian suffered side effects too, to wit, quite a deal of hair loss—something poor Sebastian had at first thought might*

*not be such a bad thing in his case. But the hair loss suffered by
Sebastian was quite conspicuously uneven. Where formerly the
ferocity of his furriness had lent a certain animal magnetism
that had served him well at fashionable dinner parties, these
new developments gave him a sad, patchy, lupine air. The pair
of them were awfully depressing to cast eyes on, leading to their
ostracization from every swank soiree in the city.*

*Nine very long months later, Sebastian and Bella found
themselves the parents of a darling little princeling, just as
sweet and fuzzy as he could be, tiny fangs starting to protrude,
all baby powder and big clumsy paws.*

*As it turns out, the pill worked as to Sebastian's side of the
family. What neither Sebastian nor Bella had realized was that
there had also been a bit of dillydallying on her side of the family, several generations back there in the Black Forest. The
golden pill, in stimulating her traits, brought forward what had
been a deeply recessive, teensy extra twist in the long flowing
strands of her DNA, replicating, alas, precisely the enchantment that had for so long haunted Sebastian's line. The risk of
this happening was so low that the pill was nevertheless ap-
proved for sale as an over-the-counter, nonprescription drug by
all government agencies.*

*"Who knew?" asked Bella forlornly, as Sebastian howled at
the moon.*

*Bella has sued Babybee for breach of contract. Babybee has
sued Sebastian for refusing to market the drug as promised. Ad-
vise them what if anything each can hope to recover.*

In truth, the actual science of cloning is much less dramatic
than the romance surrounding it. Cloning cells—if not whole
human beings—is a procedure technically not very different
from a number of more widely accepted medical manipula-
tions. But it is precisely the romance that is most troubling:
the conceit of immortality, the bioengineered market desire

for a world full of mes everlasting. We've all heard the clichéd litany of examples to be pondered. The replacement for the dying child. The replication of racehorses, treasured pets, and great athletes. The Nobel Prize winner for whom the sperm bank is not enough. But these examples only skim the surface: Just imagine what the advertising industry could do with a clone with the right bone structure. You could style humanity, like Barbie, so that all the outfits finally fit. Mozart? Give his DNA a few more codas. Bill Gates and Donald Trump? There'll be lots of them. And we'll need to clone a few more lawyers in a world where compatible organs can be "farmed." Will questions of "harvest rights" be matters of custodial or property presumption in the new litigation of microterritorial imperative? *I paid for that kid, it's my DNA, and those organs are mine for the mining. Hand over that spare kidney now.* The fight over the corpse of baseball great Ted Williams allowed a glimpse into the seedy potential for gold-digging lawsuits. It used to be that the mistress who showed up at the funeral to claim part of the inheritance was the best the tabloids could hope for. These days, we have relatives suing over the right to mine for the genetic "properties" of future generations.

Economies of genetic hoarding have already started to mushroom into new forms of wealth, family planning becoming a matter of literal genetic investment. Birth by chance or accident is recently but resoundingly ideologically passé. The biological movement of random adaptation that tends to cast off old forms as a way of lurching into the future is challenged as never before. Who knows, one day we just might be able to move past mere nostalgia for the known and literally revivify the past—clone a few mummies, say, to see once and for all whether the Egyptians were black or white and whether they really wore those little cornrows on their always-sideways heads. No more disruptive mutation, just pure calm continuation.

This musing isn't science, of course, it's science fiction. Worse, it's a sociobiological fantasy driving a market already informed by insidious yearnings for perfect bloodlines, perfect children, perfect races. These days, the religion of scientific pursuit is remarkably fraught with anxious expressions of desire to trace past millions of years to the original cellular division, the Cain and Abel of molecular beginning. The debate itself has been split between rabid sociobiology on the one hand—Einstein is assumed to be biologically reproducible because genius is thought to abide in the genes—and, on the other hand, utter dehumanization of the "replicated" being whose flesh-and-blood existence is justified as a "perfectly compatible replacement" in part or in whole for some preexisting will.

It's heretical, perhaps, but I can't help entertaining the possibility that building Barbie and/or her dream life over and over again—this investment in static forms—is a way of going against a basic life force. The contemporary globalizing of everything from our economy to ourselves strikes me as problematic because, despite the promises of diversity and choice, we are in fact capitulating to ever more stringently uniform standards and practices. This investment in template mentality is the very antithesis of nature's, if not Barbie's, notions of plasticity. Perhaps we should be more attentive to whatever caution we feel in the face of cloning. I suggest this not to "hold science back" but to infuse the knowledge seeking with a sense of its own great power to disrupt in the name of renewal. What carelessness—and what terror of mortality— must visit those creatures bewitched with the cheerful extinction of ever replaceable parts, of endless replaceable selves?

A few years ago, a man in Detroit tried to sell his ten-month-old daughter for $60,000, an act certainly devoid of ethics yet remarkable nonetheless for the father's "fair business practice" of circulating a promotional video that touted the child's "amiable disposition," her blond hair and blue eyes, and the

fact that she had had "all her shots." Most of us can understand instantly that the highest bidder might not be the one
with the best interests of the child in mind. The ethic of the
marketplace favors that highest bidder, but we prefer the ethic
of adoption, custody, and human rights law that favors, at least
in principle, the best protector.

These days there's a faddish premium upon the child prodi-
giously endowed with brains, beauty, or the sportsman's bulk,
that child who can move straight from kindergarten to college
or career, thus sparing his parents the financial burden of all
those years of private school. But we sacrifice an important
part of our political ideology when we subject what until recently was the "pricelessness" of our humanity to the pecu-
niary speculation of the market, which, like other forms of
unchecked power, turns the right just to be into a corrupted
sense of entitlement.

I am struck by the hubris—these echoes of the worst of
nineteenth-century eugenics—within certain quarters of the
scientific community. But the announcement of the comple-
tion of the mapping of the human genome makes my mind
wander in other directions as well. I wonder less whether this
new information will enlighten us than about some of its
other long-range effects. Like developments in the computer
industry, the wealth to be mined in medical products will
surely have a major impact on the economy. From Iceland to
the Amazon, as scientist-explorers plant an infinity of little
flags in this microterritorial New World, new forms of property are created. As governments bestow charters, new realms
of exploitation are licensed. And as corporate kings send expeditions into this vast interior wilderness, new subjects will be
created. That which was unmastered, unowned, now will become so. And as with all colonial ventures, the outcome is
likely to be something of a mixed blessing.

I think that such revolutionary moments of scientific cogni-
tion mark shifts as well in the libidinal, political, even artistic

energy that ties us together as a civilization. In the most general sense, when we are aware of what we don't know in the world, we humans tend to mark the spot with rituals of caution. With the loss of mystery can come a certain loss of ritualized regard. And we humans are never more dangerously prone to repeat our worst histories than when we are convinced we know everything and throw all caution to the wind.

Baby geniuses are quite the thing to have these days. We Americans, as a nation of spurned peasants so many of whom found redemption in the New World, have become, I think, crazed by our own well-meaning aspirations in this regard. The Swiss psychologist Alice Miller published a book some years ago about the terrible costs of rigid and authoritarian child-rearing practices, particularly in prewar Germany. It was a best-seller in Europe. When the book was first released in the United States, it came out under the title *Prisoners of Childhood*. It didn't do so well. So the publisher rereleased the book under its original German title, *The Drama of the Gifted Child*, and suddenly the book just leaped off the shelves. Gifted children are the new American dream, the object of new fundamentalist fervor. Only in Lake Wobegon are the children still merely "above average."

One evening, the moon came up bright and insolent, like a forgotten reckoning. A radiant tension filled the air. The elders gathered round in silent resignation. They had felt the ebb of the powers and knew that this moon was the last chance to bring magic back to earth. The elders began a slow song, a rushing, lovely hymn that gathered the waning spirits of the world into a great and greater reverberation. When the sky began to tremble like glass with the sound, they lifted their arms like wings and invoked the magic that stirred then spun the directions of the earth. When it came, that nearly invisible sound of light and air rushing, the four winds grew tangled in a knot-

ted eddy, and that twirling compass drilled a hole in time. An eye in the heavens opened like a secret door, and the elders prayed for whatever magic was near in the universe to enter the world and save it.

They were tired, this small and aged band. And some hours later, as the steely-eyed missionaries of the new magic began to slide down the moonbeams and materialized before them, they remembered too late the ancient koan that one must always be very mindful of what one prays for.

When the catastrophe struck the capital city, there was no response to speak of from the government officials. It was not what anyone had expected after all those years of worrying. The upper classes had been content; the government had enjoyed the stability of being ignored as long as they made publicized forays against the unruly lower-class boys who mugged and stole and raided the storehouses as do mice. Like a lazy farm cat, the government caught its share of mice, then slept comfortably the rest of the day in a sunny patch of the garden.

So when the smooth-faced army of monkey ghosts came gliding down from the mountains, everyone was unprepared. There had been stories of the ghosts, of course, but no one had ever seen one, no one had ever quite believed. The monkeys were strong and large, with long, flat, silvery faces and small terrifying pinholes for nostrils and flat metallic ears. They were self-made, in accordance with the canons of pure will, and clung to life by a series of wires and pumps and chattering circuits and pulleys and wheels and sharp blades. They moved with swift invincibility, with a deadly purring sound. By late afternoon of the first day, the city was in their hands.

It all happened so quickly, no one quite realized what had transpired. The death they brought did not reveal itself at once. The old people continued to drowse in their corners; the office workers felt a shadow pass over their hearts but continued to organize their files. The children fell silent at once, and they knew first that the sickness began with the paralysis of speech.

There were other signs, of course. The government func-tionaries were suddenly naked and small and on display in the public square, but the people did not notice. The monkey ghosts ate lower-caste boys whole for lunch and dinner and every meal thereafter, but to the people this was not substantially distin-guishable from what the government had always done, and so they forgot to signal their resistance.

The monkey ghosts conquered as quietly as the night. The second sign of the people's death came three days later. The monkey ghosts ran out of lower-caste boys to eat and began to devour the hearts of the remaining people. Because the monkey ghosts were excellent technicians, they left strings and paper bellows to assist the circulation. The people had no words for the whistling emptiness that blew in the space where once their hearts had been.

The actual death came quickly thereafter. The monkey ghosts were what some call body snatchers. A person pruning a tree or reading a book or playing cards would look up to find the pale eyes of the ghost so close he could see himself reflected in the steely mirror gaze for one last glimpse, too quick for fear. The prey thus startled motionless, the ghost would lean forward and, with a gesture like blowing out candles on a birthday cake, snuff the life from the body to make room for his own, the ghostly habitation.

They did not resurrect themselves as monkeys but as enor-mous sleek feline humanoids. They had stout snub noses now, with sharp gray eyes narrowed always with caution and large pink mouths. The distinctive plated ears remained, however. The ears were still ominous metallic buds.

They took skin and dust and droppings and hair, and they would re-create an entire working organism like a new suit of clothes. The people did not know of this ability, and so they were careless with their dust, which the ghosts treated as gold. But the ghosts had no feelings—no empathy, no sense of touch. They did not feel what they knew, did not know what they felt.

They tried—they invented loves and losses, crises and scandals. But all they knew came to them through their sharp eyes and excellent ears. They could not make feelings.

And so as nothing changed on the outside, everything on the inside did.

The people in the lands beyond began to notice the change and felt fear. The city dwellers had always been an elite apart, but now they seemed to exist in worlds beyond the known. The markets were filled with empty promises rather than ripe fruit. The ghost people moved among the stalls exchanging words, setting expectations, their whispery chattering voices like rustling paper, but there were no spices or smoked fish or cages of plump sparrows. When the people dared enter the marketplace, what meat there was was spoiled. Fungus ate at the hearts of the turnips, and the people grew sick and afraid and moved farther and farther away from what had been their lives.

The ghosts were voracious meat eaters. They ate all the meat that was fit to eat; they ate it raw, roasted, or cured. Since they were such lethal hunters, they had no need of markets. They took what they needed from around them. They caught rabbits with casual flicks of their arms, they snatched squirrels from the trees, they reached into the sky and stole geese from their flight. They ate until the ground was bare, the sky was empty, and their bellies full.

When there was no more to eat in the city, the ghosts looked out at what lay beyond. The ghosts harvested the mountain people and river people and island people as silently as they had those in the city, but now they brought to this enterprise a patient selectivity. They would need warm bodies to inhabit in the winter, so they farmed the people, taking parts only as needed. They ate hearts and eyes and livers and replaced them with wooden rods and putty. The people who had been thus harvested lived on for the most part but dedicated to vague ends, not fully aware of how much had been lost.

A few of the people dreamed of the danger and survived.

They fled and hid and hunted as they could. They slipped between walls and beneath floors, into basements and burrows; they hid in boxes and bins and under the eaves of houses that had once belonged to them. They began to resemble the ghosts as they became more and more invisible, always hiding and moving and sniffing the wind for the smell, the cool almost metallic scent, that the ghosts gave off, a smell of predators who kill neatly, spilling very little blood.

The ghosts in turn were able to track the people, because while they could not feel, they saw; what they could not see, they always heard. They could hear the frightened heartbeats and the wet panicked noise of their breathing. And in listening closely to that panic, the ghosts learned how to enter the dreams of the people and reproduce.

Back in my kitchen, the shelled peas formed a small pebbled mountain. I moved on to onions. I sliced them so thin they were translucent, their circles like Saturn's rings, or the damp stump of a fresh-cut tree. One of the onions had started to sprout. Its green shoots looked strong, promising. I set it aside to plant in the little kitchen garden of pots and boxes by the windows, from which I collected a small but perpetual harvest of chives and parsley, lettuce and dill.

I had never thought of harvest much beyond the matter of these small crops until very recently. That's when a student of mine raised her hand on the first day of class and said, "Excuse me, Professor Williams. I'm really looking forward to your class, but I have to miss the next session. I'm putting myself through law school by selling my eggs, and I'm to be harvested next week." I felt as though I'd entered the twilight zone, but all my other students seemed entirely unfazed by this revelation. It was one of those moments that make me feel quite old, and, as with tattoos and body piercing, quaintly out of touch. I recovered gracefully enough, I hope, although

at the back of my mind I began to calculate how many years
stood between me and an early retirement.

Life is short and weird, I thought, wiping the onion-drawn
tears from my cheeks.

And life is precious. Anyone who doubts it should consult
the price index for that most literal of stock markets, the trade
in human eggs. Recent speculation upped the price to a minimum of $50,000 for eggs harvested from tall, blue-eyed,
athletic coeds with SAT scores of at least 1400. Tuition at
Columbia Law School is approximately $30,000 (or three-
fifths of a human egg), so at three or four harvests a year, my
student has enough left over for real estate in Manhattan. Not
that it's an entirely free market: As it turns out, there was also
in that class a tall, athletic black student with scores over
1400. She too was trying to put herself through law school by
selling her eggs, but, alas, she had no takers, so she was busy
filling out the financial aid forms.

Some ethicists downplay the significance of all this. It's
how the child is valued once born, they say, not the price of
the ingredients. But money has never been more symbolic
than in this context. What sort of acquisitive rigidity is revealed by the advertisements one sees in Ivy League student
newspapers—for blue-eyed egg donors who test well—so
clearly expressed as a set of consumer preferences, of expectations upon which they place so great and precise an economic
value? There are no guarantees in gene science or in life, only
a series of infinitesimal probabilities. What happens if after all
that investment, that accounting of eggs before they hatch,
the child comes out short, "average" (whatever that means),
and dyspeptic? Do we measure this as some kind of "loss"?
What is being purchased, what sacrificed, with such an insur-
ance policy against the undesired? How do we play the law of
"averages" against the splendid uniqueness of our children's
bright humanity?

Of course, this is precisely why the science of cloning is at-

tractive to some in the fertility business. No more law of averages. Move over, smart eggs. Cloning promises genes that
deliver.

One response to this is that purchasing eggs or manipulat-
ing cell lines is no more than what is commonly done in selecting a mate. The economist Gary Becker, in an article
called "Assortive Principles in the Marriage Market," charted
patterns of spousal choice: It reads a bit like a Harlequin romance fractured into one long string of algebraic, economet-
ric equations. Basically, the availability of beautiful women
with heaving bosoms to a male of the species is posited to be a
direct function of (the wealth) + (social reputation) of the
given male.

Nothing in this equation sets us apart from birds and ba-
boons, of course, but what is sometimes overlooked is the degree to which the pecking order even for those with small
brains has to do not only with raw size but also with patterns
of social organization designed to enhance survival. What
does distinguish us as human, however, is the immense variety of invented, rather than merely instinctual, ordering our
collective creativity has brought forth—from rubbing two
sticks together to the tax code, from building huts to signing
treaties. This intellectual adaptability of human beings has
been our saving grace. But because we are a fallible species,
what has also been our undoing is the excessive attachment
we form precisely to our own inventions, even when their
practice is of limited or negative utility. We eroticize everything from "six-pack" abdominals to sport-utility vehicles far
beyond their function in nature. And if "breeding" were all
there was to creating greatness, tomatoes would taste better
and the British royal family would be known for its long line
of really great-looking geniuses.

I've been rereading Charles Darwin's *Origin of Species*. It
is instructive to look at it against the backdrop of today's almost universal sense of Darwinism as an unemotional, ultra-

rationalist triumph of scientific inquiry. In fact, Darwin writes
with an almost breathless faith that there is a sacred thread in
nature, an echo of Genesis. Very much a product of the
rhetorical gestures of its era, the book is filled with romanticized calls of the wild and the imperially heraldic discourse of
epic discovery. Indeed, this cornerstone of science as we know
it seems to employ creationism as a central, if unspoken,
metaphor.

If *The Origin of Species* would never be recognized as living up to the rigors of scientific discipline today, it is nevertheless an object lesson in how much of what we call
scientific is deeply infused by the political, cultural, and aesthetic valuations of its authors. Today's gene science, which so
many shrug off as merely an extension of "natural selection,"
is anything but. Nature favors mixture, diversity, randomness.
When Monsanto devises plants that cannot reproduce, this is
in service to its own market interests in forcing the world's
farmers to repurchase seeds year after year. When so-called
prize animals like the cheetah become endangered by human
encroachment, the problem is not made better by overbreed-
ing, and now cloning, for pure type. As of this moment, the
cheetah's gene pool has been so reduced that all it will take is
susceptibility to one bout of just the right microbe to wipe
them all out.

But whether we are on our way to breeding ourselves into
extinction or a world of the undifferentiatedly clever, it is
clear that what is at stake in this new purchase of life is the
settling of old historical arguments such as: Are we men or are
we monkeys? Are we women or are we wombs? This question
is not actually about genetics but about the dignity we accord
each other and our fellow living creatures; it is a vastly complex one in which God, history, science, racial myth, the distribution of resources, and your momma are always on the
line.

Under the current formulation, genetically engineered or

drug-induced superintelligence becomes a product like any other, subject to the same rational economic interests that govern the distribution of blue Jell-O, ball bearings, or Britney Spears, but priced as a luxury item. Racial and class superiority in a designer bottle. Nor, given the times, do I foresee such socialist tomfoolery as dumping a little fluoridated bioelixir in the water supply so that there would be equal opportunity for all to outwit each other in the advancement of our various civilizations.

What a future we face—the spoils of civilization controlled by really rich know-it-alls.

If this sounds like nothing more than a biologically literal translation of historically familiar struggles for dominance, then we should be examining the traditional risks of such states of imbalance: intolerance, a sense of infallibility, and much time expended battling those deemed unattractively underendowed, us genetically impoverished know-nothings.

Which brings us back to ethics after all.

It was an era when all the babies were cool skinned as alabaster and long limbed as spider monkeys. Their round moonish faces glowed with the peculiar waxy luminescence of the intently and thoroughly bred.

To an observer from an earlier era, the most apparent sign of the evolutionary leap would have been that they came out of the Womb equipped with perfect sets of sharp little teeth the size of water droplets. They were meat eaters from birth.

The Womb from which the new breed came was warm and clean, a peaceful host from which the world's detritus had been cleansed with perfumed jets of pink water.

The World, on the other hand, was busy with conquest, organized into missions, occupied with goals and timetables. The World was beautifully functional, with blue skies and efficient transportation. Ever since the institution of free-enterprise time zones, age, speed, and sense of direction had been profoundly altered. Parallel universes were tracked carefully, to prevent their careening into one another, and now that an hour could be mapped for multiple uses, spaces grew, along with the population, toward infinity.

That was all there was, the Womb and the World. Life was balanced and good.

It was eleven o'clock, NorthernWiley.com time, on a field of Thursdays, when the spirit children began to appear. They simply walked out from the shadows and would not be gone.

In retrospect, they acknowledged, they should have noticed something sooner. The shadows had grown thicker over time, the dark a tangled fence of voices, a ringing in the ears, a cacophonous site of random remembrance.

At first, the authorities treated them like the rest of the shadows from which they had broken off—like echoes, like the leftover wisps of another, discontented place, where people and ghosts were unmerged and at war, the scraps of a time too dense with grief. The police tried to sweep them away, as though they were dry rusty leaves, into the bins of elimination. The public vacuums were called out to suck them back into the void. Spotlights tried to reveal them. But it was weeks, and by then much too late, before they realized that the shadow children were alive, and that they were multiplying.

These new children had no teeth. Their limbs and their lives were short, terse, economical. They lived in the silent spaces of the meat-eating world, the neglected corners where the lanterns did not penetrate. They ate what had been forgotten. They played with the emptiness. Bred of and into a world of multiple dimensions, they were nonetheless bereft of any ability to orient themselves in the World. They could not tell right from north, left from yesterday, south from hot, or cold from a teaspoon. They could consider any given object only from above or beneath or by looking at it head-on. They were trapped in a land

of flat images; in other words—no, there are no other words.
Their world was flat.

The World remained round and layered, however. When the
new children came to a curve or an angle or a dip in the road,
they got dizzy. They fell into ditches. When they came to forks
in the road, they were disoriented. When they turned a sharp
corner, they walked into walls. When they reached the horizon,
they bumped their heads on the sky and poked holes in the
clouds.

Every time they bumped into something, little bits of them-
selves broke off like sparks or a shower of seeds. The sparks ig-
nited instantly into more children. Thus there were tens then
hundreds then thousands of them in no time, silent, tumbling,
disoriented, blowing and shifting, aimless and lost.

The people were terrified of these apparitions. They huddled
indoors, listening to the muffled bumps of the children strug-
gling to disentangle themselves from picket fences and over-
hanging eaves. The people wrapped themselves in thick quilts
and listened to the sound of accumulating children, a barely
perceptible sound, like drifting snow, like the breathing of birds.
They listened for the nearly imperceptible streams of light and
air circulating in hollow bones.

The onions were done. I rose to find a skillet. I put on water to
boil the pasta. Life felt good and grounded, like a solid oak
table. The house was filled with robust dinner smells and the
sliding sounds of heavy old chairs; my son's room was clean.
The boy next door had meandered over for a visit. The boy
was teaching my son how to belch the alphabet backward. My
son learned rapidly, contributing a little two-part harmony by
belching contrapuntally and in a different key. The boys have
brains, I marveled, as I interrupted their dizzy music with a bit
of Core Knowledge about the risks of hyperventilation. It's a

perfect example of what my godmother once said of Machiavelli: Sometimes having brains is not what matters most.

"Time to set the table," I counseled them, and a general clashing and thrashing of dishes and silver ensued. It was, to all appearances, a task that this particular gene pool will need years more practice to perfect.

VII

The Crystal Stair

Many years ago, I lived in a luxury apartment building in Los Angeles. One day an elderly lady whose eyesight was failing entered the elevator in which I was riding. She squinted intently at me, then smiled in recognition and apologized. "Forgive me, dear," she said. "I didn't recognize you at first—my eyes, you see . . ." Here the elevator door opened to reveal a swarthy young man in a baseball cap carrying a bag of what appeared to be Chinese food. "Take the service elevator," she called out to him in a voice gone raspy with disdain. "As I was saying," she continued, "old age has made me blind."

Old age isn't all that makes some people blind. There was a history to this woman's inability to see me in the chandeliered lights of the nonservice elevator. "I don't believe you exist!" she had exclaimed the first time she met me and discovered not only that she had a black neighbor but that I was a lawyer. It was very hard to tell if she was gladdened by the turn of events. She'd sighed with heartfelt something or other and said, "I never thought I'd see the day."

. . .

My great-aunt Mary was hardly the earliest to "rise above the odds," as she put it. There was a small stream of others before her who fled to Boston in the beginning of that great movement of blacks from the rural South to the urban North that began after the Civil War and peaked in the 1960s. Everyone knows stories of the Underground Railroad, and Frederick Douglass's memoirs have come to exemplify the status of the escaped slave during that era. But immediately after the Civil War, there was also another wave, a largely invisible generation of just-freed slaves, who migrated to Washington, DC, to Baltimore, to Philadelphia, to Boston and points northward. But without much voice or education, many of them remained "in service."

"Slavery wasn't that long ago," my mother once cautioned. "I grew up talking to people who had been slaves."

How, when, where, I asked her. And my mother described her experiences playing chamber music at Resthaven, a black nursing home founded by a man she remembers only as Mr. Benjamin. His family had also come up from the Deep South. He had gone to law school, had become a solo practitioner, and was doing well. With some help from the Episcopal Church, he opened Resthaven in honor of his mother. She had been born in slavery but ran to Boston after the Emancipation Proclamation and worked as a maid while making sure her son got a good education.

Nursing homes were a new thing then. In those days there were very few places for an elderly person other than home or a boardinghouse. But there was a new and urgent need for some kind of care facility because a whole generation of ex-slaves was growing old. These were people who had worked as servants all their lives, who had little or no family. While the feudal system of black servants living with the families that formerly owned them continued to exist for a while in many places in the South, the North was different. Their new employers didn't often house them for life, didn't dream of feeding or caring for them after they grew too feeble to work. The ones hardest hit were the domestics who had spent years "living in." They were largely a childless female population, elderly women who had coped with the demands of being "just like family," but who, at the end of their tenure, had no place in the world to go.

And that is how my mother came to offer the weekly solace of her cello to an audience of former slaves.

All my mother's siblings were imbued with a deep sense of needing to prove wrong the legacy of assumed inhumanity. Like so many children of the survivors of traumatizing human events, they carried both the benefit and the burden of parental hopes, as wide and as deep as the thwarted dreams of all who had struggled before. They were quiet pioneers—by circumstance alone—in these interesting, if complex, times. They were also blessed to have at their disposal a public school system that was excellent. As immigrants from the serfdom of the South, they sat side by side with other recent immigrants from the serfdom of northern, southern, and eastern Europe, taught by teachers who were paid a relatively handsome wage.

There was comprehensive music and art instruction. It was before white flight. It was before the Southern resentment of taxes and the federal government spread north. They were the beneficiaries of America's greatest and least cynical period of investment in public schools. A great and hopeful middle class was created.

My aunt Elizabeth turned out to be a talented pianist and graduated from the New England Conservatory of Music. My uncle Neil went to Boston College and became a lawyer; like my father he found the law firm world a hard one to break into and so spent his working life as a clerk in New York City's courts. My aunt Muriel, the baby of the family, was gifted with a particularly quick mind. She raced through school chased by the great expectations of her doting family, to graduate from Radcliffe at the age of nineteen. She was getting her master's degree, also at Radcliffe, when, apparently out of the blue, she joined a short-lived but all-consuming Roman Catholic cult, an episode about which I know very little except that she broke her family's heart by denouncing them all as heretics.

The extremity of her intolerance was something my mother has never reconciled. Apparently Aunt Muriel did not even attend her parents' funerals. Eventually, however, she did recover a sense of balance, perhaps because the cult's rigors were so extreme that its leader was excommunicated. She became a Carmelite nun for a while, whose order at that time required a very strict oath of seclusion and silence. Even harder to comprehend than her extraordinary religious fundamentalism is the notion of anyone on my mother's side of the family giving up speech. Unsurprisingly, therefore, her time as a Carmelite was brief. She has spent the rest of her life as a Benedictine nun, teaching and writing books about the lives of saints.

But the breach with her family was a lasting one. I have never met her, never seen a photograph of her, never gotten my mother to tell me more.

At the center of our family's dynamic is the absence of Aunt Muriel, the silent drama of her exit. For years I imagined that there must be some much greater mystery to her disappearance from her siblings' lives. She must be an ax murderer, I thought. Perhaps there is indeed a deeper drama, but I have come to think that it is what it is: a sad but idiosyncratic family feud with lines drawn for a lifetime. My grandmother never recovered, my mother tells me bitterly. "She had bragged so much about Muriel's great future career. After the break, she could never bring herself to face her friends."

As among so many ethnic strivers, saving face is an extremely powerful ethic for blacks of a certain class. "Putting on a bold front," is how it was described when I was growing up. "You must maintain appearances." It can be utterly exhausting, all the polishing and buffing and keeping up with the Joneses. You had to be so perfect. It can have a rigid, high-schoolish, self-hating futility to it as well, the kind of mind-set that leads to not very constructive ends, like massive clothing debt or visits to the plastic surgeon (as in author Lawrence Otis Graham's essay about having his nose and chin reconstructed after a model from the Brooks Brothers catalog). My sister and I grew up with some of that pressure to "look right" at all costs — how I hated the little white gloves! the roller-brimmed hats! — but no one in my family, not even Aunt Mary, was ever part of the generally lighter-skinned black upper-middle-class society of networked clubs like Jack and Jill. I was an adult before I met black people who kept A-lists. I was an adult before I heard of the upper-class black men's club The Boule (and even then I thought they were talking about a fancy French restaurant).

I think now that there was a freedom in that, although when my son was born, a friend told me that I would suffer for the lack of connection when it came time to negotiate the modern educational reality of private schools in New York City. And since there is indeed a kind of frothing craziness to schooling in Manhattan, I worried that she might be right.

"Do you think I'd fit in?" I asked. I meant Jack and Jill. Oddly, I had no fear at all of fitting into the private school scene itself, although fear and fear itself might have been a very good idea. Instead I worried about the "black boogie aristocracy," among whom I always feel like a complete and utter failure. I am not a fashion plate. I am not what you'd call an upbeat conversationalist. And then there's the little matter of the hair . . .

"Well, you are different," said my friend.

"You think so . . ."

"Mmmm. You're the only person I know whose dishes don't match."

That did it. There had been a small window through which I might have dispatched myself unto the designs of a good hairdresser for the sake of my son's larger well-being. But never, ever could I revamp my life sufficiently to compete at the level of dishes.

The history of the black middle class begins in slavery, the lighter-skinned slave children, usually children of the master or his sons—the favored few, the "house servants," who, like pampered pets in a Georgian tableau of upstairs-downstairs, led somewhat easier lives than those who labored in the fields. Over generations, that sense of "privilege" morphed into a kind of class system whose boundaries were patrolled by rituals mimicking the master's ways—debutante balls, secret societies, and all. Growing up in Boston, for example, one watched from afar as the Brahmin class held glittering balls for their daughters at the Ritz and the Copley Plaza, the silvery spun-sugar details reported breathlessly yet perfectly decorously in the society column of *The Boston Globe*. Growing up black in Boston, one also could follow along, in the pages of the local black press, as the African-American daughters of a certain class greeted society at events with ambitious names like the Snowball Cotillion.

When I was in law school, Harvard abounded with the kind of secret societies, populated by the white children of old money and privilege, that somehow everyone knew about anyway. (Yale's Skull and Bones, with its prodigious number of presidential alumni, is perhaps the best known of this associational genre.) There was one secret society called the Choate Club, which was always rumored as the supposed fast track to political power. The secret societies were reputed to be the ultimate mentoring programs. I still don't know how much substance to attach to the stories, but given the ideal of the level playing field assumed by us determined egalitarians, it was disconcerting to hear that your classmates Mr. X, Mr. Y, and Mr. Z had had dinner the night before with Professor A and the secretary of state, or Professor B and the prime minister of some controversial corner of the globe, or Professor C and the head of a corporation whose operations we were reading about in our textbooks.

There's no profit in being naïve about such things, I suppose; pure power isn't inherently democratic. But I still marveled at how much those secret societies were the object of covetous admiration among the student body at large; it was in marked contrast to the almost insane rage reserved for any given clump of black students who had gathered for any purpose, whether for a study group or informally for lunch. No matter how much of the rest of our lives was spent in open, friendly, integrated settings, whenever three or more of us gathered publicly—or even privately—one was sure to hear charges of reverse racism! exclusivity! self-segregation!

I sometimes think that the paranoia about gathering to "conspire" does not just have its roots in some ancient fear of slave rebellion but may also be a kind of interesting psychological projection. If the secret societies and fraternities really do require as many codes, circumventions, and hazing and bonding rituals as is made out, then no wonder the elites who make it through might imagine that every other category of humanity may be doing the same.

In law school, we, the new black admittees, were indeed conspiring to change the world. Not the secret kind of conspiring, but rather a noisy, shout-it-from-the-rooftops kind of planning for the future. These were the early 1970s and people of every race, religion, or stripe harbored public ambitions to make the world a better, different place. We were still riding high from the victories of the civil rights movement; peace and love were not yet disparaged as mere political correctness. What substance was accomplished is yet to be tested by time and perhaps will endure in accidental rather than wholly pur-

poseful ways. As far as I'm concerned, some of the most interesting postscripts to our having been granted admission fall
within the range of the unquantifiably random, even as they
are still the clear product of that gift of opportunity.

My law school classmate A., for example, would never have
met her husband if she'd had to constrain her aspirations in
the same way her father had. And the city of Raleigh, North
Carolina, might never have gotten its first black television station as soon as it did unless A.'s husband had decided to move
to Taiwan.

A. grew up in Brooklyn, where her father worked as a civil
servant because, as a classically trained opera singer, he could
find no companies in the United States that were willing to
give roles to blacks. She graduated from Erasmus Hall High
School and Hunter College, skipping a year of each to arrive
at Harvard Law School at the age of nineteen. "It was close,
though," she said. "My college counselor assured me not only
that I was not law school material but that I certainly could
never qualify for or succeed at a place like Harvard." (Three
years later, when A. returned to New York to take the bar
exam, she caught a glimpse of this counselor, who was also
there to take the exam. It turned out that he too had gone to
law school but, as far as she could determine, despite numer-
ous tries he never did pass the exam.) These days A. pursues
an ardently international lifestyle. Her husband, a Belgian national, is an engineer whose job requires him to move all over
the world on a moment's notice. Early in her career, she
founded two businesses: Applied Communications Technolo-
gies Corporation and Spectron Broadcasting Corporation.
When she followed her husband abroad, she donated an op-
erating license she had obtained through an FCC minority
set-aside program to St. Augustine's College, a traditionally
black college. Raleigh, North Carolina, thus received its first
black-owned television station.

As significant as this philanthropy was on its own, I don't really think I got a complete sense of its dimension until B., another of my law school classmates, told me of her experience growing up in Raleigh. Her father began his career in the uncomfortable position of cameraman at WRAL, a station whose executive vice president was soon to be Senator Jesse Helms. During the 1960s, her father was the one "behind the scenes," filming Helms's regular television editorials inveighing against the civil rights movement. "In a different time, Dad would have been a great media personality," B. said. "He is a smart man, a 'Morehouse man' with a wonderfully resonant voice with great sensibilities."

As integration opened more doors, her father emerged from the wings to become a local television personality—the host of *Teenage Frolics*, a long-running dance show that was a kind of precursor to *Soul Train*. Eventually, he became a respected TV editorialist in his own right, offering a perspective radically different from that offered by Helms so many years before.

How to build an institution. How to make the progress last. How to network without excluding, how to bank without hoarding, how to create a mobile society without frozen socialites and all the deep divides. B. embodies the difficult paradoxes of the attempt simultaneously to position oneself in the world advantageously yet idealistically and yet again generously.

In other words, B., as the daughter of such a prominent father, was a shoo-in for the interesting phenomenon of the Black Debutante Ball.

"It was just what you did," she said, laughing. "It was a whole production, for a year ahead of time. You learned how to waltz, how to wear your hair, and how to prepare a résumé." For her, it wasn't about imposing a class order but rather was an attempt by the small black community in which she was raised to provide its children with as many of the accoutrements of white privilege as it could afford. "It was a segregated world, one with obvious limitations," but she said that events like the debutante balls were the rituals of connection that "tied us all together, that insulated us from daily racial confrontation . . . I grew up with the room to be very self-confident. It was nothing like what I saw when I moved to San Francisco and peeked into white debutante society."

For one thing, the young ladies of Raleigh had to raise the money for their own debuts by seeking out sponsors who would buy advertisements in the evening's program. Funds were also raised to provide college scholarships, which were distributed at the festivities. The queen of the ball was the one who raised the most money. Anyone of "reasonably good reputation" could be invited. After a moment, B. added, "But it's true, they did have to be invited. And they did have to raise the money from reputable sponsors—they couldn't, you know, just throw a fish fry . . ."

C. is yet another black friend of mine from our days at Harvard. C. also grew up in Raleigh. C. is the daughter of a single mother who worked as a maid in the white homes of Raleigh, and she has never forgiven or forgotten. Today she is a brilliant businesswoman who married a perfect man and wears elegant designer clothes. But C. is very, very bitter. She grew spitting mad when I asked her to talk to me about growing up in that time and place. C. had not a single kind word for the white women who worked her mother to death. C. had no patience for the black society that held itself together with debutante balls. And I had to hold the phone away from my head,

I simply could not repeat to you here what C. had to say about the socially cohesive potential of a fish fry.

Mr. Swift, Aunt Mary's gilded second husband, was a member of a society at Harvard that came to be known as the A.D. (standing for Alpha Delta) Club. The 1936 edition of the club's self-published annual describes its formal appearance (after a few years as an informal drinking club) at Harvard: "In 1851 its accommodations were increased by enlarging and re-furnishing the old room, an aged negro was installed guardian of the hearth, and the society board, 'adorned with appropriate ribbons,' appeared for the first time on University Hall." In 1861, however, "the members, wishing to keep the fact of its continuance secret, spoke of the society as the A.D., choosing this title from its resemblance to the name of a College boat, the Haidee. The uninitiated ear, overhearing any conversation, might thus be easily misled. From this date the society was always called the A.D., and from this circumstance the name of the present club was derived."

While the mostly white social organizations dominated the invitation-only intrigue of my law school years, I don't wish to understate the degree to which there was also some clandestine social striation, based mostly on class, among black students. While black students weren't plotting against white people in the way many white students seemed to imagine, I found it profoundly ironic when some African-American students set up their own secret cliques and societies. And since there were so few of us, it proved quite divisive. I remember one famous flap about a formal dinner for fifty to which the vice president of the Black Students Association was invited, but not the president, and to which one roommate in a suite was invited but not another. There seemed to be no rhyme or reason to the invitations, and surely it was the merest of accidents that only the very lightest skinned of black students were asked to come. Since I was not among the chosen, I can speak of the dinner party only from the somewhat ungenerous secondhand accounts: There was a chamber ensemble playing throughout the evening. There were ten courses. There were roses for the ladies. There were cigars for the gentlemen. There was an aged Negro installed as guardian of the hearth.

Anyway, the world of black social climbing was and still is a shadow world whose formality and strictures are both a lovely triumph of sheer will and quite punishing. I do not want to imply that all these organizations are a bad thing—in fact they provided the structure from which an enormous degree of social progress could then be charted. Historically, they provided the stages for validation, the networking for match-making, the goodwill to start businesses, and the names of homes in which to stay (thus enabling long-distance travel in an era when blacks could not stay in hotels). But at the heart of such organizations, born of the exigencies of battling in a hostile world, was a battle of self-esteem. What drove so many successful African Americans of a certain era was a ruthless commitment to the overcoming of every single stereotype about "the race," no matter how trivial or ridiculous. "Proving them wrong" was a mission, a duty, and it led to an exhausting kind of perfectionism. Blacks were "supposed" to be dirty, so you had to slick your skin with Vaseline so that "they" could see how shiny and gleamingly clean you were. Blacks were "supposed" to be loud and incomprehensible, so we of the black middle class learned to hyperarticulate in rounded, preacherly, elaborately decorative swells. I remember the competitive ethic urged upon me by Wade McCree, the first black solicitor general of the United States, who had grown up in Boston with my mother. "They said I couldn't learn Latin, so I learned Latin. They said I couldn't learn Greek, and so I learned Greek."

I think learning Latin and Greek and taking baths and

speaking beautifully are wonderful accomplishments in their
own right. But they can't disprove others' conviction that
you're inferior—or else a mere "exception" that proves the
rule. Indeed, they are rather whimsical tests by which to
measure our humanity, when you come right down to it. And
when huge amounts of energy go into jumping through those
hoops for the sole sake of performance rather than personal
satisfaction, a kind of bitterness settles over the enterprise. We
risk a deep disappointment, an existential fatigue that can
poison the collective resolve. There is an adage attributed
to Charles Haddon Spurgeon, as cited with perhaps unin-
tentional but nonetheless delightful irony in the Levenger
("Tools for Serious Readers") catalog: "Learn to say no. It will
be of more use to you than to be able to read Latin."

Another of the complex psychic motives behind such hier-
archical formations is rooted in a kind of Cinderella complex
among the generations of slavery's illegitimate children—the
angry, confused, dispossessed orphans, the aspirational bastard
princelings born of those who, like Thomas Jefferson, thought
hybridized blacks a more advanced—and more dangerous—
species than "the pure African." It is my sense that most white
people in the United States have never really thought how it
came to be that, on the whole, African Americans today look
very different from the inhabitants of those West African
countries from which some of our ancestors came. Intermarriage rates were and continue to be much too low to explain
the phenomenon. I think it's why many more white people
were upset about the Sally Hemings–Thomas Jefferson allega-
tions than were black people. Black people just rolled their
eyes and thought: What else is new? The archetypal Mr. Big's
exploits on *Sex and the City* pale compared to his insatiable
historical pursuit of Sex and the Inner City.

Many were shocked, for example, by the announcement
that Strom Thurmond had fathered a daughter by one of his
family's black maids. For years, knowledge of her existence

circulated in black communities. For just as many years it was dismissed as sordid rumor by the mainstream press. Essie Mae Washington-Williams herself waited until she was seventy-eight years old and until Thurmond had died to come forward, stating that while her emotions had always been mixed about keeping the secret of her ardent segregationist of a father, he had not been a bad person and she wished to do him no harm. It was a sad little explanation from this hesitant, conflicted woman—this aged woman who had spent her whole life protecting a man whose venomous ideas brought such harm not only to black people but to America itself.

It was fascinating also to track the rhetorical shifts in the media response. At first the story was worded along the lines of "A black woman who claims that Strom Thurmond is her father . . . " Only after Thurmond's white family corroborated her story did the language shift to describing her as the "biracial" or "mixed-race" daughter of the late senator.

Many in the press called Thurmond a hypocrite in the wake of this story. How could a man who waxed on so about separation of the races have had a relationship with a black woman? But historically, sexual license with black women has always been a central feature of racism's double standard. Segregation only described what blacks couldn't do; it allowed white men to do pretty much whatever they wanted. Thus, to many African Americans, the little shift to calling Ms. Washington-Williams "mixed-race" seemed odd. In the United States, being "black" virtually always means some mixture of African, Native American, and European ancestry. Almost all African Americans are to some degree the taboo-saddled descendants of Great White Slaveholders—very, very few of us do not have closely guarded family secrets, sordid histories about some complex, messy relation to a famous white progenitor.

A friend used to cite her family background as an example of this invisible past every year in the college-level history class she teaches, laying out her family history on both sides of the family—i.e., the white side and the black side—all the way back to the times of slavery. One year it turned out that the great-grandson of her family's white owner was in her class. He put two and two together before she did. Unfortunately, no one had ever told him about the slave relations and he went into a rather public state of shock.

"I certainly wouldn't have used that particular example if I had known," she says. "I tell these stories to give them a sense of complexity about our current social fabric, not to put particular people on the spot without warning. He was a very nice young man, and the news took him completely off guard. He was stricken, horribly embarrassed. I apologized to him, but I know some other students felt that I had intentionally 'outed' him, and that I had meant to tarnish his reputation and humiliate him."

What was also quite interesting about this encounter was how impermeable, even today, are the boundaries of these sad, racialized public secrets. As my friend put it, "Every white person in the school seemed to know that this kid was the descendant of a respectable Southern gentlemen of considerable reputation. But even as a professor, I'd had no idea. That knowledge seemed to have circulated through a conversational network, or a class grouping, to which I and most of the minority population didn't belong. Meanwhile, on the other side of the invisible wall, just about everyone in the African-American community takes for granted the pervasiveness of white-on-black relations as a sad historical reality. But that's a body of knowledge that still seems to be a recurring source of explosively laden shock to many if not most white people, even direct family members."

Well before Aunt Muriel, my mother's godmother graduated from Radcliffe. Gertrude Mabel Baker was her name, class of

1900. For years I thought she was the authentically "first black woman" to graduate from Radcliffe, but it turns out she was the second. Miss Alberta Scott had graduated in 1898.

Aunt Gertrude spent her career as an elementary school teacher in the public schools of Cambridge, where she lived all her life. She met my great-aunt Mary through their mutual interest in early childhood development. She and my grandmother became fast friends. They formed the Fortnightly, a little group of local black women dedicated to political "uplift." It was not as exclusive as Jack and Jill came to be thought of, nor did it survive any of its original members; it was one of innumerable little circles of black women that sprang up all over the country in those times, self-help organizations dedicated to universal suffrage, racial equality, and lessons for the children.

"From the time I was born," says my mother, "Aunt Gertrude honored me as much as any godmother ever could. She gave me a desk set once, with onyx around the rim. There was a children's symphony in Boston, and one year when I was about eleven or twelve, she purchased season tickets for me, and she would come by and take me to each concert. When pure silk stockings came into fashion, she gave me a pair. But my legs were so thin that my mother had to put them away until I'd put on a little weight. Aunt Gertrude was the gentlest person in the world. No one was ever as kind as those old women of my mother's circle of friends."

Aunt Gertrude died when I was five, but I remember her as clearly and as warmly as my mother does. My most precious possession was a gift from her—my stuffed dog Cicero, named not as grandly as it might sound but after the cat in the newspaper comic strip *Mutt and Jeff*. She never married and died with few immediate relatives. Like the Delany sisters, like Condoleezza Rice, like Anita Hill, like a significant percentage of professional black women of that generation or this—

like me, perhaps—being "one of very few" seems correlated to likely status as ever-single woman.

It was my friend D., in one of our talks about privilege and community, who dragged me back down to earth with advice about the New York private nursery school scene. She and her husband have a son who is a little older than mine and had done the thing called "shopping." "I hated it!" she declared, having ultimately sent her child to an integrated public school when he was old enough, so he could get what she calls "a holistic education with real live people." But she nonetheless informed me that I had been terribly naïve; when the application forms asked for references, I put down the names of people—friends and babysitters—who knew my son.

D. laughed. "You'd better get real," she said. "Don't you know Toni Morrison?"

What a question. Despite all my class immersion, I hadn't realized till then that private schools, the really elite ones that black parents dream of when vouchers are dangled before them like bait, operate very much like country clubs. "Merit" looks an awful lot like lineage in this world.

"I shook her hand at a conference once," I said dubiously.

"Call her up now." A pause. "If you're sure that's what you want, of course. You want a school that only takes you if you know someone?"

D. is good at this sort of thing. Among the many components of her service to the community, she provides a broad network of information and support for black mothers about schools, babysitting, scholarships, educational opportunity. On one typical day, "I was asked to speak on a talk show about the constitutionality of fining or punishing parents who fail to 'properly supervise' their children. Before the show, I picked up my son from school, rushed to the station, engaged in a

heated thirty-minute discussion with another guest who favored public flogging of 'bad' children, presented an analysis
of the discriminatory impact such legislation would have on
black and poor communities, and then dashed off to the Museum of American Folk Art," where she presented a live
broadcast on representations in black folk art.

The next time we talked, she picked up in midsentence
from where we had left off the last time we'd talked.

". . . pancake-exercise birthday party," she was explaining.

My head was spinning with that sense of inadequacy I get
whenever I talk to her. "Pancakes and exercise, did you say?"

"And big bowls of fruit, with four-foot Lego boards and a
zillion pieces. Enough for everyone. Your son sure missed a
good party."

"I know, I know," I said miserably, ever the guilty mother.
I'd been traveling again, dragging my patient son through air-
ports in Tucson and Salt Lake City. "But what on earth is a
pancake-exercise party? I mean, what books are you reading?"
My entertaining skills are limited and text-based.

"Oh, I made it up," she said breezily. "The kids got here at
ten o'clock in the morning. I put on *Thriller* and led them
through my aerobic routine. They loved it, they were sooo good,
you wouldn't believe it. All these serious kids just bending to the
right—breathe deeply! I told them—and bending to the left.
Then I made pancakes and then they ate fruit and then there
was more exercise, then Legos, then birthday cake. I put the parents in a big room with toddler gates over the door so they
couldn't get out and they all had to talk to one another . . ."

At twelve-thirty, the party was over, and at one-thirty, she
was giving a speech to the Westchester Women's Club on the
racial implications of three-strikes-and-you're-out laws.

So many "firsts," so many circlings of the landing strip of those
who have "arrived."

It is interesting to ponder this history in 2004, the fiftieth anniversary of *Brown v. Board of Education*. There has been much change in the world, for better and for worse. If legalized segregation is no longer an issue, de facto segregation remains an intractable problem in housing, employment, and education, and the remedies of the civil rights era are under attack. States' rights has reemerged as the watchword, even as a helter-skelter drive for national standards drives a panicked industry of home-improved, do-it-yourself education—from Muzzy foreign language tapes advertised on Rush Limbaugh to educational CDs at Costco, to $300 sessions with private tutors from Princeton Review.

For black middle-class and upper-middle-class parents, schooling means segregation of a different sort—children who almost never encounter another black child, who are always "the" integration wherever they go. "They talk about the achievement gap, and I'm in no position to do a study, but it seems pretty obvious to me what's going on, in New York, anyway," says a friend with a nine-year-old daughter. "Her white classmates have tutors for *everything*. Tutors in Manhattan cost hundreds of dollars. An hour. One of her nine-year-old friends decided she liked poetry, so her parents hired a PhD graduate student to work with her. We're well off, but geez, we're the first generation to have income at this level. My parents can't help me with my mortgage or buy my children trips to Europe. And I sure can't afford a poetry tutor. It's exhausting, this educational rat race. Just when you think you've arrived, you discover that tennis lessons are not enough. Music lessons are not enough. Chess club is simply not enough."

But if the frenetic intensity of educational oneupsmanship is a relatively new phenomenon for everyone in our society, the sense of isolation that the thin sprinkling of blacks at "good" schools feel is not. Yet what's different, hypothesizes another friend, is that "back then, there were so, so few of us that not as many people were afraid that you were going to take over the world. They were happy to romanticize you as the most brilliantly exotic creature they had never seen. Now the whole of American culture is a lot more like the South: Every last bit of the media tells them that you and your lonely black butt, yes you, are personally sitting in a place where a hundred more-qualified white people ought to be. They are completely and absolutely convinced you don't belong there."

"Sometimes it's subtler, but still maddening," another friend maintains. She describes a meeting at her husband's firm during which a black candidate was turned down because "there were crumbs around his plate" after lunch. Her husband's colleagues were very judgmental about this. It cost him points in the elusive category of "collegiality." It might have been easier to take, she went on, "if two of the senior partners hadn't been sporting ties flecked with the bright red spatters of their own marinara wars."

Another friend worries that part of the exhaustion she feels comes from the fact that when her son excels, it drives the white kids crazy. "Not in an overtly hostile way," she told me, "but it makes them horribly insecure, like they've made him their benchmark for failure. Like, if you're doing worse than the black kid, you must really be a mess . . . It's crazy—his best friend is the one Japanese American in the class, I think because that poor kid's getting the same thing from the other side of the stereotype. I mean, Asians have been made into the benchmark for success. The teacher actually challenged the class, saying that the 'American' kids were going to be 'in a race' to keep up with anyone 'from Japan.'

"Anyway, my son's a really good student, but they've got it in their heads that he's disadvantaged and deprived and ought to be grateful to be there, and they've been awfully good to let him in and maybe even had to lower their standards to do it, so, what does it mean when he gets A's and the white kid doesn't? I know, all the talking heads keep telling us that black kids keep other black kids from succeeding by taunting them out of achievement. That doing well is not part of the culture. But I think the taunting is just as bad from the white kids who resent blacks who achieve. I've had other parents actually say to me, kind of congratulatory but also with an edge, like they're complaining, 'My son is really upset because he didn't do as well as yours on his last report card . . .'"

Her husband interjected, "They're always doing these studies of white kids who are depressed and they've put them on Prozac and all kinds of drugs and they pop a pill and then they're fine. And the sole measure of how undepressed they are is always that their grades improve. None of these studies ever talk about black children. Now, if large numbers of white kids are depressed in this society, just imagine what the rates must be among black children. Is there really a pill for that?" He sighed and shook his head. "It's going to take a whole lot more than Prozac to antidepress our children." A friend who's an educator says that one of the questions they ask children on IQ tests is what they would do with a wallet if they found it on the street. The high-scoring answer is that you would find a police officer and hand it over. But black children, especially boys, almost never say that. They'd take it to their mothers or other female relatives to have them turn it over. They tend to avoid police officers, and try not to have their names or those of any men they know in any public agency's files, especially the police's. But in the race-blind context of standardized tests, taking the wallet to your mother is a sign of immaturity. Little boys run to their mothers. Big, smart, fearless boys take things directly to the men in charge. Thus, "common" sense exists in complicated relation to value systems of coded fear, encrypted credibility.

The degree to which anxiety and achievement are intertwined is clearly not just a black problem; it is merely the most visible tip of a much larger national crisis. The degree to which our educational system fails children of all races is an issue in every election in every state of our union. Yet we seem to be frozen by terrible ambivalence. Universal public education is as necessary as air and water; universal public education is a Communist plot. On any given day, one reads in the nation's newspapers calls for smaller classes, tougher curricula, and better working conditions for teachers. On any given day, one also reads about citizens choosing to slash taxes, complaining about teachers' unions' requests for livable salaries, and eliminating art, music, foreign languages, and social studies.

On the one hand, the neoconservative Manhattan Institute has expended oceans of ink excoriating the New York City public schools for their lack of high standards. On the other hand, the very same neoconservative Manhattan Institute lit into Mayor Michael Bloomberg's plan to require Everyday Math, a highly demanding curriculum originally developed for gifted students at the Chicago Lab School (algebra and geometry are introduced by the fourth grade). As the foreword to Everyday Math's textbooks explains, the program is now recommended for all children, based on clear data that every child can "learn more and do more than was thought to be possible ten or twenty years ago." Yet the Manhattan Institute's *City Journal* subsidizes critiques like those by Matthew Clavel, a teacher in the South Bronx: "If the architects of *Everyday Mathematics* had their way, I would have placed my children in various groups, for the most part unsupervised, so that they could work on one elaborate activity after another, learning on their own . . . I'd derive bitter pleasure in watching a Fuzzy Math 'professional-development' expert try using [this approach] in an inner-city classroom, filled with kids whose often unstructured home lives make self-restraint a big problem . . . I avoided this loss of control, because right from the outset, even before I chucked the whole program, I felt that pursuing cooperative learning with my students was asking for trouble, and so I mostly didn't do it. I was going to teach; my students were going to learn."

Yet the statistics are compelling. In every school district that has actually used the Everyday Math program, scores on standardized tests have soared. If you ask me, I think Mr. Clavel's biggest problem—aside from his quite understandable yearning to be in a nice suburban school where all the kids come from homes structured enough to afford Ritalin—was not the math book but rather that he seems to have been the lone teacher in a class so large that breaking it into smaller groups meant that the children ended up "unsupervised," and "on their own."

Of course, I'm a big believer in cooperative learning. Aunt Gertrude, Cicero, and I taught ourselves to read in a succession of very cooperative little Saturday afternoon huddles. Just the three of us, she would say, which was her generation's version of "completely on your own."

Paula Penn-Nabrit is the author of *Morning by Morning: How We Home-Schooled Our African-American Sons to the Ivy League*. Penn-Nabrit's book is a kind of cult classic among ambitious middle-class parents, so many of whom yearn for the dream that *Brown v. Board of Education* promised, yet who have serious concerns about whether being the spotlighted lone minority in a largely white environment is significantly better than being one of the many forgotten in an all-black school.

Morning by Morning is a particularly interesting read because her husband's uncle was James Nabrit, who, as part of Thurgood Marshall's team, argued *Brown* in the Supreme Court. Penn-Nabrit removed her children from their very well-regarded private school because of her concern about the toll on their self-esteem. She recounts an incident when a so-

studies teacher reported that her twin sons had been
~ught "lying": "Why did they say their great-grandfather, Dr.
James Nabrit, was one of the first presidents of American Baptist College? Why did they claim their maternal great-great-
grandmother, Mrs. Hattie Edwards, was a student at Bluefield
State Teachers' College before migrating to Columbus in the
1890s? Why did they say their great-uncle, Dr. Samuel Nabrit,
received a PhD from Brown University in 1932 and went on
to serve on the Atomic Energy Commission? Why did they
claim their other great-uncle, James Nabrit, had been the
dean of the Law School at, and later president of, Howard
University? . . .

"We asked the teacher if she had confirmed the facts on the
other boys' work, but, as it turned out, none of the other work
seemed 'false' to her. She did not, however, see it as 'a race
thing.' "

I think most upper-middle-class black people face some
version of this, some clash with the myriad images that inform
everyone around you that one way or another you're bringing down the culture. With no detailed sense of African-
American history beyond Martin Luther King taught in
schools, many people are bound to be surprised by these hidden pockets of history. The problem arises when people are
not just surprised but disbelieving. The shape of such disbelief
reveals very troubling kinds of resistance. It is one thing to say,
"Wow, how unusual" or "I didn't know," but it takes an unbecoming allegiance to one's own preconceptions to leap out
there and say, "You're lying."

"We spent the summer in Australia, where my husband was
doing field research," says an anthropologist friend whose
child attends another toney private school. "At a school tea,
one mother told me that my son had a reputation for telling
whoppers. I asked why on earth . . . ? 'Well, he claims he's
been to Australia and New Zealand and that his father speaks
three languages, and that he's driven in the Outback.' Now,

you have to understand that this is a woman who has a house in Brazil and an apartment in London. It's not like no one at this school ever traveled beyond the county line. So why was my son's life so hard for her to imagine? She thinks coming to this school is the first time we ever ventured out of the ghetto?"

My friend the anthropologist continues: "If it's this hard getting heard when you're pretty well-off, just imagine how hard it must be if indeed you've got a kid who's really never been outside the neighborhood where he grew up and he's 'chosen' to attend one of these schools and they try to set up a support program to help him adjust, but then all the other parents start complaining because they think it's 'preferential treatment.' And if the kid has real learning disabilities, it's genetic inferiority, not some 'alternative learning style.' There really is no winning."

Of course, this is "no winning" at the very luckiest end of the social spectrum. But I put it forth because it represents a wider concern among many of those African Americans, regardless of socioeconomic status, who are trying hardest to make integration work. Consider what "being black" means in the variation offered by a mother who worries about her son who is growing up in an almost all-white environment. "He yearns for a black culture that exists only in his head. He feels different to begin with, so he puts on baggy pants and slouches when he walks, and he feels 'black.' And he's more popular with the white kids when he does this because all their heads are locked in MTV land. So he likes thinking he looks scary, and the kids like thinking he's scary, even though they've known him since kindergarten. So it's safe to be scared by him. But I don't think this is a good thing, his 'styling' blackness to fit into the white kids' expectations. I mean, they actually want him to be a little bit dangerous. Isn't that something? A nice safe middle-class black kid who's learned 'blackness' from Eminem CDs instead of the mean streets—what a convenience. But what's it costing my child to act as the proxy street black for his middle-class white classmates?"

It is not just the children who serve as proxies from central casting. A black friend who works in the corporate world was recently divorced from her never-present husband. When they separated, she downscaled her job so as to work only during school hours and moved from her apartment to a house with a large yard, close to the proverbial good school. Yet the divorce court gave her husband full custody. The judge acknowledged that she was an exceptionally devoted and well-educated parent but still gave custody to her workaholic husband, a high-flying executive who travels seven months of the year, solely because "an African-American boy needs his father."

"Can you beat it?" she asked in tears. "People are so afraid of what they read in some magazine—that fatherless black boys are a danger to society, that black mothers are insufficient role models who'll ruin their manhood. So he turned my son over to his father, even if he's a father in name only. He gave my son to his father's empty house rather than to me."

She regularly gets calls from the child, home alone but for the live-in babysitter.

This kind of media-driven stereotypification is what compelled conceptual artist damali ayo to create her Web site, rent-a-negro.com, which offers to "promote your connection with a creative, articulate, friendly, attractive, and pleasing African American person" who "can make diversifying your life a pleasure." The requests she has received are very funny, although it's not clear that the erstwhile clients intended them to be:

> i can't seem to get along with my black roommate here
> in college. we live in the same 4 bedroom apt. there

weren't enough people to fill our apt. so they put her in the apt. with us. i realize that i have never really had to associate with black people, but now i am being forced to, but i just want to see if i can rent a person to be a friend of mine from high school and maybe she will think that she relates to me more and that i can relate to her . . .

I wanted to bring an African American with me to this event because so many of my friends think I'm racist. I might tell a joke or two, but I'm really a good person.

I am interested in procuring your services for a black-tie corporate function. May I see both head and body shots of the available resources. This person must be able to converse with the wives of financiers as well as the financiers themselves. High-ranking government officials will be present. This person must conduct herself in a very professional manner as well as be very informed of current events. I must ask that this person say nothing critical or defamatory regarding the Bush administration . . .

I think this search for black proxies for white dreams of blackness is a phenomenon that is largely responsible for the supposed "void" of black leadership. It's just so hard to find good black leaders these days, the kind who laugh in all the right places and won't criticize George Bush.

"I integrated the Shipley School," my elegant friend R. was saying, speaking of the elite, formerly all-girls prep school in Bryn Mawr, Pennsylvania, from which she graduated. "And I am only now dealing with all the scars."
Scars? Shipley? "Isn't Shipley the kind of place that guar-

antees you'll emerge a scar-free flotation of gentlewomanliness?" I asked.

"I came the first year blacks were enrolled," R. replied. "They took two of us; the other one was a senior and looked white. They admitted one Jew the next year, and they made the two of us roommates. We became like sisters. But it became part of my character to be marginal, to always feel myself looking in from the outside. It pulled me in two. I never felt part of the world in which I was immersed. Imagine. They had dance cards. Partners would see your name and disappear. I wasn't invited to most of the debutante balls come twelfth grade—partly because of the parents, partly because few of the private clubs would permit blacks to come in the front door. Once, one girl actually asked me to be her roommate, but her mother wouldn't let her."

R. went on to describe the painful issue of black hair, which "you couldn't talk about." It took Shipley's legendary retired headmistress Margaret Bailey Speer to help out with that: Miss Speer had personally arranged for the scholarship that permitted R. to attend Shipley. "She really put herself on the line to get me admitted. I always wanted her to see her courage had paid off." And it was Miss Speer, "the stellar human being," who used to drive her across town to the black hairdresser.

When R. was a senior, some of the staff at Shipley tried (unsuccessfully) to discourage her from applying to the Ivy League, even though she was a student leader and had very good grades. They said that she would be "more comfortable" at a smaller college. R. and I were conversing by telephone, and R.'s mother murmured something in the background. "Oh, yes," R. added. "After Martin Luther King's assassination, they apologized to my mother about this. They admitted that it was race that kept them from thinking of me as going to Stanford." She paused. "You see, that's the upside, the beauty of the experiment. They were decent people, but they had these images. But in the end they also had the courage to see themselves and to transform."

I enjoy a very fortunate life, notwithstanding the tragedy of my mismatched dishes, there is no doubt about it. I think there were very specific ingredients that allowed me to accomplish as much as I have, all proceeding from intergenerational gifts of learning from progressively well-educated family members. (This despite externally difficult times and even though the earning power of their combined degrees never allowed the generations before mine to live in any but very working-class circumstances. Except, of course, for Aunt Mary.) That they were so relatively well-schooled was in turn the product of at least two things. First, they were beneficiaries of a world that did not then hoard learning like water in the desert. Learning gave them a plan and a sense of being able to "rise above" small setbacks. Second, the teachers who most influenced the course of my family's history believed, luckily enough, that even illiterate, newly freed slaves were "qualified" and "deserving"; they believed that genius was spirit, spirit was inspiration, inspiration was a kind of confidence.

The word "confidence" itself comes from the Latin root meaning faith with, or faith among. Let me clarify: I do not dispute that intelligence may be in large part a biological or chemical endowment. But I think that the ability to make manifest any level of that endowment is almost entirely premised on each individual's faith that there is a community willing and grateful to receive it. We are free individuals only to the extent we are not miserably atomic islands of isolation; we are most expressive when the smallest errancy does not threaten to send us twirling downward to the pit of perpetual punishment.

When I was growing up, if you made a mistake there was time to think about what went wrong; there was willingness

among most of the adults around me to consider how to re-
connect with a better path. I never had a fear of flying because
even if you couldn't get off the ground in one realm—like
music lessons—there was so much else to accomplish. There
were never paralyzing regrets, and there was always something
new waiting to be done.

"You were good enough to have played in a symphony," re-
peats my mother insistently when she thinks of the hoedown
derailment of my first cello lessons.

I smile at her and think: *In your dreams, momma bear.* She
sails on: "But instead you became this wonderful writer."

When I listen to her, I sometimes really do think I could
have been a cello-playing unicyclist teetering my way across a
circus high wire while dictating appellate briefs and balancing
the perfect child atop my shoulders. In real life, however, I
am just a lawyer who writes, and just another anxious mother
who watches hopefully as her own baby bear learns to balance
on the great unicycle of life. If I am not as wonderful a writer
as my mother envisions, I am not as bad as *The Daily Mail*
imagines. At least I am one with the fortitude to push on
come hell or high water, buoyed as I am by the internalized
exuberance of my mother's and my extended family's faith in
me. They always insisted I work hard, but not that I be perfect. They worked hard with me, on me, for me. And we all
profited from learning the good side and the bad side of all
kinds of people on the mini–United Nations of our street. I
was lucky, lucky, lucky.

From the Great Depression through the beginning of the
1960s, the Boston school system was seen as a public good,
unquestionably worth investing in, particularly since the city
has always enjoyed a proud heritage as home to the nation's
first public schools. I grew up before the drain of resources
brought about by white flight. It was before the fights against
school integration that sapped so much from urban schools,
and before the cynical reversals that have recast segregation-

ism as a bulwark against the "undeserving" as opposed to the historically unwanted.

I enjoyed wonderful, experienced instructors in elementary school, several of whom had taught my mother. I had a fine classical secondary education at Boston's old Girls' Latin School, six years of Latin, four of French, with the sort of committed teachers who didn't think twice about reading us *Beowulf,* Chaucer, and Milton in the seventh and eighth grades. And my years at Wellesley College were a gentlewomanly model of serious education—small seminars, Gothic architecture, crackling fires, time to think but for small frazzled moments of horticultural emergency—nothing worse than the wrong flowers—sit-down dinners with linen tablecloths, silk-suited housemothers and solemn high teas. But neither did it really resemble a temple to the joys of domesticity, as depicted in the film *Mona Lisa Smile,* for example. Those high teas had less to do with the cult of true womanhood than with laying the groundwork for power lunches and state dinners. Wellesley had a lush refinement to it that was easy to parody—and we did—but it was also a deeply respectful place and remains so to this day.

Indeed, I don't think I ever had a really unpleasant confrontation in any academic environment until I got to law school.

Law school was a different world. It was much worse than *The Paper Chase* made out. From the very first white-tented gathering on the lawn, people were running around asking each other their LSAT scores. People talked about the rates of suicide and mental breakdown with little smiles playing on their lips, as though death and dementia made the place more desirably exclusive. When I moved into my dorm, there was a blind woman on my floor who kept setting the kitchen on fire. People said she had lost her sight only the year before and was still learning how to cope. The story circulating was that she had been studying so hard for a business tax exam that she had ignored a retinal inflammation and finally her eyeballs had exploded. Just popped right out of the sockets. The tale certainly had the ring of mean exaggeration about it. But during very late nights when I'd be up toiling over a thousand-page hornbook in secured transactions and I'd hear her crashing about in the kitchen like destiny knocking, it seemed so impossibly right, this miserable, perfect apocrypha.

I still don't know the real story. I never had the courage to ask anyone anything in law school, not even their LSAT scores.

Sometimes, however, the real story is at least as intriguing as the apocrypha. My friend A. was sitting in my living room, her "Democrats Abroad" scarf thrown jauntily over her shoulders. In town only briefly, she had been telling me about her latest project: She was the European representative of the National Brotherhood of Skiers, a post–civil rights organization of some fourteen thousand African-American skiers. (Who knew that there are officially more blacks on skis than there are followers of the White Aryan Resistance? Who could have guessed at such a fortuity of distributed obsessions?)

A. was responsible for inviting them to Innsbruck some winters ago, and she described with pride the sight of a thousand black skiers marching down the main street. This place—only sixty-some years after Hitler refused to shake the hand of a "monkey" like the Olympic gold medalist Jesse Owens—was filled with the fluttering flags of a parade led by a Tyrolean band of welcoming Austrians. "Oompah, oompah, oom-pah-pah. You should have seen it," she said. "There are the Austrians leading a procession of a thousand black American skiers intent upon 'conquering the mountain' and 'going for the gold.'"

I suppose there is a danger here: This happy scene is only an image, a frozen slice. The picture it crystallizes is highly atypical in a time when Europe's anxiety about dark-skinned outsiders is very much on the rise. But it is also an image of the possible. It is a monumental moment precisely because so few in our society have ever imagined that it could occur. And behind the image is another small "first"—the reality that there are black American children, for the first time, enrolled in the elite Olympic ski academies of Europe.

I meditated upon a photo A. showed me of a young boy dressed in racing stripes and sitting on a platform beside the mayor of Innsbruck. He began skiing when he was two; he was "the great black hope" of the group and would stay to train when the others had gone home.

Chatting with A. is always a bit like hopping aboard some sort of intellectual catapult. One minute you're talking about the weather and the next you're taking a walk in a cool mountain stream and the snow-capped Alps are gleaming and you're boarding a train for who knows where and then the sun is rising over the China Sea and your children are all speaking perfect Dutch.

A.'s three children do speak Dutch. And English and French and Mandarin and a little of a lot of other things. Her eleven-year-old daughter, who was traveling with her, had taken my son and led him to his room "so our mothers can talk." She emerged half an hour later, announcing that she had cleaned his room, made up his bed, and was "teaching him his mathematics."

"If you please, may we have more paper and perhaps a pencil sharpener?" asked she.

"You betcha," I responded in my best American vernacular.

A. stood and stretched, then began to pore over my library of out-of-print books, written by generations of forgotten black thinkers—this generational forgetting of black contributions an American ritual, like seasons of oblivion following upon the cyclical renaissances of discovered "darky wit," "Negro wisdom," "black power," and "African-American public intellectualism."

"This sounds like me," she said as she pulled down a volume titled *The Black Expatriates,* published in 1968. The book fell open in her hand. "No," she exclaimed. "It sounds like F.'s family!" And indeed it was. The book had fallen open to a chapter devoted to Mattiwilda Dobbs, a relative of F., another of our law school classmates. Mattiwilda Dobbs was a black opera singer who moved to Stockholm and married a Swede. "She knew my father," said A., referring to the years her father sang in Europe, before he returned to the United States to raise her and her brother. She also knew my globetrotting godmother, Marguerite. "It's a small, small world," we agreed.

Really, really, far too small.

I am part of a generation that went to law school not just as a result of the civil rights movement but because of it. We were creatures formed in the crucible of civil rights, the Kennedy years, Vietnam, and the women's liberation movement. It was the tail of a remarkable era, but we didn't see it as the beginning of the end just yet. The bright balloon of optimism that had buoyed us in our educational careers thus far had a slow leak and a few patches but basically had survived the events of those times. Kent State, Jackson State, love-ins, and the Democratic National Convention in Chicago had dominated our college years. Hillary Clinton graduated from Wellesley the year before I arrived on campus; Yale's undergraduate school admitted its first women the next year. Lani Guinier's father was the head of Harvard's African-American Studies Program. Derrick Bell was the only black faculty member not only of Harvard Law School, but of any major school in the country. There were no women on the faculty. I gather it is much better today—Harvard Law now has not only female professors but a woman as dean—but back then watching the men interact was like watching one of those English movies in which the students just love to wrestle one another nude. They were all so involved with one another, always one-upping one another and tripping one another up. Hazing at Harvard Law School was legendary in those days—our professors made fun of people with Southern accents, people who were overweight, people who disagreed with them. The misery the men visited on one another was different in lots of ways from what the women—particularly the black women—went through. They advertised it as the kind of jockeying that makes one think sharply and fast, but to some of us, the men looked like an eternally roiling mass of puppies, always chewing on one another's legs. It was bewildering, particularly to those of us who had grown up without brothers—all those flying sports images and hunting metaphors, those "seminal cases," "red-meat eaters," "dropped balls," and "spilled blood."

And how we "double minorities"—people like me, black *and* female, "two-fers"—must have looked to them: We were the object of much double-taking during the first few months of law school. There were so few of us, yet so many in comparison to past years, that we stood out like sore thumbs. Or accent pillows, as I recall someone analogizing. Let's just say that they didn't altogether know what to make of these new faces. They were flustered by the novelty of us, embarrassed by us, maddened by us. We were years away—and still are to some degree, I think—from that happy day when we would be just a normal part of the landscape, years away from the nirvana of no one even thinking twice about our presence.

Almost all of today's visible black public intellectuals are of this generation, this first of us having access to those Ivy League passports to power in numbers beyond one or two every few years or even decades. It should be no surprise that Henry Louis Gates, Anita Hill, Marlon Riggs, Lani Guinier,

Stephen Carter, bell hooks, Clarence Thomas, Paula Giddings, and Cornel West were all hatched from more or less the same institutional moment.

Traditionally black colleges like Howard, Fisk, Morehouse, Spelman, Tuskegee, and Wilberforce had brought forth the lion's share of civil rights heroes like Thurgood Marshall from just after the Civil War until the 1960s. They continue to do so, but after the 1960s there was a sudden lurch to integrate among many of the nation's most elite schools, and schools like Harvard and Yale were able to attract many of the children of the black middle class—those whose families, like Anita Hill's, owned a little land, or, like Clarence Thomas's grandfather, ran small businesses. Even as there remained many exclusions from powerful secret societies and unmentioned social hierarchies, the Ivy League thereby delivered to these new numbers some of the extraordinary network of jobs, support, and investment opportunity that my parents never dreamed existed.

Yet the emotional liminality of the newly, conspicuously "included" is reflective of a measure of isolation, and being an outsider remains the defining feature of this period of most of our lives. And if indeed we represent some part of the so-called talented tenth, then perhaps our experiences can shed light on why we remain not even a tenth almost a hundred years after W.E.B. DuBois coined the term.

There are people who love every minute of life as a law student. I don't know any personally, but I saw them in law school; I see them now as mature lawyers. They have a certain clubby, convivial, glad-handing spark that goes beyond just studying hard: They love corporate life too—the dinners and drinks, the deal making, the long billable hours. They double as very fine politicians. But back then, very few of us, especially the few of us who were women, were particularly happy in law school. Polling just black women, the needle dips farther yet down the scale toward unhappy.

We didn't spend much time together back then, though each of us, I learned, had imagined that the others were off nurturing tight friendships and circles of support. "I thought it was just me," everyone said. We had all battled a soupy mush of uncertainty, loneliness, and some fear. Judith Richards Hope, class of 1964, has written about the years when there were only ten women of any stripe at the law school in her book *Pinstripes and Pearls*. She and her classmates, including future Supreme Court Justice Ruth Bader Ginsburg and Congresswoman Pat Schroeder, were summoned to dinner by Dean Erwin Griswold, who then demanded to know how they could, in good conscience, take up the space of better-qualified men.

Even decades removed from the shock of admitting women, my friend F. remembered her time as a partner at a firm in Palo Alto, specializing in computer law. Shortly after the birth of her second child, she was told about a business meeting where one of her colleagues began to rail against female lawyers who breed "like rabbits." She sighed, "There have been times like that."

When she had her third little bunny, she left the firm with a few big clients of her own and, for a while, set up practice in her living room.

Some of that is changing, as my friend B. observes: "Now that women are breaking into the corporate sector, now that a few of us are the clients to be courted, there are many more people at many more firms running around at lunchtime saying, 'Where's our woman?'"

Back in the early 1970s when my class arrived at the law school, women were greeted with quiet resignation if not open arms, the question of qualifications having shifted with a vengeance to the expanding numbers of racial minorities. Allan Bakke filed the first "reverse discrimination" suit against the University of California at Davis during our law school years, and we were repeatedly put on the defensive about how we could, in good conscience, take up the space of better-qualified white candidates.

African Americans were told that Harvard had lowered its standards to endure us—but not to worry, we were sufficiently plucky and lucky to pick up a thing or two. Back then, before the backlash against affirmative action had risen to a bitter boil, it was somewhat easier to grit one's teeth and not take it too personally. After all, Harvard officials were always making pronouncements implying that Harvard had lowered its standards by the mere act of admitting anyone at all. It was common lore that on the first day of class, some professor or another would greet new students by reminding them that Harvard could have accepted a class composed only of those who received a perfect 800 on their LSATs. But they didn't—no school does that. I know of only one university that briefly instituted a policy of automatically admitting everyone who received a perfect score. They discontinued the practice after they ended up with a class just a teensy bit too tilted toward compulsive hand washers and those who fell to sobbing if they stepped on a crack in the sidewalk.

Admissions committees look for a balance of qualities, in the individual student and in the class collectively. As paradoxical as it sounds, that kind of balance means that everyone in the class will be a little bit worse than someone else in some category or endeavor. Or a little bit better. It is in the nature of our nonrobotic human differentiation that half of any class will always be below its own collective norm. But this reality is complicated when you add race: Woe betide any African-American students who fall below that midpoint—they risk being seen as thieves, imposters, pretenders to the throne of some "better-qualified" candidate's just deserts. Indeed, unless a black student is first in his class, it's very hard for many people to imagine that he or she is anything but last.

It is that sort of prejudgment and condescension—plus a recent resurgence of old-fashioned, Southern-style, unapolo-

getic, in-your-face resentment—that sustains my conviction
that affirmative action remains a very necessary remedy in the
struggle for a fairer society.

"Mommy!" The little call echoed in the background of a conference call I had organized to catch up with the nine black
women who were in my class at law school, who, like me,
were among the first beneficiaries of affirmative action. For
hours, these nine classmates and I had talked into the blind
intimacy of telephone space, into the jumble of background
sounds transmitted with crystalline fiber-optic veracity—
rustling pages, dripping water, dishes clanking and computers
clacking, office doors opening and shutting, toy trucks being
driven across kitchen floors. All of us felt that we had spent
our lives exploding stereotypes, some of which we thought
had been long since undone by our grandparents. The precariousness of our privileged social position as "honorary
whites" or sometimes "honorary men" is filled with paradox:
We were the product of grassroots efforts that with each generation have launched just a few more of us just a little bit
higher onto the narrow plateaus of power. Yet we are a generation whose very accomplishments are now being advanced as
one of the reasons that affirmative action is no longer needed.
    All of us have experienced the contradictory categoriza-
tions by which the appearance of one of us is a marvel, two of
us a miracle, three a mission accomplished, and four—hey,
time to sell. All of us know loneliness, even as we are said to
be taking over the marketplace. We're said to be undeserving
because we're the underqualified product of an inferior value
system; at the same time, we're resented as the overqualified
children of a mythically endowed, imaginary tribe of Huxta-
bles. But that glib resentment of the few who have succeeded
seems to have distracted us as a nation from the data of widen-
ing disparity between rich and poor and, most alarmingly, be-

tween blacks and whites. In February 2004, for example, large numbers of conservative college students in New York City were busy protesting affirmative action for its supposedly unfair burden upon white people—against the backdrop of the city at large, where almost one-half of black men ages sixteen to sixty-five were unemployed.

One more thing—a concern at a very high level, but it is important when considering the ultimate distribution of power. Successful as we all were, it is perhaps difficult to think of any of us as having encountered "real" glass ceilings. To get a sense of that, one has to look at our black and white male counterparts, for whom the Harvard Law School passport launched careers as ambassadors to nations, chairmen of stock exchanges, presidents of banks, CEOs of major global corporations. It is the sort of concern that when expressed is not heard as a real question about the glass ceiling but rather one that gets you labeled a peevish malcontent. But it is for the next generation that we strive as we contemplate what consistent integration at those highest levels of control might mean.

In our last conversation, D. said, "We all go through what [former head of the Civil Rights Division] Deval Patrick calls the indignities du jour, but we don't say anything—we're just accustomed to it. You know, when you live where I live and you take your child to school, they want to know whose child you're there to pick up."

The indignity in this example is not that we are misidentified with respect to class. In this regard, we are probably somewhat different from my parents' "ethnic" neighbors who cringed at being taken for "peasants" or my great-aunt Mary, who passed her life behind a mask of heavy white powder. The indignity to our generation is not about feeling "lowered" in some hierarchy of class comparison. It is rather in the experience we share with those who are indeed there to pick up someone else's child: that people feel free to talk down to you, make assumptions about you that both blind them and imprison you in the limitations of their imagination. It is this edginess, this deeper dimension of W.E.B. DuBois's "double vision," that feeds an artesian sense of conscience, of social commitment to a more inclusive America that is still trying hard to realize its own best vision of itself.

This is not to say, of course, that there aren't substantial differences between D.'s life and that of the women who do earn their living as nannies; it's just to observe the generalization that freights the life of each. It is hard to imagine, perhaps, no less for blacks than for whites, a black woman who has a Swedish family and a degree in mathematics and whose religious faith inspires her as she carries out her duties as a judge—and as a mother.

But if it is easy to miss these parts of the half-seen brown women who come and go, riding the elevator while carrying laundry and speaking of Michelangelo, that doesn't mean that they don't exist. It means we've lost a vital part of ourselves in denying that they do.

VIII

The Dusty Parlor

On December 31, as the old year waned, the sky was full of omens. The world was poised for cataclysm. The sun was in perihelion, the moon in perigee, perched like a giant golden egg atop my neighbor's garage. Probably because of this unusual alignment, my various selves and different faces, my pieces and parts, my atoms and divisions, came together and huddled like old friends. The weather was outlandishly warm, lettuce-growing weather, balmy and moist. Chives and daffodils sprouted in the window boxes. In the park, still-foraging squirrels flopped about, huge bellies dragging on the ground, so fat they were close to exploding.

Like me, they were waiting for the hiatus that somehow had not happened, the little stoppage of time we expect of the solstice, the hinge in the year that seems increasingly old-fashioned in a world of seamless commerce and streaking motion. The forces of nature, the fatigue of the last tumultuous century, inspired both awe and the hunger for a quiet season in which to catch our breath.

Like the squirrels, I was inclined to forage, storing up things for hard times. Thus it was that on New Year's Eve, my larder was packed with water, duct tape, canned goods, and extra batteries for the flashlight. I was ready to be snowed in, ready for contrast, and ready for sleep. But hunkered down for a rest, there was no rest. The phone rang, deadlines closed in, and the stock market soared and then fell; the game shows jacked up their jackpots, the shops were online 24/7, and the night sky glittered with a thousand man-made objects.

The insistent warmth was enervating, the rat race wearing, and so despite weather reports of the snow to end all snows, as well as governmental proclamations that civilization as we know it was about to end, when the second hand crossed midnight, I put black-eyed peas in a bowl to soak and soon was sound asleep.

I woke up at dawn, January 1 of the new year, to discover that things had gone off without a hitch. Fireworks and only fireworks exploded in every major capital and the sun came up all round the world. Time hurried on exactly as it always had, only maybe just a little warmer, maybe just a little faster.

By breakfast of January 1, the brand-new year was already boring. I made pancakes while my son and a little friend wrestled happily in the kitchen, mock karate chopping one another and shouting ungentlemanly things like "Heee-yah!" and "Eat my dust!"

"Did you know," said a neighbor who had dropped by to help me finish off the night's champagne, "that ninety percent of household dust is just dead human skin?"

"Some orange juice?" I said, putting down the spatula and eyeing the dust, the little heaps of human detritus that nestled conspicuously in every corner.

"Yup," he continued, helping himself to a heap of scrambled eggs. "We're not snakes, you know, the kind who can slough it off all at once. We shed all the time."

I must say that there are some facts I could just as well have lived the rest of my life not knowing. The dust in my house rested in the corners, wrapped in shadows. The shadows made it hard to see, except when illuminated by neighborly insight. I made a mental note to sweep . . . soon. And I imagined myself like Mrs. Darling in J. M. Barrie's *Peter Pan*, rolling up Peter's shadow after it snapped off in the nursery window; I thought of Mrs. Darling tucking it deep inside a drawer so as to keep the nursery tidy.

My tired son came over and leaned against me, moist with the exhaustion of racing in circles, of happy rough-and-tumble. "Help me! I've been flabbergast," he sighed.

"Do you know what that word means?" I asked.

"Yes," he said uncertainly.

"It means shocked, overcome with surprise, startled."

"Yes!" he responded, confident now. "It's like when Sam knocked me out with a big shot of flabbergas."

My son was wheezing slightly, a swirling, juicy sound within his chest. I rubbed his back and patted it, rub and pat, rub and pat, listening for the evenness to return to his breathing, still absently thinking of Mrs. Darling.

I remembered that being one of the most disconcerting storybook images I read in the whole of my childhood, that description of Peter Pan trying to reattach his lost shadow, his faith "that he and his shadow would join like drops of water; and when they did not he was appalled. He tried to stick it on with soap from the bathroom, but that also failed. A shudder passed through Peter, and he sat on the floor and cried."

This fragile skin, this dust. This holy wrapper of such consequence and such inconsequence.

My son was breathing easier now. He let out a loud whoop and ran off to play with his friend.

"No running in the house," I called, but they didn't hear. "Did you hear me? No running!"

Once, the father of one of my son's classmates told my son

to stop! Stop running down the sidewalk! "A police officer will see you and think you're a gang member fleeing the scene of a crime," he said, meaning to be helpful, I suppose.

"Why?" asked my son, straining to see what this man saw, straining with the work of double vision. Straining to rise up out of his body and look back at himself. In that moment I saw my son straining to leap out of his skin . . . to see his own reflection.

"I run so fast, all they would see is a shadow," he concluded.

There is a wonderful tale in Natalie Babbitt's collection *The Devil's Storybook*: Once upon a time, a very bad man died and went to hell, where he fit in very well indeed. Up in the world, his wife placed the vessel of his ashes upon the mantelpiece, where they sat until the housemaid accidentally knocked the urn over. The ashes spilled onto the hearth, where a pig had been roasted recently. The housemaid swept up the bad man's ashes, inadvertently gathering also those of the late pig, and replaced them all in the urn.

Back down in hell, the bad man suddenly found a pig trotting after him everywhere, turning large fond eyes upon him, resting its large head upon his lap, and snuggling beside him when he lay down for bed. The bad man complained to the devil, who explained that the only remedy was to separate the two sets of ashes, and so he set out to do exactly that. For the next several eons, the man sat with tweezers and a magnifying glass, separating each molecule of dust into two piles: his own remains and those of the pig. Gradually, the pig became less and less of a nuisance, speck by sifted speck, until the process was almost entirely complete and the pig spent most of its time wandering happily elsewhere. At this point the housemaid died, descended to hell, saw two big piles of dust, and swept them up and disposed of them in a place no one ever found. The man and the pig spent the rest of eternity cheek by jowl.

I suppose it's completely unfair to say that this story makes me think of the Human Genome Project, but it does. I think of those teams of scientists, with their high-tech magnifying glasses and high-tech tweezers, deciphering the jigsaw puzzle of life's building blocks, earnestly sifting men from beasts, blue eyes from brown, strong from weak, life from death. I celebrate the intriguing scientific insights and look forward to the potential medical benefits as much as anyone. But there is also something mythic about the moment: It is the kind of triumphalist scrutiny of grand design that almost begs the Goddess of Unintended Consequences to come sweeping through with a very large broom indeed.

By lunchtime of the brand-new year, my son and his friend had settled down and were playing a gentlemanly round of indoor soccer with a deflated ball. Their score was amiably tied the entire game. If one scored, so did the other. One to one, shouted my son, as he shot one into the goal of the wastepaper basket. Two to two, shouted Byron, as he shot one back.

In the background, on my little kitchen radio, the millennialist doomsayers had gotten their second wind. They were prognosticating about forest fires, crop failures, the melting of the polar ice cap, and the weather getting ever warmer, time marching ever faster.

Years ago, I remember hearing a story about an extended family of Vietnamese refugees who had fled the war and ended up in a one-bath, two-bedroom apartment in downtown New Orleans. They were faring well enough, given the trauma they had been through—but for a misguided attempt to improvise a thriving rice paddy in a series of large buckets, pans, pots, and tubs in the aforementioned very small bathroom. It was the eternally running water — rice needs constant irrigation — that led the neighbors to call the police. And when the soggy ceiling in the apartment below collapsed a few days later, they were summarily evicted.

I thought about them recently when I found myself wondering if I could squeeze in some corn over by my mother's petunias. I found myself mentally homesteading space for radishes out on the balcony, herbs in the kitchen window, some dwarf citrus over by the bookcase. I imagined Rubbermaid receptacles in the laundry room, full of seeded topsoil, pushing up sprouts for soup greens. When someone told me about a woman who's raising turkey chicks in a box beneath her kitchen sink . . . for the longest minute, it struck me as a quite sensible thing.

But as for lunch. There was a plate with two little leftover lamb chops in my refrigerator. They looked lonely and cold, those ridiculous frilly paper socks dressing the ends of their elegant arches of bone. Their presence reminded me of a TV program I once saw about hunger and homelessness in New York City. The reporter interviewed endless numbers of middle-class New Yorkers who don't want to look at the homeless, who want them removed from the bus stations, from the parks, from the streets, from the common view, who gave reasons such as they're unsightly, they defecate in public, they might attack young children, they smell, they're *so* depressing to look at.

Then the reporter interviewed policy analysts about why the homeless should be permitted to stay. They gave reasons such as they have a right, where else can they go, it has always been thus, and besides, they perform an ecological function by scavenging through garbage cans for recyclables.

The one time the reporter talked to an actual homeless person, the exchange went as follows: "Why would you rather sleep on the street than go to a city shelter?"

The old man snapped, "Don't you put words in my mouth! I don't want to sleep on the street. I'd rather be sleeping in a penthouse on Fifth Avenue overlooking the park, with a maid and a chauffeur and a cook who could make me a dinner of lamb chops. What's your address?"

The program closed with some observations about how "aggressive" and "hostile" these homeless can be toward innocent, vulnerable, middle-class victims-waiting-to-happen unless we Act Now to prevent our own slaughter.

Anyway, those chops lay at the back of my refrigerator for the longest time, like a moldy existential offering.

After lunch, I took my son to the zoo. I am not loads of fun at zoos or football games. I tend to theorize.

"Lions and tigers!" crowed my happy son.

"Oh, my!" I said brightly. I know I should have just shut up right there, but I couldn't help myself: "In contrast to the inanimate steel monumentality of most of the rest of Manhattan," I continued, "the zoo is the embodiment of nostalgia for nature. Look at those blinking computerized displays flashing the decreasing acreage of rain forest, so reminiscent of the blinking computerized displays of national debt. These are the racing convergences of our time."

And so we made our way through simulated jungle waterfalls heavy with the scent of wet Plexiglas and the heavy sweat of troubled tropical animals. We meandered past a stillness of ostriches, yaks, tigers, camels, and owls. We rode the shuttle while a prerecorded voice told us what to see: "Here we have the North Pole, where the polar bears live. Rounding this corner, we come to India, home of the Himalayan tiger. Now we are in East Africa, on the slopes of . . ."

There was no irony in the prerecorded voice. It was bright and slightly schoolgirlish. The shuttle passed only the portals to various exhibits, so that while the voice prattled on about great white bears and the nearly extinct down-bellied, fish-foraging, yellow-billed bog bird, what I actually saw was a parking lot, a popcorn concession, and, floating like a shadowy cluster of fish just beneath the surface of a clear sea, a large family of brown-skinned, almond-eyed people, pressing their way against the flow of the crowd, three generations, grandparents to infants, the women elaborately bedecked in gorgeous Guatemalan textiles and beautiful beads, the men in duck-billed baseball caps and clean white Nike sneakers.

We disembarked from the shuttle at the reptile house. Inside it was very warm, and everything moved in slow motion. The crocodiles looked dead, the lizards hid under their lettuce leaves, the snakes lay frozen among their palm fronds. The giant tortoises were lined up by their little pool; they looked parked, like a row of golf carts or a used-car lot. But at some unseen signal, the tortoises started moving, groaning, creaking, a snoring sound, an ancient elephant sound, the motion of ancient rocks; they were like a thudding, clumping, clomping, walking wall of bricks.

A prison riot, I thought. They are going to make a run for it. But just as mysteriously their motion slowed, their rumbling subsided, they were parked once more, solid, silent, and inscrutable. I was vaguely disappointed; I had wanted them to rise up, cast curses, make war. I had wanted them to fling themselves against the walls like a herd of slow stone buffalo and break free.

Animals used to be more proactive, I guess. During the Middle Ages, there were a number of recorded instances in which animals—such as mad dogs, rampaging bulls, and swarming locusts—were prosecuted for various crimes and misdemeanors. In 1474, in the city of Basel, a raucously deep-throated hen, apparently suffering from "hydropic malformation of the oviduct," was mistaken for a cock and burned at the stake for laying an egg. As anyone knows, real cocks' eggs are rich in the lipids, proteins, and amino acids so necessary for authentic witches' brew. And, when left to incubate in the heat of the noonday sun, they're known for hatching baby basilisks, those evil-eyed gargoylish things with the deadly breath.

Thanks to the vigilance of our methodical forebears, roosters who lay eggs are a thing of the distant past. Yet given a postmodern world still beset by unnatural creation, there are times when I pause to wonder what lessons might be gleaned from those latter-day trials by fire in which poor Chanticleer was purified into wispy, crispy medieval McNuggets. It is intriguing: The authorities didn't just kill the offending bird but rather executed it in a manner befitting the Inquisition, with full magisterial process, pomp, piety, colorful headgear, and legal formality. Those were days when the consequences of an act meant so much more than the motivations of the actor that it didn't much matter that the actor in question was a creature incapable of forming intent. Our rationalist modern jurisprudence makes motive the cornerstone of criminal culpability, but back then unexplained phenomena in the natural world were mythologized either as miracles—that is, "acts of God"—or so unnatural as to upset the order of things—i.e., the work of the devil.

We humans have always needed rituals to draw like curtains over the chasms of the unknown. Without them we go mad, I think. I mused upon the odd moment in history when the Heaven's Gate science-fiction cult committed mass suicide under the direction of a particularly loopy charismatic named Marshall Applewhite, whose beady, starry-eyed gaze bored its way into the bucolic high ground of our collective slumber. Heaven's Gate, if you recall, was a cult of ascetic computer programmers (of all things) who, rather than dreaming of their first public offering, envisioned a spaceship coming to earth to rescue them from the confines of mortality. So, on Applewhite's advice, some forty of them donned new Nike running shoes and identical purple shrouds, and then committed suicide. President Clinton brokered the religiosity of the moment by appealing to Americans not to engage in "copycat" versions of the cult's mass death. "It's important," said Clinton, that "we get as many facts as we can about this to try to determine what in fact motivated those people and what all of us can do to make sure that there aren't other people thinking in the same way out there in our country."

Thoughtfully enough, Applewhite left video records describing the group's "motivation" in precise detail. He and his followers were "caterpillars," on their way to their true status as intergalactic butterflies. They videotaped themselves assuring the world that they knew what they were doing. One woman "anticipated public bewilderment" and expressed deep personal angst. " 'Maybe they're crazy for all I know,' she said of her fellow disciples. 'But I don't have any choice but to go for it, because I've been on this planet for thirty-one years and there's nothing here for me . . . ' "

Applewhite had scheduled the moment of metamorphosis from chrysalis to butterfly to coincide with both a lunar eclipse and a clear comet sighting.

According to Chinese legend, a solar eclipse is a hungry dog devouring the sun. If you gaze upon him he will devour you too. It helps to have a few explanatory myths at hand, I suppose. Many articles were written in response to the phenomenon of Heaven's Gate, articles about the dangers of spending too much time watching *Star Trek* or playing computer games or generally fixating upon the fiction of cyberspace. We postindustrial Americans tend to tell ourselves legends in which the hungry dogs work decidedly closer to home than the heavens. But perhaps Heaven's Gate had as much to do with the limitations of earth space as with the intoxications of cyberspace.

Some years ago, I went to an exhibit at the DeCordova Museum in Lincoln, Massachusetts. On display were various works by artist Vico Fabbris from his series on "the botanical unknown." Lovely illuminations of "invented-extinct" plants, plants that might have been. This evocative compendium of pharmacological fantasy, of long-lost alchemical ingredients, of horticultural hot-dish surprise. Their form as innocent as nature, their biology as improbable as a peacock's, their beauty so inexplicably useless, their function as mysterious as God. As art it made me think about the invented-extinct dimension of a cyberkinetic, genetically engineered world. The current state of science grants us the conceit that invention of actual life-forms is as simple as teasing it out upon the drawing board. As though we might think and thenceforth it is. But life is always more art than artifice, more magic than manufacture, resurrection more than mere invention.

I paused to reflect. Perhaps the most truly transformative moment of my own adult life was a small, odd event: the morning I killed a squirrel. I was living in an old Victorian house at that time, and I'd had a problem with squirrels nesting in my roof. I'd had a friend come and seal up all the holes and vents, and he'd sworn that he'd seen "the" squirrel exit before he closed things up. The following morning at five a.m. I was awakened by a squirrel that had been trapped in the roof and had somehow found its way into my bedroom. It was hissing with fear. It scared me too, half to death, and I went into a kind of primordial trance. First I reached for my socks and slowly put them on. For some irrational reason I was most terrified that it would bite my toes.

Then I seized a curtain rod and beat the life out of the poor thing. And what was odd was that I felt a sense of victory afterward, a kind of clear-headed competency, like I had survived against great odds and was ready for the wilderness. It was such an unbidden and lusty sense that it's taken considerable reflection to reconcile the passion of that killing potential within me. I'd never killed anything before, even avoided stepping on ants. But nothing before or since has made me feel so strong or so humbled. I had not known there was this side of me that could be so all-out unbridled and dangerous.

I buried the squirrel with great remorse and more ritual than any squirrel has ever been buried before. I can understand how shamanism grew out of psychic necessity: I grew superstitious about squirrels in the days afterward. I imagined they were circling my house and casting spells. I would see them leaping from branch to branch in counterclockwise circles around my house and it would make me shiver a little. I didn't really believe they were out to get me, but if confidence is a kind of faith in and with oneself, this incident expanded my thinking of what that means in very complex and uncomfortable ways. It changed my sense of how I might behave faced with threat. I know it sounds like such an unlikely context for this kind of self-examination. But I was terrified by this small squirrel. It wasn't just that the squirrel was close to me and that it was dark but that it was hissing. I was still half asleep, and that sound plugged into some fear deep in my autonomic system. There was no thought at all involved.

Maybe I was suppressing some other anguish that came out just then. My son had been extremely sick and had just gotten home from a week's hospital stay, during which I had slept by his bedside and held myself together like the well-controlled model mother I so desperately wanted to be. So I was pretty wrung out when that squirrel crossed my path, just inviting sacrifice unto the gods. I was, I admit, quite on the edge of falling apart to begin with. But because my response was so deeply visceral, it did make me think about how soldiers are trained or become accustomed, even addicted, to the adrenaline rush of the kill. It made me think about mob responses, mass panics, the kind of thoughtless hysteria that does great harm before it shakes off the spell. About people who are trigger-happy or easily spooked. I had always found some of that incomprehensible, but now I think I understand how the stressed body could respond without a hoot for superego or rational individualism. I thought about what it might be like to live perpetually in a state of stress or fear or chemical imbalance where one is always as edgy as I was in my alarm. It's a dangerous place.

Yet the complication for me as a hopefully benign social being was that the sensation was also one of self-preservation: I was fighting off lions. It gave me a heady pleasure that would have served me well in prehistoric times: My aim is spot-on! I am a huntress! We'll never starve! It inspires some shame, living the cosmopolitan life as I do. So it made me really think about how societies have always tried to channel that sense, control it, civilize it, surround it with ritual, walk gently, raise our children calmly, wisely, and without the adrenaline-fired inflammation of sustained distress. How much we need to prime the body for peace.

I guess it also made me take stock of all the coexisting values in our very diverse society. When I started talking to friends and coworkers about this, I was startled to discover a wealth of odd animal death stories among them: from one who skins roadkill, then stitches the fur into nice warm mittens that he gives as Christmas presents (he learned this in the military), to a friend whose new bride, a fashion model from rural Bolivia, had to be counseled against snatching the fine hand-fed, Dipsy-Doodle-fattened geese who roosted round the little decorative pond in their Long Island town, then wringing their necks and serving them proudly for dinner. A lot of friends, many of them dressed in three-piece suits, had recipes for squirrel—stewed, braised, jerky, you name it—at the ready. Talk about the secret lives of lawyers. It's a dark little world out there. It was also a dark little world inside me at the time of the squirrel murder, however. As I said, my son had been very sick and I was quite beside myself.

It began with a fever, a sore throat, and sluggishness that late October day. My son was sent home from a school outing—a little something going around, surmised the school nurse. But by Halloween night we were old trusties at Children's Hospital in Boston, and I was watching my son receive a blood transfusion under a full moon.

My son had contracted something called Kawasaki disease, an inflammation of the blood vessels that can result in permanent damage to the heart. It's a rare condition whose cause is unknown, although it does appear to have a seasonal cycle (cases tend to cluster in late fall) and a strong genetic component (it strikes those of Japanese ancestry ten times more often than anyone else). It starts with a sustained high fever, cherry-red eyes, unusually flushed palms, and often a rash around the groin and midriff. Soon the lining of the mouth and intestinal tract become sore, with excessive discharge of mucus, diarrhea, and vomiting. The urine can become discolored, a rusty red-brown, the sign of hydropsis of the gallbladder. Liver and platelet counts become elevated; the heart races, the blood pressure drops, the body dehydrates. The nose bleeds; the skin peels, snakelike, in sheets. If not treated within seven to ten days—massive infusions of immunoglobulin seem to work best—there can be scarring of the heart muscles, and what the literature describes as "giant coronary aneurisms."

Luckily my son was diagnosed on the sixth day. It has been ten weeks since the onset, and he is entirely recovered now, whooping and wrestling in the backyard with his friends as I write.

But we have both changed. He is brighter and lighter (literally—he lost twenty-two pounds in the first two weeks). And I feel it as a kind of permanent inner snowstorm. The trauma is still inside me, like an immense snowdrift in which everything is still and all I can hear is my son's heart beating at that

incredible galloping rate. Some part of me is still reliving our
time at Children's Hospital on Halloween night. My son
had a hemalytic crisis that evening—his red-blood-cell count
dipped to dangerously low levels. There is a muffled, under-
water quality to my recollection of those hours when I sat by
his bedside on the green plastic Barcalounger and watched
the blood drip into him. Beyond the door of his room, a sad
parade of gravely ill, wheelchair-bound children were being
pushed in slow motion by staffers dressed like dalmatians and
Pooh-bears and fairy princesses.

"If the time ever comes when you have to put me in a nursing home," my mother says of that evening, "just don't put a
party hat on my head and a tambourine in my hand and then
have my picture taken as though I'm having a good time."

I promised her I would read to her from dark Dickensian
dramas and sneak in a Thermos of sherry instead.

But I couldn't do that sort of thing for my child. And so I
lay stretched on the green plastic Barcalounger next to his bed
in silence and in shock for what stretched into seven days and
nights. He slept, burning with fever. I did not sleep at all,
frozen with disbelief and apprehension.

When friends called, they'd ask how he was and I'd break
the silence, babbling at length. I'd tell them every last bit of
how he was, I'd unburden in a serious way—I held every last
detail up for public examination in case there was something
I'd missed. Help! Help! was the subtext to these exercises. But
it only made most people shrink and cringe and shiver and
gasp, until they joined me in the reverence of silence and of
shock.

At night, the wonderful, wonderful nurses would help me
pull out that plastic-covered, linoleum-colored Barcalounger
till it was flat, then cover it with sheets and a blanket, and I'd
lie there fully dressed, swaddled in hospital linens like a co-
coon waiting to be born. I'd lie there with my eyes wide open,

watching his oxygen saturation rate and feeling bright prickles of burning distress bubble just beneath the surface of my skin. The exhaustion visited me like that—like a kind of painful carbonation just beneath the skin. A busy surging of fiery disbelief and urgency, reminding me that I had a body, that I was still in the real world.

But the fear was the worst. The fear was so peculiar—it made me numb, it slowed time, it made my body cold on the outside, yet hot just beneath the skin. I became old. I felt my mortality as well as his. I could not bear to hear the news on television or radio—all the world's catastrophes became too personal. Fire, flood, avalanche, war—they were all happening to me, and to my fevered child with all the tubes and wires running in and out of his poor body.

Friends brought odd, intuitively wonderful things, things I could never have thought of and appreciate in retrospect because then I couldn't think. I couldn't hope. I could scarcely breathe. My friends M. and N. came by with their two sons and they all sang "Dona Nobis Pacem." It was lovely, just what was needed not only because it was prayerful but because it roused my son enough to make him giggle and cover his head with a pillow. My son's friend S. came with a pocketful of rubber bands and taught him how to shoot them across the room.

Despite it all I did hold it together at very specific moments. Early in his hospital stay, I remember telling my mother, "You pray, I'll do homework." And then I plugged in my laptop while I sat by my son and went online to research everything I could about Kawasaki, going to Web sites, e-mailing doctor and scientist friends of mine, and so on. Overnight I had a PhD in my son's illness and the chemical composition of every last drug they wanted to put in him. But it was the very process itself that also calmed me. "Homework," like prayer for my mother, is a practice, a ritual, with me, I think, something I was always good at since I was a very little girl. So in crisis, that's the mode I went to. Homework, the well-worn path—like a meditation.

Perhaps the most valuable gift I received was advice about what to expect: My friends R. and T., whose own son has been through a few hospital stays, predicted the cycles that I would go through—particularly that I would fall apart a few weeks after it was all over. Which I did. When my son was out of the hospital and on the road to recovery, I went through a period of deepest despair. I wasn't numb anymore. I felt every last frisson of horror and became completely nonfunctional. Whatever had held me together theretofore came unraveled then.

Someone once said that children render us hostages to fate. If so, then having a sick child is a bit like being a prisoner of war. Without the warning from friends, I don't think I would have known what was going on inside me—it was so roiling, enraged, and murky. It helped immeasurably to have been reminded that now it was okay to do all the falling apart I had not done during the time of greatest crisis. I could let go without fear. And so I slept a lot. I ordered Chinese every day. I let the house descend into epic mess. I stopped trying to write thank-you notes. I didn't do the laundry. My job piled up around me. I didn't read e-mail. I let my son play more computer games than he ever had in his life. I stopped everything, I took long hot baths, I lay around admiring the ceiling. I did that for a full week, until my sanity returned. Then for another week, I got up, did enough work to keep my job, but spent every other waking hour reading nothing but non-Dickensian comedic novels—Carl Hiaasen, P. G. Wodehouse—as a kind of ladder back to a world where I could be upbeat again, and laugh. My mother bought me a party hat and a tambourine.

But regaining my sanity involved another kind of effort as

well. I had to stop playing computer solitaire, and that took as much willpower as I have ever had to muster in my life. It was so soothing—it emptied my mind, blocked out the world. But it was numbing to the point of narcotizing, and hour after hour flew by painlessly. I wish I could say I found an easy way out, but it was surprisingly hard. "Move, legs!" I finally ordered from command central of my inner adult. Inanely, I thus made myself get up and exercise, whipping myself with the faith-based proposition that a little sweat is also calming and addictive.

Then too I had to consciously rework how I was envisioning everything that had happened. I had repeated dreams that my way was blocked by a large, dark, avalanche-prone mountain. If there was residual distress in my life, it was embodied in that image; it was as though I carried the weight of that mountain in everything I did; it was on my back when I climbed the stairs, it cast a shadow as I did the dishes. I realized I had to picture this crisis as something that I could surmount without ropes and pitons and cleats. Better yet, I had to get the mountain behind me.

Now, you have to understand that I am someone who prides herself—no doubt unduly—on her competence and tremendous independence. But I kept coming up against that mountain. It loomed black and unyielding, it occupied a place I was beginning to recognize as depression. So I did something that sounds simple, maybe even simple-minded, but which was actually very hard for me—hard because I had to reach beyond my own head. I'm an academic; I *live* in my head, and usually it's quite warm and cozy in there. I don't venture out much past the ears. But when my son got sick, I realized I had to rely on other people to help me think things through.

I asked a series of friends who'd been through bad times how they coped. Then I took their suggestions and drew them out, like a child, with crayons and a big pad of newsprint. I turned their self-helping metaphors into literal pictures and instructed my subconscious dreaming self to wake up and pay attention. My friend H.'s idea was the one that took: She said that hard times are like sailing along when the wind starts blowing the wrong way, so you just have to tack in order to keep on course. I'm no kind of sailor at all, but in this case ignorance probably helped, since sailing exists entirely in the realm of romance for me. And so in my dreams, the mountain melted and in its stead I found a nice sturdy little boat with a strong mast and a good sail. I bounced along the waves with a stiff breeze across the imaginary prow, plying my crooked course, invigorated, salt-encrusted, challenged, but not afraid.

Around this same time, my sister sent me an article written by Erma Bombeck when she was dying from breast cancer, about how much less of a perfectionist she would have been if she had had more time: She said that she would have had more dinner parties even though the rug was stained and the sofa was faded. I too am a perfectionist sometimes, constantly postponing the good times because my carpets are unvacuumed, my curtains askew. But my son did not die and neither did I. We still have time, if never enough. I ran out, got an industrial-sized package of frozen buffalo wings—I think Ms. Bombeck would have liked buffalo wings—zapped those suckers in the microwave, and held open house.

And then I felt better, as though I had survived some ancient ritual of rebirth, some ceremony in which I had been trapped in a dark cave, and was coming out a new person, the world of sensation sharpened a bit, the adjustment to bright light making the world look different, precarious, precious. Life was shorter but clearer, the order of things undone, then reassembled. This reemergence, this climb back to the surface, had a gorgeous shimmer to it, and the warm awareness of water and air and sun and hope and the lovely bounty of growing things.

In the late afternoon of New Year's Day, I decided to go uptown and drop in at a gathering of old friends. I donned my expensive flame-red nubuck walking pumps and set upon my course, treading lightly, skimming across the asphalt surface, tense with the premonition of surging, hydra-headed, alien revenge from every manhole.

Earth skimming is hard work under the best of circumstances, however, and I grew exhausted long before I reached my destination. At the corner of Broadway and Fifty-first, I jumped into a cab. Almost immediately we were caught in gridlock. I watched the stoplight turn red then green then red. The taxi driver was tuned to a radio station that seemed to specialize in soft Christian rock. "For He so looooooved the world," sang a folksy female voice as a guitar strummed along melodiously, hypnotically, like the purr of a cat. Finally, miraculously, the light changed, the traffic cleared, and we were off like a rocket . . .

"That He gave His own-leeeee begotten son . . ." We careened from left to right, from lane to lane and back again. "Life everlaaaasting . . ." We narrowly missed a group of pedestrians. ". . . O Son of Gooooood . . ."

"Fuck!" shouted the driver at a man whose body we missed by a hair's breadth. And then, turning his head 180 degrees away from the road so as to attain a full measure of warm, expressive eye contact with me, the driver said, "Excuse me. I was speaking to that shithead, not to you."

New York is overflowing with such gallantry these days, and scarcely a pundit alive has missed the opportunity to record the various sightings of civility. Our city's niceness against all odds has everyone united in the enjoyment of a New York so pleasantly ordered. Indeed, if you just pin your money to your underwear, squint a little, and strap on your gas mask while clapping your hands over your ears, a certain sense of the Platonic ideal will well up at once—even though the more dour of the citizenry will always render their comparisons to the Disney corporate handbook.

I am always, I confess, on the dour side of things, even in the encounter with my gracious cabdriver who was so generously accommodating my delicate sensibilities. I know a cheery mien is all for our own good—got to get tourism back on track and all that—yet I couldn't help noticing that the driver's first name was Mohammed. I saw how hard he was trying to be simultaneously friendly Christian American and profanely cosmopolitan New Yorker. But I wonder if the vulnerability and fear that beset many "ethnic" Americans in the wake of September 11 at all motivates the kind of theatrical efforts at assimilation that so distinguished my great-aunt Mary.

The taxi deposited me at my destination. There were twelve of us gathered. We, as a group, had lost a lot of friends in the last several years—premature deaths, all people in their forties and fifties. Our wonderful friend Jerome Culp, the first tenured black professor at Duke Law School, had recently died after a long battle with kidney disease. He was the kindest of men, in addition to being a brilliant and prolific scholar. The last time I saw him he was weak from multiple operations and the need for constant dialysis. But he found the strength to come to my piano class and listen to me try to discover rhythm. When my piano teacher's dog, ancient and toothless but aspiring to belligerence, barked at him, Jerome was genuinely hurt. "But . . . but . . . dogs always like me," he said with such sweet, injured surprise that we all laughed. Realizing the magnitude of his mistake, the dog snuffled abjectly, curled up, and went to sleep on Jerome's feet. We lost our friend Kellis Parker to a septic blood infection. He was the first tenured black faculty member at Columbia Law School. Our friend Dwight Greene, one of two black professors of law at Hofstra University, had been murdered brutally in his home. In what was rumored to be a contract killing, our friend Mary Jo Frug, a feminist theorist at New England School of Law, had been stabbed outside her home one early spring evening some years before. Her murder, like 60 to 70 percent of all murders, has yet to be solved. Feminist theorist Teresa Brennan, one of the first women to teach philosophy at Cambridge University, died after an apparent hit-and-run in south Florida. Haywood Burns and Shanara Gilbert—the entire black tenured faculty of CUNY Law School—had died in South Africa when a truck ran a red light and hit their car broadside. In an apparent suicide, Denise Carty-Benia, the first tenured black person at Northeastern University Law School, was found hanging in the attic of a friend's house. And Andrew Haynes, the first black tenured professor at Salmon P. Chase School of Law, had drowned while successfully rescuing someone else.

As my grandmother used to say, people were dying who had never died before.

We had traveled thousands of miles among us to meet and eat and give each other ideas and inspiration. We were not very good at it, I think. Over drinks, the conversation spiraled around subjects like utopia and the Supreme Court, the nature of ideology and the USA Patriot Act. It was a stressful profession, this legal career we had all chosen. We felt threatened, mortal, despondent. We mourned our friends and celebrated our good fortune with all the trepidation of those who are testing fate. We discussed what kinds of funerals we wanted. Drums, bagpipes, Buddhist bells, loud lamentations, nurses in white gloves, two thousand in attendance, a High Episcopal service with a lot of Baptist noise.

After a while, we agreed to talk about one thing that makes each of us happy. It quickly became evident that, like me, everyone would rather talk about what was making us miserable. Every sentence started off optimistically, then withered into a "but" clause: My children are my greatest joy, but I have no time to see them. I love my husband so much and yet I want to kill him. I'm at the height of my career but all I want to do is kill myself. I'm incredibly happy but all I do is sleep and cry.

I left the party after a colleague turned the subject to the one thing that, despite his recent divorce, really did seem to perk him up, to wit, discussing the finer points of the Uniform Commercial Code.

"The core doctrinal rule is that a transferee of goods acquires such title as the transferor had in the case of a good faith purchase, as provided in 2-401, subparagraph 1," said this friend, his spirits brightening visibly.

"It was recently reported that Miss Waldron's red colobus monkey has become extinct," I babbled back miserably.

My colleague, restored to his customary ultrarationalist, econometrically inclined stance, paused for only a moment and then warned me not to be too sentimental about these things. "Life evolves," he said briskly. "That beast was big, noisy, and colorful. Predators go for easy pickings like that. There weren't a lot to begin with—I'll bet you'd never even heard of a red colobus before its demise."

Not that it's relevant to much of anything, but as a matter of fact I had. Both its name and its appearance were unusual enough for me to recall its description in an encyclopedia we had when I was little. The monkey was named after the lady friend of an English explorer who collected specimens for the British Museum. When young, I had a very romantic image of this creature, something straight out of Dr. Doolittle: the gentle monkey bobbling across the waves from West Africa to Britain in a sailing ship, bearing a message of eternal love from the handsome leader of jungle expeditions. I pictured all of them living out their days in Cornwall, in a stone cottage with labyrinthine gardens, green velvet bell pulls, and clattering teacups—a colorful menagerie over which the red colobus, dressed like Babar in a very tailored suit, would reign wisely and supreme.

It was this silly, innocent, elementary-school image that came flooding back when I read *The New York Times*—obituary, do we call it?—describing a rather different scenario: "The monkey was first described by scientists in 1936, based on eight specimens shot by Willoughby P. Lowe . . . It was named for Miss F. Waldron . . . a traveling companion of Mr. Lowe." Images of taxidermy, monkey stew, and Bonnie and Clyde on safari rose in my head as I read *The Times* account of the ecological imbalances wrought by farmers, loggers, and "bush-meat" hunters. John Robinson, a vice president of the Wildlife Conservation Society, was quoted as saying that "[p]eople don't really worry about cockroaches or newts too much, but when you lose a large primate that's a culmination of lots of years of evolution and with which we share a lot of genes, the consequences to humans of that kind of loss—both practical and emotional—are much greater."

It scarcely needs stating that the ecological devastation of tropical forests is a matter of considerable practical import to the survival of all primates, but I was intrigued by the suggestion that this represents an emotional loss as well. I do not propose holding up as models either my own childish anthropomorphizing or the relentlessly disengaged views of certain social Darwinists. But somewhere between the ideologies of primate-eat-primate and Curious George, there is a symbolic realm where play our various images of the world and of its inhabitants. And that symbolism—or sentimentality, if you will—perhaps reflects the patterns of other of our human relations.

My colleague is a good person, and kind for an ultrarationalist. As I left, he patted my hand and told me that I was just having reentry problems. He blamed my mood on too much sabbatical time spent writing in the country, holed up in a rural retreat with only bread, cheese, and olives to eat, a diet that, according to him, "has thinned your blood." Urban life was proving too rude a shock for my system, he said, and we went our separate ways.

For months, it is true, I had been running away from life in New York City. But in the process I had learned small things, like the fact that spiders can't crawl out of porcelain bathtubs by themselves, because the sides are too slippery. (I had always thought spiders in bathtubs were just hanging out to better plot human demise.) I learned that in some parts of the world people hang "spider ladders" over the sides of their tubs so as to help the little creatures make their escape. This is unimaginably alien to me, yet such a gentle gesture that it gives me hope for . . . well, for . . . "Think carefully—for whom, exactly?" snapped my colleague.

When I got home, I boiled water for tea and checked my e-mail. A friend had sent me a joke: Down at the local elementary school, the children are coming in from recess. Little Johnny comes into the classroom, and the teacher asks, "What did you do during recess, Johnny?" and he says, "I played in the wading pool." The teacher responds, "If you can spell 'pool,' then you may have a cookie."

Next little Sally comes in, and the teacher says, "What did you do during recess, Sally?" and Sally says, "I played in the sand." "Very good," says the teacher. "If you can spell 'sand,' then you may have a cookie."

Then little Tyrone comes in, and the teacher asks, "What did you do during recess, Tyrone?" And Tyrone cries, "Johnny and Sally kicked me out of the wading pool, threw sand in my face, and then they called me the n-word."

"Heavens," exclaims the teacher, "that sounds like blatant racial discrimination! If you can spell 'blatant racial discrimination,' you may have a cookie."

Poor little Tyrone. This is probably why they don't have recess at many schools anymore. Trouble lurks like a shadow when children are allowed to go out-of-doors.

Thus it is, perhaps, that the preponderance of play spaces in big cities are indoors these days, where the osmosis of who goes in and out can be regulated, the skin of urban walls a defense against those multiple personalities, that multiplicity of selves, who would fill those cool private places past the point of containment, to overflow, to eruption and disruption.

A reverential, half-sad sensation settles over me. When I was growing up, children streamed out the schoolhouse doors and into the streets. We played on those streets, outdoors all day, every day, until we were called in for supper. Almost every block had a vacant lot to play in, with clover and poison ivy and skunk cabbage. Boys whiled away their time exploding those little paper-wrapped dots of gunpowder known as "caps" on the curbstones. Girls played house and dressed dolls. We all read comic books. We made war with sticks from the huge old oak trees, we fashioned forts out of refrigerator boxes with doors woven of honeysuckle vines, and we made plenty of mud pies to feed the imaginary troops. After supper, the fathers smoked Lucky Strikes on the front steps. The mothers stood, always with their arms folded comfortably, and chatted in pairs. It was a time before mercury vapor lamps, and even though we lived in the heart of Boston, there were fireflies and stars visible in the early evening sky.

Forty years after mud pies, I'm raising a son in a city where there is no mud. Perhaps there never was mud in New York City, just pools of water from backed-up sewers settling into the asphalt until that seismic shift known as a pothole rends the ground, sending hubcaps, bicycle wheels, and Rollerbladers arcing through the air like tumbling semaphores of distress.

"Look," said my son as we walked past a formerly vacant site in Manhattan where bulldozers were digging a deep pit. "They must be making a swimming pool."

"Wouldn't that be nice," I said, even though I was thinking: fat chance. But as it turns out, the new building will indeed have a swimming pool, albeit on a high floor with a membership cost of more than $100,000 a year.

"Pesticides!" shrieked a mother past whom I strolled in Central Park not long ago; she was chiding a child who was jabbing at the patchy grass with a plastic spoon. "Medical waste" is what another friend of mine worries about when her child works in the community garden near their apartment. (She doesn't have to worry for long. The city has sold the garden to developers and it's scheduled to be plowed under any day now.)

Today, play areas for children are probably safer, cleaner, and better supervised than when I was a child, but the preponderance of them are private and indoors. There are indoor gyms, indoor game arcades, indoor soccer fields, indoor discovery centers. Kids in search of a good time in New York spend half their lives in museums and theaters. Few children haven't memorized every last dinosaur at the Museum of Natural History, every last bit of armor at the Met, every last fish in the Aquarium. Few haven't had a personalized backstage tour of Lincoln Center.

For all the fear allayed, there is a price, of course. Not only does such a lifestyle cost buckets, but to the little hothouse humans it breeds, sun is a threat, birds carry disease, and butterflies are nothing more than roaches with interesting wings. Before September 11, my own little boy, cocooned beneath the fiercely bright night skies of New York City, used to see airplanes plying their course toward LaGuardia, pretend they were shooting stars, and make a wish.

Some years ago, I remember reading an article by a woman whose name I can no longer remember who had taken in her homeless teenaged niece. The niece had suffered many privations growing up in a warren of high-rise project housing, but perhaps most poignantly, she had never seen the moon.

When it rose, great and glowing, over the low-rise horizon of her aunt's suburban neighborhood, she was dumbfounded, and, struggling to name it, cast it as some peculiar kind of street lamp. The niece, according to her aunt, had never had time or opportunity to lift her eyes from the meanness of the streets in the neighborhood where she had grown up.

I used to think of that story as an illustration of extreme deprivation. These days, I wonder if it is not exemplary of a more general experience shared even by the privileged. My son's is a generation to whom "fresh air" means air-conditioning that works and for whom the forces of nature exist somewhere past New Jersey. I wonder how these children will see themselves in the world. When I was growing up, naming and nicknaming were related to traditions of specificity and the timelessness of connection—little Johnny Junior, Sarah After Her Great-Grandmother.

Today's wired global village is peopled by Jason62493@ aol.com. Yet within the packs of clones one can only hope there dwells some more poetic sense of the infinite. Indeed, I was inspired to see one such little Jason, bright and autonomous, huddled beside my son. The two of them were composing fantastical and chimeric e-mail addresses. Birdboy2000@magictree.com, Laughingfishleaps@foodchain.org, Moonmindedearthling@glowworm.smile.

That these youngsters still tie themselves to the earth while sighting moons in cyberspace is strangely comforting, even redemptive, to this mommysixtrillion@homegirl.edu. It gives me hope, somehow, that the children of our relentlessly panoptic millennium will find at least a few heavenly bodies to guide them in their exploits through inner worlds and outer limits, then home in time for supper.

By suppertime of January 1 of the year 2002, I was tired again. I pondered the matter of dinner. I decided to begin with a frisée of young California greens in malathion drizzle. Next, a nice genetically enhanced, fat-free New Zealand piglet in transgenic fruit compote, accompanied by tender seedless baby corn crossed with the hormones of a jellyfish to give it that beautifully blight-resistant glow on the plate. To finish off, Quadroon Surprise, a medley of café au lait, white chocolate, mango, and high-yellow lemon sorbet . . .

The passing from one era to another has brought forth the desperate, the paranoid, and the romantic in all of us who are apocalyptically inclined, or just ambivalent about change. If we are now at a moment when the genes of an eel can be injected into a monkey or a soybean, it seems pretty likely that the next époque's survivors will look back on something like a battle of the life-forms.

Our world proceeds at breakneck speed, in nanoseconds, with no room for remembering. Yet a thousand years is a season so slow, so immense, we probably ought to feel more insignificant and endangered than we generally do. Instead we seem afflicted by complacent but devouring consumerism on the one hand, and on the other, wild acts of fundamentalist theological fervor.

That night I painted my toenails an iridescent green. It was a silly little thing to do, frivolous and self-indulgent. My toes glowed like the lights of a landing strip for very small alien spaceships.

At midnight, my son woke up, coughing, congested, a touch of a fever. He wanted tea, and I went to the kitchen to put the kettle on. It was the simplest of acts, one that slows time. Life is a mystery, the body's growth a miracle. I took the tea to my son and watched him breathe in the steam as he sipped it slowly. He was so young and gap-toothed.

"My left canine is loose," he told me. "I think I may lose two teeth at once."

"That will set a record," I replied, rubbing his wheezy little back.

I wonder if, in all these busy, busy days, in all this sowing and reaping, this hoarding and hiding, there is a certain eros at work, some spirit of desperate desire. It's not all that hard to understand the appeal, actually—like the worst of the millennialists, I too harbor a sick little longing to tuck into a nice warm bomb shelter, my loved ones around me, snug and protected against the drifting atomic snow outside. I imagine sleeping late every morning. I dream of having time to read my never-sulky child all the great classics as defined by me, and I see myself lovingly presiding over candlelit dinners of Spam, dried apricots, and distilled water. How grateful and warm we would be, like bunnies burrowed in for the winter. Come the nuclear spring we would emerge from our lead-lined warren into the bright, silent, decimated landscape and begin to repopulate the earth with new generations of lawyers (for surely rocks, rivers, and lawyers will live forever).

When I give free rein to these fantasies of apocalyptic grandiosity, what is obvious even to me is not only the nest-as-neurosis thing but also a childish nostalgia, a literal yearning for global disaster as the only excuse for a day off from work, no questions asked. This hope of return to an emotional womb reconfigured as political state, a bit like Walter Benjamin's angel of history blowing backward into the future. In these fantasies I recognize all my own disappointments and resentments. Through fantasy, it is so easy to purge the world of all enemies, all debts, to say nothing of such necessities as hewing wood and toting water.

Years ago, I lived in a house in Berkeley, California, behind which two peacocks lived. They'd belonged to an Italian restaurant down the street that had acquired them with the idea that they would wander among the clientele in a dignified and picturesque fashion. But the owners hadn't clipped their wings, so the birds had flown over the back wall and settled in my backyard, where there were cats—and here's a little-known fact: Peacocks like Purina Cat Chow. Anyway, it was magical living in that house. I used to dream that giant emerald- and diamond-studded peacocks were roosting on the roof, guarding the house by wrapping their gorgeous tails around it.

During mating season, the two of them would stand in the driveway and spread their feathers and do the shivery, shimmery circle dance that signaled their desperation for peahens, of which there were none. I used to sit in the big bay window of the living room and watch people scurrying past the house on their way to Herculean labors, from the looks of it—brows furrowed, jaws clamped, eyes glazed. Based on their response, I came to divide the world up into two kinds of people: those who expected to encounter peacocks in the driveways of life and those who did not. I could never understand the depth of the preoccupation that allowed so many people to go sailing past that miraculous swirling blue spectacle without noticing anything at all. Years later, long after I had moved back to the East Coast, I heard that Berkeley had passed a noise abatement statute that the peacocks, being quite noisy, had failed. Last seen, the authorities were carting them off to the zoo.

So here I am, back in the urban jungle, walking the streets, riding the subways, observing large, colorful primates battling for dominance, chewing, clawing, spitting, swinging, long limbed and glittery eyed, chattering senselessly to the voices in their heads—or their cell phones. Even at the graveside funeral of yet another dear friend, beepers were beeping and those primates of the subspecies lawyer could be seen diving behind great granite monuments to retrieve their messages. I imagine a world where these are the only creatures left, and my brain feels suspended, anesthetized. I imagine the quiet starlit night when not even that remains.

Then the eye within, yearning fiercely because that is what we do, lifts beyond the grave, beyond this little rusty tub of doomed souls, and scans for evidence of life: I find and cling to a wide road, the color red, mountains, a feather, thunder, the taste of iron, splinters, mud, and breath after breath after breath.

I suspect the search for high ground or a low bunker signals retreat from community that cannot be found in real life, and in this I'm awfully lucky, I suppose, for my sense of disconnection comes not from war or from trauma but from great fatigue alone. I yearn for a good long holiday, and not just a weekend with alternate-side-of-the-street parking rules suspended. Perhaps we as a nation need a rest too—a breathing space, an amnesty, a season of mourning, a month of indulgence, a year of reprieve, a century of celebration. A laying down of arms, a laying on of hands. A long, cool rain of forgiveness.

Acknowledgments

I wish to thank first and foremost Anna Deavere Smith's Institute on the Arts and Civic Dialogue for its inspiration and insight. It was my great good fortune to be a fellow at the institute for all three summers of its existence, during which the ideas for this book came into being. I am indebted to the sponsors of the institute, the Ford Foundation, and the W.E.B. DuBois Institute at Harvard University; it was with the direct benefit of their resources and support this book was written. I am extremely grateful to the John T. and Catherine D. MacArthur Foundation, whose fellowship enabled me to take the time to write this book. I thank my dean, David Leebron, and Columbia Law School for allowing me the leave time in which to write; and Katrina Vanden Heuvel, Victor Navasky, and *The Nation* magazine for providing a consistent outlet for my thoughts. I am also grateful to Hamilton Fish and the Nation Institute, and Robert Pollack and the Columbia Center for Religion and Science, for sponsoring seminars and support that also inspired parts of this work. Some ideas in this book were first developed in essays published by *Callaloo*, *The Nation*, *The New Yorker*, *O*, *Opportunity Journal*, and *Transition*.

I am particularly indebted to the following friends and colleagues, all of whom took time to share their thoughts and wisdom: Marlene Archer, June Baldwin, Maurice Berger, Charles Blank, Nancy Blank, Teresa Brennan, Cynthia Cannady, Stanford Carpenter, Alex Case, Ann Case, Frank Case, Merry Conway, Jerome Culp, Lynn Daniels, Angela Shaw Decock, Elsa Dixler, Troy Duster, Michelle Fine, Julie Dobbs Gibbs, Jackie Goodrich, Ariela Gross, Michael Harris, Richard Harvey, Bill Hing, Gail Hochman, Marilyn Hutton, George Joseph, Melanie Joseph, Isaac Julian, Oliver Lake, Evelyn Lewis, Richard Lingeman, Bradley McCallum, Barbara Parker, Kellis Parker, Deborah Post, Noni Pratt, Dawn Raffel, Kimber Riddle, Maggie Roche, Suzzy Roche, David Rossinow, Laura Rossinow, Sam Rossinow, Jack Sheehy, Jake Sheehy, James Sheehy, Valerie Sheehy, Bernestine Singley, Bernard St. Louis, Constance St. Louis, Jaqueline Tarry, Matthew Wilkes, Carol Williams, Gail Wright, Joanne Wypijewski. And my wonderful editors at Farrar, Straus and Giroux, Jonathan Galassi and Ayesha Pande, deserve special medals for their patience and faith that this book would one day see the light of day.

Finally, I have taken the liberty of suppressing the identities of certain characters in the book as well as changing small details of some events so as to respect the interests of privacy.